Travels, Challenges .....Marc!!

Lyndell Heyning

© 2022 Lyndell Heyning

Travels, Challenges…..Marc!!

All rights reserved. No part of this publication may be reproduced, stored in a retrieval system or transmitted in any form or by any means, electronic, mechanical, photocopying, recording or otherwise without the prior permission of the publisher or in accordance with the provisions of the Copyright, Designs and Patents Act 1988 or under the terms of any licence permitting limited copying issued by the Copyright Licensing Agency.

Published by:

Madhouse Media Publishing | www.madhousemedia.com.au

ISBN: 978-0-6455695-1-3

Written and distributed by:

Lyndell Heyning

www.inmyownlittlecorneroftheworld.com

Printed edition IngramSpark 2022

Travels, Challenges ….. Marc!!

(Travels with my husband and other challenges.)

If it doesn't challenge you,
it doesn't change you …

Every challenge is an opportunity to learn,
to figure out problems and tasks,
to invent and reinvent …
in more ways than one.

Fred DeVito

To:
Helen Fletcher:
For your initial suggestion of putting together these stories
For your wisdom of words
As my editor, mentor, and advisor
I would not have completed this book without you!

For:
Marc Heyning:
My love
My inspiration
If I had not met you,
My stories would not have existed at all!

Thank you to
Sarah Kennett for your artistic contribution to the book.

Chapters

Chapter One - When I Met Marc!..1
Chapter Two - A Wee Walk..5
Chapter Three - A Sting in the Tale...12
Chapter Four - Out of My Comfort Zone..................................21
Chapter Five - Flights of Fancy...34
Chapter Six - Tour De France...44
Chapter Seven - Can I Take a Rain Check?.............................60
Chapter Eight - If The Shoe Fits...73
Chapter Nine - Why Walk When You Can Slide...................93
Chapter Ten - Why Walk When You Can Ride?.................109
Chapter Eleven - The Call of The Ride..................................122
Chapter Twelve - On the Flip Side of It All..........................140
Chapter Thirteen - Something In The Air............................151
Chapter Fourteen - Celebrate Good Times but….............160
Chapter Fifteen - Taste of Family...168
Chapter Sixteen - Not all Plane Sailing..................................192
Chapter Seventeen - The Turn of The Key...........................205
Chapter Eighteen - Too Hard To Hold..................................219
Chapter Nineteen - Just Look for The Lake
Ok, Which Shade of White Shall I Look For?.....................234
Chapter Twenty - Frozen in Time...243
Twenty-One - Sometimes You Win, Sometimes You Don't!....264
Twenty-Two - The Lighter side of Travel.............................268
Twenty-Three - Here Comes the Sun....................................281
Twenty-Four - The Calm Before the Storm........................300
Twenty-Five - The Old Grey mare..309
No, she definitely aint what she used to be..........................309
Twenty-Six - Then There Was Covid!...................................326
Epilogue..332

Prologue

There is a saying that the most important turning-points of life often come at the most unforeseen times and in the most unexpected ways.

But what happens when sometimes life manifests in ways that catch you completely off guard? When you feel or think your life is planned the way and direction you want it to go, but suddenly the unpredicted occurs?

What do you do when someone enters your life unexpectedly? A someone who brings diverse challenges, encounters, and unimaginable risk-taking behaviours into your world.

Did I know what I was doing?

Did I know where I was headed?

No - not at all … in fact I had absolutely no idea!

Oh, please do stay with me and let me tell you my story.

And with a smile I glance up to his face and ask ….

"Do you know where we are going?"

With a mischievous grin he replies …

"No, but let's find out!"

Chapter One

When I Met Marc!

Those five words above swirled inside my head as I stood on the rocks in freezing conditions.

The foreign mist shrouded me in its cold wet arms, as the thundering torrent of the waterfall cascaded downwards, sending icy water streaming through my once beautifully coiffured hair. My back was aching, my arms were sore, the huge backpack was tilting high on my small back and most uncomfortably slowly digging its straps into me, The frostiness of the air around me, permeated all through my rain cover, my jacket, and my many layers of clothing. Just like the water from the waterfall was pulled inexorably downwards by gravity, my sense of humour had now been sucked completely away!

This was not normal!

I was chilled,

I was wet.

I was definitely not happy.

I was thinking, what was I doing here?

What on earth made me get out of my warm snuggly bed, where my body once luxuriated in mindless dreams and comfortable slumber;

the cat napping beside me, radiating his warmth to my body, the bed covers nestled happily under my neck. Where I was, once upon a time, so warm, so relaxed, and so, so happy! So, please tell me again, whisper it to me, or better still, shout it loudly to me so I could hear, "What on earth was I doing here!!!" This was not what I generally do!

You know, I did once have a *normal* life.

I grew up in the most conventional family. The family that had two parents, siblings, lived in suburbia, attended Church and Sunday school, went to the traditional public school, living and maintaining a sedate family life in the suburbs of Sydney. I conventionally moved through the channels of high-school and teachers' college. I worked hard and really enjoyed my teaching. I followed the assumed natural path of relationships, fell in love, got married, had two beautiful children, and survived the 'normal' family trips, the weekend outings, those few days away. You know, all those sorts of things that we generally know as 'Traditional' or 'Routine' or in colloquial terms - *Normal*.

In that conventional life, I also had travelled and enjoyed adventures.

As a child, I had completed the annual camping trips with family. I mean the kind of family adventures where you slept in tents all decked out with camping equipment. My parents slept in the trailer and us kids were head to toe on canvas stretchers three tiers high, or on a mattress on the floor, complete with mosquito nets, cooking fires, burners, kerosene lamps and all the luxuries that could be brought along in the back of the family station wagon. Then later, as an adult with my husband, our 'holidays' or 'travelling' were the usual type, 'to go see the family', or to enjoy miniature weekend camping trips with friends and family, or to be with our children as part of scout or guide camps. But always, with whatever comforts we could squeeze into our then little Suzuki Vitara 4-wheel drive vehicle. Then there were of course, the few traditional weekends with our special friends and their kids; a couple of short business trips overseas and our one wonderful special family holiday to Italy. I certainly enjoyed all those family trips.

But the normality of life and its predictability always subsequently returned. Once more, laboriously but lovingly running my children around, attending school and after school curriculum activities, graciously assisting my husband in his work, and being involved in our community commitments. All the while, working full time and following my own musical interests. You know … that normal pathway of life … anticipations, dreams and hopes … all adding gracefully to my cheerful, ordinary, predictable life as a suburbia-raised woman now approaching middle age!!!

And I was genuinely happy.

However, I knew I was not one to just be content to see my own home country, although there is nothing wrong with that. Believe me, Australia is such a great place. I am Australian and very proud of it and would not wish to live anywhere else. I love living here. But have you ever sat with a coffee in hand, flicked through those Sunday morning papers to the travel section and gazed longingly at those sun kissed beach scenes or the snow-capped mountains with the brazen captions of, "You must see"? I did! I knew that I really wanted to travel.

I used to dream of roaming to those far away, exotic destinations and being swept off my feet in the glory of its scenic beauty and grandeur. I wanted to see more. I wanted to share myself, my proud Australian culture, and my own perspective with the rest of the world! I truly wanted to see how other people lived; to see different elements of nature; to engage with the people themselves. I wanted to see the physical infrastructures combined with a completely 'different' from what I knew 'natural 'world. I genuinely wanted to face the world as I knew it, by travelling outside and away from my home to unknown destinations. I wanted to explore the culture of places where English was not the language spoken. Where you simply revelled in the excitement of that new, confusing unexperienced place stretched out before you.

How many times when shopping for those mundane boring essential groceries did I meander slowly past the travel centre in the plaza? How often did the illuminated bold print beckon to me, coaxing me into their store, luring me with their whispered courageous phrases of, "*We have cheap flights*", "*Come on, you can do it*", "*Get away from it all …*". But of course, I did not. I looked. I breathed in their phrases and scenery, but I walked away. It was just not on the practical agenda of my life at that time. My husband and I had both said that once retirement came, we would do it 'one day'. So, after immersing myself in those far off dreams, shaking those alluring images from my head, I would always merely hurry home.

But unfortunately, those futuristic plans we both had of travel and holidays scheduled for retirement did not happen. Life regrettably, took a different turn with the unexpected, unplanned illness and eventual demise of my husband. Obviously, when that happened, those proposed dreams dramatically and naturally flew out the window because that 'One Day' would now not ever happen. Things had changed.

Being a conventional normal mother, homemaker, and worker, I slipped back into the familiarity of life as I had known it. I retreated to the normality of my conservative world. A world that was safe, secure, warm. That was a welcoming haven in facing my now same, but different, world before me. I simply picked up the pieces and for a few non-descript years, moved on with my life. Calm. Sheltered. Comfortable. The only bold addition being two cats to now share my bed.

And Then I met Marc.

Chapter Two

A Wee Walk

Yes, I met Marc.

So – Who is this Marc?

Well, as he is the primary reason for these stories, I guess I should introduce him to you.

Marc is someone I knew a lifetime ago. He was someone, only associated very briefly from my past, with whom I never really connected, and was basically insignificant in my previous life. I guess I knew him more as an acquaintance, as a professional person and we did not have much in common. However, one day, in the local township we shared, I literally bumped into him again, and from that first unintended collision, we commenced to chat. Encounters at first were via unplanned get togethers that then became intentional arrangements. And I guess my 'story' with Marc began! Most conventionally, in our hometown, sharing coffee. That was how I met Marc!

Of course, I can see you looking at me with an amused expression. However, at that point of time, there were no 'dinner dates or 'romance'! It was merely a foundation period, of establishing a friendship between two people in their late forties. A common ground created solely through suitable conversation of our now shared professional background of teaching, being that he taught medical students and I taught pre-service education students. Basically, we were purely two people who had both been through disparate hardships and this was a time when we delighted in shared laughter and countless varied dialogues over many, many, many cups of coffee! Undeniably, it was fun!

Plausibly, we developed further into our relationship.

But you know it is not as easy as in the movies or in romance novels to start 'a new life', or 'a new story'. In fact, it is quite the opposite. It is actually extremely hard! I mean you are not that silly 18-30-year-old flirting with life, dreaming of your pathway ahead, foolishly thinking that you could control and choose your route and not yet wise enough to know that the destination is not the goal.

Well, plainly put, I had already gained my hard-won wisdom!! I had a path that was comfortable and rewarding me in its own way.

In my past life, I was more than content with the road I had been travelling. I had already defined my own significant stories complete with easy clear corridors, obstacles, and fences and my path had already been dug with clear well-worn grooves! So, for me, starting a new story with a new man was not an easy task.

Truly questioning myself, did I really want to start an unknown, unscripted narrative??

We were two single adults with grown up children of our own, who shared time talking, drinking coffee, chatting about life, but realising with each new cup of coffee chat, we actually did '*like*' each other. Perhaps, even a little more than '*like*'. We were two adults who started to tread onto ground that was a little unsafe, rocky, and possibly a little dangerous for both of us. After all, one person had been through a marriage breakup with their partner and the other in buried theirs (now that's a true breakup, believe me. No return from that one!).

Did we both want to tread that uncertain path? Do we move back to the safe known uncomplicated ground of before, simply stay where we were, both comfortable, both protected? Or do we take it a step further and add more variety, more involved periods of time together?

So, what do we do?

Well, that questioned was answered.

To shift away from that safe world of social coffee platforms, I was asked by my new 'friend' if I wished to do something different by accompanying him on a small walk … a different kind of 'chat"

Now, I did enjoy walking! Fresh air, sunshine, and the joy of being outside!

Being 47 and suburbia-bred, my mind took me away from our safe common coffee shop ground and the people we knew, to a delightful picture of us walking and talking together, surrounded by nature, in a totally different environment. I even was bold enough to think that if it felt right, we might hold hands or link a finger or two! My imagination took me to the image of the two of us enjoying a coffee at the end to finalise our 'first date', called a 'small walk' and this in my mind as so idyllic!

"I would love to go!", was my reply. So, we did!

We had ideal conditions. A beautiful sunny day. The drive was friendly, pleasant. Both of us obviously a little hesitant and nervous at the change of mode, but as we ventured off to explore the countryside ahead, we both slowly began to unwind and relax more in each other's presence. There we were, two people, in their late forties, … the two of us walking together, A gentle amble within nature in that perfect scene set of a small walk. So romantic?

Right? … Wrong!

I guess, on reflection, the obvious word here that I ought to have noticed should have been the word *'small'*.

Tell me, what is your concept of the word 'small'?

This word generates the meaning, "*not great in amount, extent, duration, and of limited size*". Well, you would think this official dictionary definition should be correct. But after this first 'date', I realised my understanding of that word was SO wrong. My definition, as well as the dictionary's and likely yours, did not equate with my new friend's definition. His translation was quite different. I guess I should have considered the fact that as a Scout Leader he was used to taking his 'troop' on 'extended 'strolls' and that the word 'small' was relative!! I think even today, many,

many years later, Marc has still yet to learn the correct definition of that simple word when applied to walks!

In truth, our 'small walk' was actually a hike in the country, scrambling up, over and down a mountain. And this 'small walk' went on and on, eventually adding up to being twenty-three kilometres long! Not even halfway through, my wished-for vision of a 'Small Romantic Walk' vanished along with my breath! (I did not know any better at that time, but I can now hear my now-sister-in-law laughing as she herself knows what *small* means to her brother. She has her own stories to tell!)

Here was the scene.

We had perhaps walked about halfway. We had one small bottle of water and one muesli bar between us – this being Marc's idea of adequate rations for a 'small walk'! The sun was hot, the track became steeper, the breeze picked up, the clouds started gathering. Marc's response was to increase our pace.

But I was there, going up and over those rocks clambering on mountain tracks. Vainly attempting to further develop the friendship between us. Endeavouring to get to know someone, whom you don't know all that well, in a beautiful, natural outside environment, away from everything else.

My little legs were following behind his bigger legs and becoming more painful and stiff the more I walked. In front of me were two long male legs striding out, strutting up and down over uneven terrain while in contrast, my own little legs were following, scrambling, tripping, and catching on the same uneven terrain. As the sun got hotter, my panting became faster. Our conversation now had completely run out of breath – literally - on our first date, my envisioned 'small romantic idyllic walk'! To top this all off, I now had to go to the toilet! I really needed to wee!

Of course, I am on a mountain with no public amenities anywhere to be seen!

So, tell me, when you are on your very first walking 'date', alone in the bushland with a man who you really did not know that well yet, what do you do?

For convention's sake and to avoid a plainly embarrassing position, you *hold it in*. I mean, I did want to get to know my new friend *better*, but this was way too fast for me! So, I held my 'problem in' for as long as was physically possible and then abruptly, I came to the point where there was no way I could endure my discomfort any further. I simply had to wee!

Espying no other fellow humans on this track, politely, discreetly (and painfully), I tactfully informed my new acquaintance that I really needed to 'attend to nature'. He, of course, was quite the gentleman and gave me distance - but not before asking me did I need any help to which I most profusely answered, "No thank you". He then left me to do what I urgently needed to do.

Alone on a mountain track in the middle of the unknown, that seems an easy task, doesn't it? Well, to the average person, yes. You just get on with the job you have to do and go! You finish your undertaking, pull your pants up and go back to your date! But for me it was not quite as easy as that! You see, years ago I had an operation on my left knee, which meant that when in a certain bent or squatting position, my knee tended to lock up.

As you guess, it locked up!

Now I will paint a completely different picture for your imagination!

I am alone, just off this dirt track, in the bush, squatting awkwardly in a contorted position. My bad leg was stretched out to the side, the other good one was bent somewhat normal and taking my full weight. Of course, in this clumsy position, my knickers and walking pants were down and floating around my knees and my backside was displayed openly pink and very bare. But most happily, my once strained bladder was extremely pleased as it was now empty. Appeased, I commenced the concluding process with one new problem. My left knee had now locked firmly in place. I could not move! Awkwardly Contorted, Bent Over and Stuck! Oh, such a wonderful 'position' for a first date! Don't you think?

And then I hear words most unobtrusively, hesitantly float over from my friend who asked me from his polite distance: *"Are you ok??"*

Was I okay? Not on your life! But what did you think I was going to do?? Ask him to assist me? Ask him for help on our first 'date" ... in that kind of physical position? Would you?

I seriously don't think so!

Yes, I am quite sure that in his profession as a GP Obstetrician he would have previously seen the nether regions of many women in various poses, particularly in child-birth stances. He would not have been at all embarrassed and I guess I could have asked for assistance. But right there in that situation, at that particular moment in time, I really didn't care how many different or unique positions or poses related to OTHER females' anatomy he might have seen! On that day, I was quite determined he was not going to see MY pink 'tush' and nether region in ANY position at all! And most definitely not on this first 'date'. I had my pride, not to mention how that unexpected visual acuity might affect him! He may not want to come back! So, there I was, jammed, the hot sun beating down on me, my pants down to my knees, my bottom pink bare and extremely well revealed, my legs skewed in a distorted position of weight bearing and I had to find a way to extricate myself and return to my friend who was silently waiting for me further up the hill.

Now, I knew that all I had to do was release my knee and return to my original upright stance. From previous experience the only way to remove myself from this situation was to literally roll my body sideways out of that locked position. Easy? Well, you would think so! Before that day I would have said yes! However, given what I had just been doing, with an immense wet patch beneath and beside me, I had to make sure I rolled sideways and UP the hill! Yes, effortless!

You think???

I looked up ahead on the track to where he was standing with his head respectfully facing away from my dilemma. Accompanied by many cries of exasperation, short bursts of loud breath and enormous effort, in a most unladylike fashion, with my knickers most ungraciously colourfully flapping between my legs, I eventually managed to fall over and roll, amazingly sideways and astonishingly UP the hill. This wonderful antic all just to unlock my knee, cover my visibly pink private areas, regain my normal standing position, and most importantly of all, regain my style and grace.

But it worked!

Pulling my undergarments and walking pants up, and as if nothing at all had happened, I brushed the dirt from my hair, fixed my clothes, tucked everything back to where they should be. I then ambled back onto the track and made my way to my new friend. I smiled brightly again like nothing unusual had occurred.

What was my reply when I re-joined him? *"Yes, thank you. I'm Fine".*

What else could I do on our first date?

(*What else could I say really????*).

As evidence and as a 'fond' memory of the day, I still have a photo of me on our first walking date, perched on a rock, dressed in a red T shirt, my face glowing, reflecting the colour of the shirt from the exertion of our 'Wee Walk'. I mean, after all; this was just our first small romantic walking date where we covered a mere *twenty-three (23) kilometres* by foot with only one bottle of water and one small muesli bar to share between us! Easy!!

Strong Coffee and cake, where were you? No - come to think of it - a bottle of red wine and clean fresh toilet amenities would have been a much better reward!

But I was still smiling! And of course, as the saying goes ...
" Good things are coming ... just keep walking ...
... It is Just a Wee Walk!" (Literally for me!)
Of course, that was merely the very beginning!

Chapter Three

A Sting in the Tale

"The rain has eased as sunshine breaks the dawn. Last night's freezing weather has gone, and the only reminders of the heavy rain are the dripping leaves outside our window. The fire has gone out, but the heater is on. I lie in my large bed and watch the sun rise slowly in the sky. I resist the morning light peeking in through the windows as I lay snuggled beneath the warm covers. My eyes gradually close again, luxuriating in the warmth as sleep overcomes me once more.

The aroma of coffee awakens my senses. I leisurely open my eyes. A body encompassed in a white robe stands beside me. No … I am not dreaming that I am in heaven … it is my darling man with that most important cup of welcoming coffee to assist me to greet the new day. Such a wonderful start to the day!

He smiled at me as the aroma arising from the cup melts away the remains of sleep and I positioned myself higher on the pillow. I return his smile and reach for my coffee. Taking that luxurious first sip, breathing slowly, enjoying the serenity, his cheeky face then grins at mine

"Ready for a walk?"

I groan as I forget the coffee, crashed down on the bed, and pulled up the covers over my face.

Another day ... another walk. I can hear you say not another story about walking!! But do stay with me, for the reason that this was slightly different. Because sometimes 'Life has a way of payback', she says with a laugh!

Getting to know Marc a little better, we decided to try a weekend away together. Of course, it meant that I would be enjoying more 'walks' but deemed that was ok. I was slowly getting used to this side of my new relationship. So, after an indulgent sumptuous breakfast of freshly baked bread, jam and butter provided by our host in our weekend retreat, off we set.

The weather seemed perfect, sun shining brightly, not too hot, not too cold. A little different for me this time because I was now beginning to learn what I needed to do, what I needed to wear and what I needed to bring! I actually was feeling quite proud of myself, because on that particular day I felt I was sensibly attired with comfortable clothes, proper shoe apparel on my feet for the walk, nice bright colours so I would not get lost and 'Vicks' on my ankles to stop the leeches. As much as I myself enjoy walking, I am getting smarter in understanding more about what I needed to do when walking with Marc.

To commence our day trip, we talked pleasantly while driving through a beautiful undulating landscape before me. I noted that we were rising, and secretly felt pleased since any rise in altitude in the car was altitude I did not have to climb later on foot! I breathed happily knowing I could handle this! I thought, I am more prepared. I am ready for today. I can handle whatever he presents to me, and I know I am becoming more confident in my older age, in my own ability.

Eventually, the car ride ended with the sun still shining brightly after last night's winter's chills. Even better, Marc was carrying the backpack. So, grabbing my walking poles, off we ventured.

My first comment for the day. "This is a track?"

Maybe it might have once warranted that appellation but what I was seeing in front of me was not anything you could call a track! What I was walking on was lost completely in overgrown vegetation, trees, clinging vines, and brown and red clay underfoot. Let me explain.

To begin the track, we had to climb through two lots of barbed wire fencing and cross 'no man's land' – the one chain of land reserved between the entire length of the border between NSW and QLD. Of course, just like in war zones, 'no man's land' is booby trapped.

We ventured through waist high grass, and lantana, as thousands of farmers friends reached out to grab me and hang on tightly to my clothing penetrating their friendship through what I had thought was appropriate attire for a 'walk'. For those that do not know what a farmers friend is, they are seeds on weeds that can reach over a metre in height and have a burr that sticks on to your clothing, so that if you brush against a plant in seed, you will end up covered in those seeds and have to pick them off one by one. The name "Farmer's Friends" comes from the seeds sticking to you, "wanting to be your friend".

Marc is now walking happily through that waist high, sometimes shoulder high vegetation, clearly convinced he is on the correct 'track'. He stated informatively to me that 'nature is nice in helping us,' because did I know that it had been ten years ago when he last walked in this area with the scouts, and he was quite sure the *track* was still there! Really! Ten years?

In his army pants, boots, and T-shirt he is strolling quite well through the vegetation. But I have to admit that while nature has a way of helping you, it also has a great way of slowing you down. Amidst that waist high vegetation were numerous long arms that came out to slowly grab me and hold me in their not so tender embrace. They clutched on tightly, their long slender tendrils grabbed me, hung onto me, enfolding me securely, not wanting to let me go. Along with the farmers friends, so many times, I became entangled with those finely thorned vines that I now know are called 'wait-o-while'. They just wanted me to stay and *wait with them a while.* With small cries of displeasure, I frequently tried to loosen their hold and forge onwards, but it was not to be. They literally held me fast and I certainly did wait!! Yes, I 'waited a while!'

And from the distance I would hear the words "*You're not here ...*"

"No .... *I'm stuck again*".

And once more, my hero, to the rescue!! (Many times, to the rescue I might add!)

But true to his optimism the trail widened to what I personally considered was a 'track'. Well, my version anyway! Something doable! I

strode out stronger, more confident of this 'nicer' version. Unfortunately, it was not for long as once again I was confined to single file, tramping uphill, on a narrow path, complete with barbed wire fencing on one side. This would be of course, if you tripped and reached out for control, those sharp thorns would then greet you warmly in your flushed tender skin. But I did it. I walked on. And after what seemed an eternity of up-hill trekking, slipping on the red clay underfoot my friend informs me, *"We are almost there".*

Where?

All I saw before me was a large rock shelf which is euphemistically called, 'Bush Rangers Cave'. To me, all I could really see were rocks. Yes, it was deliciously large and cool after the heat of our walk and could be used as a shelter if you got stuck in the rain.

"Shall we go on?"

The usual doubts rushed through me. Do I continue?? Do I listen to that part of me that challenges me to go on? Or do I give into my fear and say, "I have had enough?" Probably the latter but the stubborn and the more confident part of me won and stated mentally, *"Yes, I can do this. I want to prove I am not a wimp. That I am learning about this new life I am embracing, and I can, and I will, do it.".* So determinedly (and rather stupidly I might add) I continued on to climb up and down over rocks past the cave, following Marc to find the next part of the trail to begin to earnestly climb even higher.

But there I was met once more with nothing my own mind could visibly call a track. That rock track I was familiar with, had now disintegrated further to following threads of what I could see to be yellow ribbon tied on tree trunks or ribbon wrapped around vines indicating a path to walkers who dared to enter, that so-called track. Marc is at times before me, climbing nimbly, helping me over hard patches of terrain as I clenched his hand tightly, the other on the walking pole and pulling myself up over the rocks, over the vines, while slipping frequently on the red clay underfoot. My eyes were watching my feet. My teeth were clenched, so rigidly. My breathing was sharp, staggered, and I climbed so, so slowly. The ground before me was full of climbers, roots, tree branches and dirt. Earthy, wet dirt with rocks that slipped underfoot. I really could not believe this was a track?? I was not sure it was even a trail. Oh, did I mention it was straight up? How silly of me! But I pushed on. Stubbornly I was determined to do it. Small single step by steps, 'one foot in front of the other' as the adage goes, and I kept going.

My friend called out cheerfully to me, a voice high up in the skies.

"Found it ... another piece of yellow ribbon ... we're going the right way."

Did he really say Yellow Ribbon? Was he really being guided by a yellow ribbon? This was what was leading us on the 'track'? I knew there was a song from the 1970's about tying yellow ribbons around an old oak tree? *"A simple yellow ribbon is what I need to set me free"*. But I think that was for love! Not sure it meant a track! But what other way could we go, and we dutifully followed those yellow ribbons! I kept going. UP!

And then came those words I so longed to hear: *"Ok - I think that is high enough. We are not going to make it all the way as the weather closing in, I think it is time to turn around. "*

But, if I thought 'up' was hard, down was quite impossible to really describe. I guess you could say that vertically up meant obviously vertically down and I mean vertically down!

"The trees are your friends, trust them," calls my amazingly happy man as he leapt down the trail swinging Tarzan-like from one tree to another, confident that each tree will stop his possible fall on his downward run. I followed behind. But quite a different story!

No, I was not leaping.

No, I was not trusting the trees to stop my fall.

No, I was not embracing the downward slope like a happy skier plunging headfirst into danger.

Instead, I was treading gingerly, watching where to plant my feet all the time as I felt stones slip out from under me. I could see my foot being rolled, my body became unbalanced, and my frame would then plunge in front of my feet!! Probably, not the way it was supposed to be as I traversed those rocks and vines. Struggling with the concept of the descent, I felt it would be easier if I lowered myself down by squatting deeply on one knee then the other or sometimes, just sitting down on my bum to assist my way down, while balancing unsteadily on the edge of this slope. This slope that was supposedly a somewhat marked (with yellow ribbons) walkers' trail. Yes, the 'trees are my friends', and I preferentially was hugging them tightly in a close embrace, not wanting to let go of their comfortable offer of safety. I was getting there, in my own way, slowly! All the time convincing myself - I could do this! My breathing was harsher as once more, those tears of fear entered my eyes. (Very annoying, do you know that wet eyes made it so much harder to see!!).

"Remember, the trees are your friend," once more calls my friend up to me.

Well, they are, until they attack you! Here is where my story changes!

Marc was swinging from tree trunk to tree trunk, descending gracefully and nimbly. He was so agile, so confident being Tarzan, flying beautifully through the air, using the trees as his break, until he embraced a 'Giant Stinging Tree' on his downward plunge.

Now if you don't know about stinging trees, these are trees that grow in rainforests throughout Queensland and northern NSW - where we were. They grow in light-filled gaps in the rainforest understory and come in many different shapes, sizes, and species within Australia. The thick covering of the hairs makes the leaves look as though they are covered with soft, downy, fur and may give the impression they are inviting to touch. But the sting is caused by stinging hairs that contain toxin and these hairs densely cover the leaves or the stems. Of course, if you have never seen one, you would not know what it looked like. I was one of those people who had no idea until this happened and believe me, once I knew what they were, I kept an eye out for them on the rest of the track!

Obviously, Marc is more nature knowledgeable than me.

He knows so much about flora and fauna.

But guess what he clasped?

You guessed right! A Giant Stinging Tree.

In his swing from one tree to another he had trusted the wrong tree to break his fall. Yes, it stopped his descent but at a cost as he cried sharply out in pain.

It stung! It hurt!

A lot!

Did I laugh?

Oh, most definitely! *(Well, wouldn't you?)*

Of course, don't you know that *"Trees are your friends!"*

As I finally descended to meet him, pulling the tree stings out of his hands, Marc hugged me and remarked, *"You know you should regularly do something that scares you. I would hate for you to get bored with me!"*

Bored??? Boy, that is something that could never be said of this oh so new relationship!!

Wrapped in a hot clean towel after a lemon myrtle oil massage later, accompanied by sighs of relaxing muscle aches, we settled back into our warm dry cabin. As I looked at the photos of where we had been and sending them electronically to my other best friend, I once again informed her:

" *Yes, we did it again ... walked on a track that was not really a track, climbing straight up from Numinbah to something called Bush Rangers Cave - will I never learn ???*"

She replied straight back with a smile emoji in her SMS ...

"*Lock the cabin door tight in case he wants to go for another little walk tomorrow*".

And with my hot chocolate in hand, I silently walked backwards to the outside door and quietly turned the lock and hid the key!

'Yes, Life's story does have a way of payback!

Such an innate Sting in this Tale!

At least this time, I can say, with this walk, there was some 'natural' justice for him too!

Chapter Four

Out of My Comfort Zone

Life with Marc had certainly begun!
What we had started, was definitely the commencement of various moments of times, places, and above all, adventures. There was so much in this new life that was different for me. But, do you know, at almost 50 years old, even though hesitant, I wanted to 'have a go'. When I reflect now upon some of the things I attempted, I am not sure that I should have tried a few of them because while some were enjoyable, others were not! I think I was quite mad to even consider them!

Let me explain.

In my many previous years of living in a comfortable conventional world, I had faced and survived trials such as financial emergencies, health crises, family, and friends' events, bringing up kids (that one quite a challenge all in itself), geographical and workplace changes and, of course, my late husband's premature death. Along the way I dealt with it all as I knew how, and each time, opportunely moved on! But in meeting Marc, I was introduced and challenged to new and completely different experiences.

I knew I had met a *different* man. I knew I was now in a world where I would be confronted with new and distinct experiences. No, they were not horrendous or life-threatening experiences but fundamentally in meeting Marc, I was introduced to *taking risks*, something that had not been part of my previous 'conventional' life. You also have to remember that as an almost 50-year-old woman I was not used to taking risks of any serious kind, yet there I was, attempting things that were quite out of my comfort zone! Marc's love of outdoor activities found me facing new physical and mental challenges. I need not have attempted them, and it was my choice to say, "Yes" or "No". Sometimes I hugely questioned my own sanity for even thinking about them let alone trying them! In pushing me out of my pre-defined 'happy world', he definitely propelled me away from my previously predictable suburban life!

It was not all 'new' experiences. We continued to do the conventional 'safe' dating activities of going to the movies, having our coffee dates, … This was an informative time, as we sat, talked, walked, and shared more things about ourselves. With both of us coming from different relationships of many years and other lives with children involved, you can imagine the naivety and inexperience both of us felt being with someone new!

To 'get to know each other even more' my 'new- found friend' planned a special trip away, this time for a week in Tasmania.

As a learning curve in that early part of our developing relationship, with an attempt of blending the old with the new, we spent a few days exploring this southern-most part of Australia; of talking, walking, dining, enjoying each other's company. It culminated with our final few days being together at Cradle Mountain.

For background information, Cradle Mountain forms the northern end of the wild Cradle Mountain, Lake St Clair National Park, itself a part of the Tasmanian Wilderness World Heritage Area. The jagged contours of Cradle Mountain epitomise the feel of an untamed landscape, while archaic rainforest, alpine heathlands and colourful deciduous beech trees provided a range of environments for us to explore. According to the tourist web guide, we should see icy streams cascade out of rugged mountains, and ancient pines mirrored in the still waters of glacial lakes. Doesn't it sound beautiful?

In the travel brochure and photographs of this particular area, it certainly did! Tasmania itself and parts of what we had seen briefly that week, were intriguing both naturally and historically, but after a wonderful time of relatively easy walks and exploring, what I experienced on my last day of this week away, was 'slightly' different to what the tourist poster presented.

Our 'walk' took us on part of the Overland Track which is Australia's premier alpine walk. In its entirety, it is actually a sixty-five kilometre, six-day trek through the heart of the Cradle. No, oh no, we did not do the 65-kilometre walk, we were only out for the day, it was a 'simple *day walk*'. Now - do remember those words!

Our day started out like any other hiking day with Marc, and I came prepared including correct attire this time! Remember I was still learning! I was also now carrying my own backpack with my own food and water not relying on Marc's idea of adequate provisions. The sun was bright and glistening as we left our warm cabin. The sky was blue. Our smiles were on our faces and off we walked. This was the last day of our 'learning' holiday and we wanted to enjoy every last minute together that we could.

Leaving the safety of the tourist area, we saw a wooden boardwalk that stretched out as far as the eye could see. That boardwalk led us pleasantly, and importantly, safely, and dryly, across water-filled trenches and green marshes at the foot of the mountain. We were both journeying forward and onward! I smiled. We looked at each other. Enjoying the sunshine, the aimless chatter, the scenery, and breathing in of the friendship walked. Together.

The tourism brochure suggested that this walk was only *one walk, but it has a million moods*. Well, I can certainly attest to that! Our boardwalk came to an end. The path deteriorated to a dirt track interspersed with rocky climbs. I climbed, he talked. I was starting to breathe more heavily, heavily enough to not waste air on words, but I was still smiling! Not a bad adventure for 'getting to know my new friend'! I could certainly think of worse things to do! It was doable, it was pleasant. We were still even holding hands when they were not being used to pull ourselves up the rocks!

But the day turned colder, and the sun-drenched blue sky disappeared and turned grey. A grey mist slowly moved in and enveloped us. I continued to follow behind my friend. His footsteps were still quite steady while mine were now starting to slip and flounder on the track. The smooth safe boardwalk we were previously walked on had been left long ago and was replaced by uneven rocks and dirt turning to mud. But our expedition upwards continued. I was proudly still progressing quite well and satisfactorily I thought!

But it became unpleasantly cold, and the track became wetter. Somehow my God of Nature had decided to thicken the mist allowing it to soak its way into my hair which now unattractively lay flat and wet across my back. Silly me, because, for this, our last day together, I had made a genuine effort to attempt a radiant, coiffured look for my long hair (which I was very proud of) but was now dismally resembling a drowned cat draped down my back. I thought I was supposed to look 'nice' on this day, for those final photographs captured together, not bedraggled, and sweaty! Apparently, that was not to be the case! My jacket was now zipped high to my neck as I walked through the wet fog, climbed up rock faces, boulder after boulder, torturously asking my knees to lift my body up 'once more time' on this Cradle Mountain *Day-walk*.

It became colder.

It became mistier.

It became murkier.

It became extremely hard to see in front of you.

My mood grew deeper. I experienced a few of this mountain's 'million moods.' Not sure which ones they had been describing, but I knew which ones I was feeling. I am generally a happy person but have realised when I am tired, stressed, or hungry, while trying to elicit my, "I-am-okay-face" to the world, my internal mood slips! But, as always, I was surprised by the fact that Marc's mood had not changed and he was still the same bubbling, ebullient man I had started out with that morning. It had not been altered by the loss of the sun, the loss of its warmth, the loss of its 'mood-uplifting effect'. To his credit, he just continued to smile and talk while he climbed up and over the boulders. Sometimes stopping and coming back to assist me when I became stuck with one foot up, one foot down and unable to move forward! To my credit I was still progressing upwards! I was still moving forward!

Hot body sweat was now mixing with the icy fog dampness, oh, such a great combination! But what do I do? I knew it was hard work, but I had chosen to be there, doing that activity, so did I complain? Should I have complained? Should I have said "I would like to stop now"? Yes! But did I? Instead, this silly woman kept moving, determined to keep going, as she wrapped herself more warmly in my '*I thought they were correct but now I know they are not quite the right* walking clothes. Knowing they will have to do!

Yes, I kept moving! But I was NOT smiling now.

I stopped holding his hand.

Cradle Mountain huh!

It was such a great name I might add because the mountain was definitely cradling me, as we now ventured into a rainforest! The dirt tracks up that so-called cradle mountain had changed to muddy, slippery tracks and had adopted a zig-zagged vertical feature. On these tracks, my feet were slipping, my hands were grasping onto whatever vestiges of safety overhanging branches offered. My breath was heaving as I wound my way more vertically up that most majestic mountain scape! And oh, they were such long 'steps' up in between widely spaced footholds. I realized that my 'Stepping Up' gym classes were nothing compared to what I was doing now. I was so glad I did not wear G- string underwear, or even tight undies as right at that moment, I would have been quite badly highly strung in all the wrong places that had absolutely nothing to do with a G! With all that 'stepping up', by rights my underwear should have been working its way north to strangle me!

Truth be known, with Marc, what else should I have expected! I definitely had not imagined this type of vertical climb on a *day walk*.

Of course, it was a beautiful landscape, enriched in its natural grandeur. Cradle Mountain had its splendour and majesty but at that moment I thought 'who cares'!! Who cares what it looks like! Who cared about the beauty, the rainforest, the colourful beech? Right then, my positivity was lessening with each step as I was too busy trying to climb up the wretched thing! I just wanted it to end. And then that male voice floated to me in a fog of moisture …

"*Going ok?*", he asked.

I looked up, smiling into the blurred world above.

"*Of course, I am*", through brilliantly clenched teeth was my reply, as I grabbed his arm to get my foot finally out from the rock it was wedged in and as I moved my twisted contorted middle-aged body from one rutted place to the next. What else could I do? I was not going to complain.

"*Yes, (pant, pant, pant pant,) I am fine!*"

But I made it! I did it!

Arriving breathless at the top, we stopped to admire the view and pause for breath as the sweat ran down my face. The sun was actually shining as we emerged from the mist and fog. A good omen! Yes, it certainly was a mountain of a million moods because in case you think I am whining and complaining too much, the views were quite exhilarating. It was worth the climb, even though it was hard going at times. Taking in my effort, the beauty, the peace, the landscape, and the fact that I was now extremely proud of myself, that I was 'not that old 'and had actually climbed all that way UP, I sat and relaxed and breathed in the glorious views as radiant sunlight warmed my damp cold back.

It was peaceful.

It was calm.

My irregular breathing slowed to a calm steady beat breathing in the world around me. Together, enjoying the peaceful reticent environment. I looked at Marc smiling at me and then I heard his words …

"Shall we go on? There is a much higher point we can climb to?"

Are you kidding me?

Then as I look upwards, I knew I was rescued by God because the weather had quickly started to close in again. The sun was rapidly disappearing from view and fog was covering the mountain top once more. Scrutinizing the grey clouds sliding into place, instead of more 'up', my new friend surveyed the skies and made the decision to go down. No complaining from this woman about that! OH, thank you, thank you, thank you God! Happily, I descended!

Now, on our downward descent there was a choice to make.

Reaching a point on the wet mountainous landscape, my handsome friend informed me, we could either meander our way across the face of the mountain, which was a longer, but safer route given the souring weather, or instead, we could take the shorter path which was much rougher but definitely quicker to get off the mountain. Oh, wasn't that sweet. Oh, I did like this man. Such a gentleman. He actually wanted my input into what would I like to do.

Of course, I had to think about it!

I had to make the decision between continue snaking around and around and around being 'cradled' by the beautiful beech and icy streams jutting out and snatching at me and my already cold wet clothes as we hiked until we, eventually, a few hours later get off the mountain? Or take the quickest, shortest route down the mountain, much less time in the cold and the wet, and get to the *warm dry* cabin early. Tell me, in my position, which one would you choose?? Did he even have to ask?

"I will take the shorter route down thanks!"

And down we went. Onwards to that cosy, warm cabin with its hot shower beckoning and warm dry clothes to drape around me!

Did I mention it was down?

Did I mention it was straight down?

Did I mention it was more like sheer vertically down???

So many times, I slipped and slid down on my rear end, bumping precariously over rocks with my bruised derriere becoming blacker and bluer, as I made my way 'down'. I should have been used to this by now with experience from previous walks, but this was quite different. Hand holds only when I could find them. Foot holds only when I could find them. When I could find neither more slipping, more sliding, more jolts, and bounces. Meanwhile, my friend is literally bouncing all the way down ahead of me – very much imitating Tigger from Winnie-the-Pooh. He is happy. He is safe. He is so used to this!!!! But like the ad on television …*'But wait there's more!'*

Silver chains gleaming with moisture from the mist appeared ahead of me.

No, I was not hallucinating. The park rangers had attached chains to posts bolted to the granite rock on the edge of this mountain cliff face. I assumed the rangers thought the appearance of bolts would reassure the walkers that all was okay. You could feel safe. Now, did I see that? While my logical brain was saying, this was acceptable and I could do this, my sceptical brain intent on survival was internally speaking to my body saying, *"Really? Come on! How securely can those posts and those chains really be? How could they have drilled a reasonable hole in the rock this far up the mountain and how rusted were the bolts be by now?"*

I was desperately trying to just keep a sensible head about me as I traversed cautiously this 'charming' 'beautiful' 'picturesque' mountain scape. Fear makes me cry. I was trying so hard to keep my fear contained, to stop the tears that had brimmed in my eyes from dripping down my face because I really needed to see where I was going. Believe me, as I made my way down, my creative brain was working overtime, viewing visions of my body rolling like a bowling ball, tumbling, plunging down that mountain in one great round human avalanche style to hit the valley below. Silly thoughts I know, but that is what I do. Eventually I lost my internal battle, and the tears of fear torrentially fell down my face as my breathing became more ragged. Feeling very much alone in the world, standing on the edge of that mountain gorge, and holding on for dear life those steel shackles that were supposed to secure and support me on my way down! Who was I trying to kid?

I clenched even tighter that metal chain as my body leaned outwards over the cliff. My head informing logically, *"Come on let's go, get off this mountain,"* with my feet gripped resolutely to the uneven terrain. I was praying so hard that I would not slip and that their solidity could hold my weight. One more step ... come on, I could do it ... come on, foot move ... that's it ... we can do it ... we can do it ... no, no, no, no I COULD NOT! My arms wrapped firmly around the icy steel chains. My fingers tightly interlaced into their linked strength. But after one more slip downwards on this un-inspiring Luner like landscape, I literally froze! I could not physically move anything at all. I was STUCK! Not from the cold but from Icy Gripping Fear!

My mobile phone rang.

So now, I thought I was hearing things! The shrill tones kept echoing throughout the valley below me! Who, on earth, would be ringing me in the middle of this jagged landscape with my two feet frozen on the edge of this cliff, holding on for dear life? Who would be ringing me here in this place at the end of the world?? Do you think I could answer it?

Slowly, I disengaged one hand holding tightly to that steel lifeline tethering me onto the edge of the mountain and spoke into the mouthpiece. (Do you know how *long* I actually took to answer it?)

'Hello?'

'Hello', says the familiar cheerful voice of my best friend. *"It's Friday and we usually chat at lunch, so where are you, what are you doing?"*

I looked around, I looked down and answered slowly. *"Oh, nothing much. I am just standing here in Tasmania on a track, holding onto a chain that is on the edge of a jagged mountain as I am looking over the side into a deep cliff trying to make my way down. I am quite frightened of falling and … and my feet won't move – they have stuck. That's all".*

"PLEASE COME AND GET ME- A HELICOPTER WILL DO!!!"

Silence from the other end. Abundant laughter erupted!

"Okay, I will call one now! He has done it again hasn't he!!

And I lost mobile connection!

Standing there with my feet wedged precariously, the disconnected phone in one hand, the other hand tightly strangling the life out of that steel chain, I then heard a gentle male voice call back up to me, from the safer depths of far below, *"Is everything ok?* Do *you need a hand"*? *Do you want me to come back up and help?*

Did I need a hand? Did he really ask me, 'did I need a hand?' I think I needed about ten hands or a parachute and don't forget to call the ambulance for a much bigger hand at the end of the journey!

* * *

Do you know as we get older in life, we see advertisements that encourage us to continue to 'engage in life' 'to enjoy social interactions;' 'to manage stress' and to 'feel good and make statements about those choices' we make! Well, I can say that on that trip with my new friend, I did all that! Let me see. Being outdoors in a physical activity- I was clearly' *engaging in life* 'when I had to get down a mountain, but my feet would not move! I was *'engaging in social interaction'* when my phone rang in the middle of that wilderness and definitely *'managing stress'* by clearly saying what I thought aloud to my best friend. I definitely had *control over my choices* because all I wanted to do was leave the mountain that was cradling me intensely! That was unquestionably my choice and I felt soooo good about that choice!! But what did I answer to my male friend? *"No thank you. I'm fine".* Stubborn aren't I! No one to blame for my foolishness but myself!

Eventually, we did get off the mountain.

Once my head and the logical side of me finally realised that my feet could actually move and they were not stuck or frozen forever locked in solid stone on that granite rock, we made it to the bottom of the ravine. I have to admit, it was more from sheer determination on my part as I willed my feet to move and my hands to breathe life into the silver chain again to hold me tight and firm! But I did it! We stepped off that mountain smiling at the fact I was safe and sound on the *flat* ground again. What was even harder to take, waiting for me at the bottom of the track, was a red and yellow sign, complete with large black arrow pointing upwards.

Do you know what it said?
"Caution! Track steep and rough"
Really??
I would never have guessed!

And Suddenly you know.
It's time to start something new.
And trust the start of new beginnings.

Meister Eckhart

Life moves on ...
so should we.

Chapter Five

Flights of Fancy

Life begins at the end of your comfort zone.
Well from one comfort zone to another!

I truly understood I had now left the comfort of what I previously knew my life to be and had absolutely ventured into something completely new. I was not sure where that was going exactly but there is a saying that *"we are the very doors through which we enter and where we walk is who we want to become."* So, where was I going? Which door was going to open? What was I going to find out? Who knew, but I had moved there willingly and that was okay by me!

You have probably gathered by now that our first coffee date moved us from that initial mountain trail path of twenty-three kilometres to walking down the path of marriage!

We found we were suited to each other and the fact that we liked each other as well as being in love - well that was a definite positive. Most of our compatibility was in both of us discovering and attempting a variety of experiences that time gave us, or I should say more correctly, gave me, from that very first day I had met Marc! But do remember, it was not one sided and a learning curve just for me but for both of us! In romantic terms, at the ripe old age of 48 and 50 we both, together, changed the 'known' willingly to the 'unknown'.

It wasn't all challenging adventures. Some of it was much more leisurely and pleasurable! Some ventures that I had never encountered before, were even simple pleasures of luxury where I felt like such a young girl.

The wedding day over, (which was a wonderful happy day I might add … organisation being so different from both our first marriages as we were so much older and did what **WE** wanted to do!) Excitement plus fluttered in my stomach as the honeymoon travelling day loomed and I stepped happily out of our friend's car who had taken us to the airport at some ridiculous hour. Waving goodbye, I entered the departure terminal, walking closely beside my new husband. We were heading to a wonderful, exciting, romantic destination. The place for lovers … even ones as old as us! That alone was so exhilarating!

There I was, excitedly walking to the check-in counter at the airport only to see the long lines of fellow passengers immediately ahead. People with heads down, playing with phones, reading, moving slowly as they shuffled down the long line waiting for their turn! A little despondent, I thought of the precious time wasted at airports by initially enthusiastic travellers who, as they shuffled through the 'airport process', turned into tired, negative disparaging people just wanting to board their plane.

Well, you know how it goes.

You line up like cows and sheep, moving slowly through the parallel rows of anonymous people, sliding your bag, or numerous bags, in front of you, as you appeared to be eternally locked in between those metal bars and dividing tapes, creeping backwards and forwards. The whole process I believe is actually designed to keep everyone feeling like they were moving forward even though in reality; you are really not going very far at all. Yes, you could be lucky and use the electronic or online version check-in, but ultimately you still have to line up to deposit your bag! In particular, when you are heading on an international flight!

As you move slowly you see that same smiling anonymous person again. That unknown person you were looking at before – but - now they are in front facing and looking at you. Have they moved quicker? No, not really, they are only one lane over from you! It is just the way the sheep-yard had you progressing! I must admit that every time I have been in this situation it has reminded me of the drenching sheep or cattle as they are corralled into ever decreasing spaces until 'crushed' and wormed. At airports, we are herded in the same fashion! When you think about it, all we need is someone to start mooing or baaing. Now I wonder if I ever started mooing or baaing, how many others would join in feeling similarly dehumanised? Can you imagine the uproar (and smiles)!

After surviving the 'crush', there is that further nerve-endurance 'sport' of luggage weighing. Of course, you stand there and perilously tremble inside that the luggage weight will not be *over*, knowing that if so, you will have to open your bag in front of all those passengers who are still waiting in the continuous lines behind you. You can feel their eyes boring into your back because *your* overweight bag, with all its intimate contents is now open for all to see, knowing, it was you who had caused the line to stall *again*! The thought of removing or transferring heavy objects from one bag to another, while thinking all the time where I put those dirty knickers, or items that you really don't want others to see, is just not worth considering! What a horrible thought!

But then, eventually, you finally escape with wondrous release from those metal bars and tapelines come prison aisles, feeling like you could soar through the airport sky. You are set free as you rid yourself of those heavy suitcases that weighted your arms and your mood down! Now armed with that all-important talisman, your boarding pass, in hand you start the next challenge of the pentathlon that is 'the airport process', walking quickly to security, eager to approach your departure gate.

Ah Security! That magic word of security reaches out for you in your enthusiastic promenade to STOP! Since 911 in USA, security in most western countries has tightened up so much.

Once more those parallel lines! Yes - there those analogous 'cattle yards' for us to shuffle through and wait our turn to be inspected! Your once fast-excited pace implying you were actually getting somewhere, slows to a sluggish, languorous pace as yet again those metal and tape lanes entrap and funnel you towards those anonymous security guards with their latex gloves – enough to make anyone's anal sphincter clench tight in precautionary primal reaction. Baby steps slowing even more as cabin bags are opened, liquids placed into trays, cameras, iPad, belts, laptops, keys, phones, hand luggage scanned and searched ... all in the name of 'security'.

As a passenger, timidly, you approach the guards, watching their eyes, afraid to smile, wondering if the correct amount of liquid is in your bag, pondering if you look like their profile of a terrorist. You walk through, not breathing, afraid of that buzzer to sound that 'this person carries something illegal'. Exhaling slowly, you gather your personal belongings - now scrutinised and deemed officially benign. Free! But just like when you were at school and a teacher pulled you up in the hallway but then told you to just move and hurry on to class, another disciplinarian pulls you up, stops and asks you to open your bag again and then gets a bit personal as he strokes various parts of your anatomy and clothing with a stick with a piece of paper attached to it ... hmmm ... looking for explosives they say ...

Now that point of the airport trip is always a sore (now funny) point with me. No matter how many times I have flown, I am the one who is taken aside to be searched! I am the one who has had to stretch out her arms, spread her legs, even being taken to a private booth for privacy to be 'searched' and 'scanned', 'frisked, 'or whatever you want to call it for items that should not travel with you on the plane! I must have something on my face that says - *"Here I am pick me -, Pick me, Pick me, I'll simply spread my body ... now frisk!!* It always happens to me! But with security finished and the Customs in the 'airport process behind you', you then rush to your departure lounge gate not wanting to be left behind.

At the departure lounge, if you are lucky, you sit. Breathing quietly, you adjust to the final challenge of the 'airport process', enduring further waiting in the terminal. You attentively listen to that loudspeaker blaring in a language you can hardly understand, even though it is supposed to be English! Sipping that overpriced tasteless coffee from that brown paper-cup, flipping pages on that magazine, reading that boring book, 'enjoying so impressively' the bedlam of noise and scurrying people that defines this realm, you are all the time watching the clock as the hands tick so slowly because you were 'told to be here for X amount hours prior' to the much-awaited time of boarding.

Finally, through your stuporous brain you hear a trumpet from heaven ... your plane is ready to board, it has been refuelled, the food is ready, and the crew and pilots are on board with their practiced smiles of welcome and bravery.

Up the stairs or perhaps zig zag through the ramp into the plane you climb. You escape your departure lounge gate with the noise of many others surrounding you, but as you are now actually in the plane, you decide you can tolerate more additional waiting for all passengers to arrive and board and place their luggage in the overhead locker. Of course, there is that person in front of you who is trying so hard to do exactly that, even though the bag is really too big and will not fit properly and hits you hard on the head as it falls down. You smile politely, rubbing your bruised head as they offered profuse apologies and then scramble into the seat beside you, initially fighting you for the arm rest. All the while, the air steward is asking everyone to hurry and take their seats. Eventually you are smiling, not in politeness or feigned happiness but brilliantly as you buckle up and fly out to your destination, quite a number of hours after you initially stepped out of your house. Yes, that is the normal drill of aeroplane travelling! Yes, we all know it well!

So, you can imagine what a lovely surprise I had on my honeymoon ...

After our friend had dropped us off, I followed my normal practice and began to take the usual route to the check-in counter, ready to stand behind in those lines of people already amassed in front of me. I didn't care really. I was going on my honeymoon! No longer slim as a young thin girl waiting for her dreams of life to begin, but as a middle-aged, curvaceous woman continuing with life but in quite a different direction from before. It was all new and it was exciting and a pleasure to be there behind all those people ahead of me! I honestly didn't mind!

However, my new husband reached for my hand and directed me to another line.

This line did not have a collection of people ahead. This route was basically empty with only one or two people chatting and smiling with each other in front and now grinning happily at me as I made my way to the end of what could hardly be called a line. I smiled back hesitantly with an inquiring look on my face to my new husband who simply laughed and shrugged his shoulders in a loving gesture. I followed his cue walking attentively beside him along this almost empty line, but not at all sure what I should be doing! I looked at the sign in front of me – 'priority passengers.' Priority? This was me? Obviously, it was!

Walking up to the checkout counter I glanced sideways with an excited smile at the lines of metal poles and tapes holding their massed intertwining prey captive. However not one smile was returned. Really? How rude! I could not understand why! I mean after all, I was only being polite and friendly, excited by my new adventure clearly showing on my face. But instead, glaring, venomous eyes from the adjacent line manifested their feelings towards my *priority* line as those passengers contemplated their own endurance trek ahead. But I kept smiling because do you know what, right then I could forget the long waits in unending lines. I simply held my head up high as their toxic eyes attacked and their jabs and darts of envy bounced off. I was this person given access to special check-in areas and priority boarding. I felt special because today I could forget those long waits in unending lines. It was at that moment, I realised this was something I had not ever experienced before, because for the first time ever, I have been given a business-class ticket for my international flight! A new adventure. Definitely, one I was really starting to like!

Checking in for our flight was actually delightful.

A lovely smiling attendant behind the counter, examined our tickets, even addressed us both formally by using our actual surnames, weighed our bags, (they met the required weight, and I realised then I could have taken SO much more!) Even better, there were no other people in front of us as we headed to security armed with a 'priority' pass to access the shortcut avenue designed for 'significant' people like me! Indeed, as snobbish as it may sound, I felt like royalty!

I must add here however, that I was still frisked, but that was okay. The guard who performed this service was exquisite and not to mention extremely good looking. I admit I kept looking at him the whole time, holding my arms up and out, spreading my legs, turning sideways, forwards. He had beautiful eyes, beautiful brown curly hair, and gorgeous body in that security uniform. Please excuse me, so overcome with the excitement of everything, I had forgotten I was recently married, and this was my honeymoon. Smiling fetchingly at him and drinking in that one last gulp of his uniformed security manliness, I found my husband and made my way down the steps to the departure area. I was free of those lines, so quickly after commencing!

Now this new bride took her husband's hand and walked across the floor of the main terminal area. It had been so many hours since we had consumed a coffee and eyeing a café, I suggested we buy something to drink and eat in order to assist the long waiting time ahead before our flight left. I thought I was being practical, but my husband uttered just one word to me.

"*Buy?*"

He then walked away! I watched his departing persona exiting my side. As you can imagine, I rushed after him not sure what I had stated and confused as to why I had seemingly upset him with this question? I mean I was just hungry! Wasn't he? So, I followed his retreating figure a few steps behind thinking of what I had said as we crossed the floor amidst the throngs of other travellers with their scintillating smell of coffee, muffins and screaming children.

He then led me upstairs to a faraway secluded area.

Two beautiful attendants like guardians of the gates of heaven greeted me at the entrance of a closed door leading to an unidentified world. They glanced briefly at the tickets presented, waved their arms graciously and opened the exquisite door. I ventured inside. There I was greeted by a magnificent combination of aromas and scents, of sweet smells, of delicacies, of finger food, of brewed coffee, tea, of hot and cold meals, of various categories of alcohol! Oh my!

Roaming my eyes around the huge room I saw a stylish food service area, lounge areas with computer terminals, free wireless connection, comfortable seating and relaxation areas, secluded areas for two, shower facilities, concierge services and exclusive meal offerings ranging from buffets to a- la- carte dining catering to everyone's tastes. Uniformed attendants served food on elegant plates and there was not one cash register to be seen! Here, in this never-before-realized world by the likes of me, I was encompassed in a luxurious sanctuary away from the general, 'hoi polloi' far below me, visible through a closed curtain but only if I wished to look. I am not a snob at all, I am unquestionably a commoner in my normal world of reality, but in those surroundings, at that particular moment I was not one of them. I had been transported to airport heaven! No wonder my husband had laughed at me when I suggested 'buying' a coffee from the terminal café. No wonder he had walked away!

Then there was the plane itself.

Now we have all been in economy class … or cattle class in Australian slang. Remember that feeling of having to walk through, past business class seats and seeing those bigger seats with their bubbling champagne flutes, as you kept trudging your way to the back of the plane mouth feeling parched? Remember those long-haul flights of hours of seats all squashed together, no leg room, compacted bodies side by side, meals served on plastic plates complete with plastic knives and forks where you have to take it in turns with your neighbours to use your utensils? Remember trying to sleep without letting your head fall onto the passenger's shoulder beside you? That embarrassed scene where your head nods slowly, your neck relaxes and you roll sideways to that comfortable shoulder beside you, only to wake unexpectedly and hugely mortified as you felt saliva dribbling down your cheek onto the accommodating stranger's shoulder! Reciprocated as you fight to keep your space away from your other fellow passenger drooling and nodding beside you!

There in my business class seat, I had so much extra space. I did not have to worry about the passenger in front of me reclining. I too could lean as far back as I wished, in fact there was so much room that my husband and I could have danced together in front of our allocated places! I did not feel crowded in by the person sitting next to me, I could instead pack away my belongings in convenient-to-access concealed storage compartments, stretch out my legs as far as I could and enjoy this newfound travelling space. There were footrests and knee rests in various positions and within the chair itself were hydraulic controlled lumber rolls and massage devices to suit your body shape and comfort. Award-winning menus crafted by famous chefs, an on-board cafe service and boutique wine lists were given to me, followed by perfectly prepared food, fresh bread rolls and steel utensils and to complete the scene, warm towels to wipe away the remnants of uneaten food. To finish the picture, the chair of course turned into a bed for sleeping, complete with sensory lights privacy. I must say that a spacious seat that reclined into a lie-flat bed is an incredible way to glide through the sky for thirteen plus hours. This had never happened to me before. I had to pinch myself as it was such a dream! I was sure I was going to wake up soon. With the excitement of flying in business class, it was impossible to get myself to shut my eyes and rest. It was too exciting, but of course, I did!

Flying business class to me was a whole new world. A world of lounges, leg room, proper champagne, celebrity chef-prepared meals and sleep – actual, full body reclined sleep! That particular day I had walked up that initial flight of stairs into a travelling class so unlike anything I had ever experienced before and had emerged into a different world, one of which I had no previous knowledge. At the age of forty-nine years, I was like a little girl experiencing a fleet of birthday wishes all rolled into one collection of brand-new surprises. It was definitely a new adventure, and it truly was such a simple thing that gave me immense pleasure.

For an average middle-class girl like me it was such a sumptuous extravagant delight. All I kept thinking was, "If my children could see me now!'

Every girl should have at least one time when she feels like a princess. This was mine.

What a way to start my new life!

This was not a challenge at all! This was an adventure!

I did like this adventure.

Very Much.

Chapter Six

Tour De France

"I take you to be my best friend. I will forever be there to laugh with you and to love you unconditionally through all our adventures of life together"

Who would have imagined me, no longer a widow anymore but wedded again!! It just did not seem real, but yet it was! Even more unbelievable, at my ripe old age, I was actually on my 'honeymoon'!

Honeymoons are wonderful inventions … so romantic, so peaceful, so tranquil, and extremely loving. It is another way to get to know more about my new partner in a slow and relaxing manner. So, at this point of my story, I have to ask you what is your understanding of a honeymoon?

Do you perceive it as the traditional holiday taken by newlyweds to celebrate their marriage in intimacy and seclusion? A chance for a couple after planning their wedding, to get away from stress, from work, from family and friends. Is it that special period for just the two of you to relax and spend some idealistic quality (and intimate) time together in a very special amorous location, often celebrated in destinations considered exotic or romantic? Obviously, that was what I had considered as my own definition of a honeymoon.

My heart was quite excited by the prospect of a romantic holiday abroad with my new husband. With both of us embarking on our second marriages, it was exhilarating (and nervous too,) but a wonderful way to consolidate what we had begun by just the two of us, alone, away from reality, in another destination. In our case - Paris! But somehow, somewhere along the ride, my interpretation of a honeymoon became distorted or mismatched by the reality version given to me by my new husband. Marc's view of a romantic honeymoon was to navigate me around streets and ultimately race me up and down and all over the stairs and steps of Paris!

I am not complaining about the destination.

Oh, no there was nothing wrong with Paris! It is the city of love and such a wonderful place for a honeymoon. I was thrilled to be there! I loved Paris! I mean I *really* loved Paris. I loved the buildings, the city skylines, the grey colour mixed with green, the gold and sandstone colour, and most definitely, I loved the huge metal iron lattice tower monstrosity that dominated the city skyscape, to symbolise the global cultural icon of France! It was an amazing piece of art! I literally fell in love with the Eiffel Tower the first time I saw its metallic face beckoning me. No matter how many times I saw it on our holiday or see it now so many years later … the words exclaim from my mouth, …"*I love the Eiffel Tower - I love Paris!*"

Moving on, here is my first question for you: Do you know how far you walk each day? I do not mean as in exercising … but in general walking! Without a Fitbit or an Apple watch, do you really know how many steps you walk each day?

Did you know that the average person takes between three thousand to ten thousand steps a day? That is such a vast number of steps we take without even thinking about it. I guess it also depends on the kind of occupation you do each day. Personally, I know that my husband in his medical work does more 'sliding' up the office hallway' in his socks than walking, whereas I am up and down walking those same hallways. (*Yes, to answer your question, he wears out so many of his socks*)

Here is my second question: Do you know how many steps up there are in Paris?

The definition of a step is to put one leg in front of the other in order to walk somewhere or to move to a new position, whereas a stair is seen as a 'set of steps' leading from one floor of a building to another." So, as you put both words and definitions together, I will ask you again. "Do you know how many steps there were in Paris?"

Now for my third question. What is your version of a holiday?

If you have gone overseas, you definitely want to see as much as you can. You do not sit around in your overseas hotel and watch television. Instead, you prefer to enjoy soaking in the new sights and culture, breathing in the difference, the newness to you. But somewhere in there is the actual word *'holiday'* - which to most is also a time for rest, for a break, and in my case - 'my *honey-moon*' ... a time for recreation, rest, and love. Naturally, I imagined in our walking around Paris, we would have a 'restful 'time of passion and romance. I was quite Wrong! Because do you know how far we walked and how many steps as honeymooners we actually did? Do you know how many stairs we climbed?

As you follow in the footsteps of famous people such as Hemingway, Oscar Wilde, Victor Hugo, and Picasso you walk past homes, cafes, studios, parks, places associated with historical events and traditions. Believe me, you can walk so much in Paris. There is always something new to discover. For example, there are the white cobblestone streets of Montmartre where the famous building and windmill of Moulin Rouge resides. There are the bustling street markets with their wide expanses of thoroughfare mixed with numerous lanes and alley ways to find petite and some not so petite coffee shops. With every step, you can slip into the discovery of new worlds and atmospheres as you enter into the mysterious, seductive, hidden, romantic courtyards that Paris preserves so carefully. There are so many stairs that go up and up and up into the heavens and of course have to descended again! There are stairs that are old and huge in size. There are stairs so small that you do not know where at all to place your feet!! I would imagine there would be many a slippery story to tell about these!

Let me begin.

Our hotel room was small and petite - the flavour of Paris - and outside you could see the tower summoning you to its glory. So of course, on our arrival, flinging open our windows breathless from hauling our bags up the spiral hotel stairs (no elevator in this old hotel), we both drank in the vision of Paris with its huge metal icon dominating its skyline We could only see the top of it, but it was huge. We of course did not stay there looking at it from afar for long but rushed outside to step closer to this amazing sculpture. I was so excited to be in the city of love! So happy to be with my new husband in this romantic place of adventure - two 'old' honeymooners stepping out!

However, to start with, our room in the hotel was three flights up and you guessed it - all stairs. Those stairs wound around and around, carpeted in a funny green colouring. Perhaps originally designed to give you a peaceful feel as you entered the province of your room? Who knows? The effect on us was more to augment the nauseating vertiginous effect of our circular saunter - weaving, weaving, actually slowing to a crawl at times on all four limbs, before arriving at our room. This was even before adding the complicating factor of imbibing possibly a little too much French wine as may also occur on one's honeymoon.

Our stairs down from our hotel on that first day of our honeymoon took us to the Palais de Chaillot. This was also named Palais du Trocadero – (funny- this was the name of our hotel … probably because we were just around the corner!) A bit of trivia will tell you that it was once a large concert hall with two wings and two towers! However, history aside, personally standing on the frontage of Palais de Chaillot you were greeted with an absolutely magnificent view of the Eiffel tower. It really took my breath away! I took so many photos at contrasting times of day of this particular skyscape façade! It was at that moment, I discovered what was the awakening or 'enlightening' of what I was to endure over the next four days.

Even the Palais de Chaillot had stairs!

These stairs down' led you into the foot of the terrace which held ten-hectare large gardens known as the Trocadero gardens. They were laid out around a large rectangular pond. Of course, going down the stairs and into the gardens to make your way to the city and to the Eiffel Tower itself is relatively easy when it is the beginning of the day. However, coming back the same route when your legs are tiring, your body is groaning from the exercise you did all day, your breath is wheezing and your desire for that luxurious bed to throw yourself upon, particularly when you are a little unsteady on your feet after indulging in a bottle or two of red wine (but that is another private story, maybe I will tell you about later), was, I had to admit, completely different!

We visited the Notre Dame Cathedral.

I am so glad that we did, with it being destroyed in present day, but what we saw was an exhibition complete with mental images of Esmeralda and Quasimodo in the bell tower (yes, we went 'up 'to the bell tower as well). This is where you met and contemplated for the first time those numerous ugly but intriguing gargoyles. But do you know this structure has three hundred and eighty-seven stairs right to the top of the South Tower? Even more stimulating, (and as I found out …), it is all stepped in an anticlockwise direction. A sign at the beginning of the stairwell was displayed as you entered the cathedral depicting the words "*It is best to be in good shape".* Was I in good shape?? Of course, I was, I thought as I took off at a good pace! I can show my new husband what I could do. After all, prior to the honeymoon, I did those 'step classes' and I would do myself proud. So off I went, following right behind him. I could do this!

We climbed.

Up.

We climbed some more.

Oh, did I tell you they were spiral stairs?

Up, up, more up, now leaning forward, carefully watching the narrow stairs further narrow and tighten their circular motion as I ascended. I continued higher, around, and around, and around! Finally, breathing heavy, we were there - at the top!

Excitedly, we arrived at this highest part of the cathedral, so thrilled to be there, to see the views, to look at that monstrous bell that Quasimodo pealed, to be part of the romance of history … to feel and see the city below you. You stop and attempt to stand up straight, tall, ready with the camera, focus and all of a sudden you cannot stand up. Instead, your body prefers to quiver and stumble, and you fall down in a heap! No, it is not because of the effort of going all the way to the top; no, it is not because your legs do not want to carry you any further; it is purely because you are dizzy from that continuous anticlockwise circular motion up those flights of stairs that you coiled around and around and around and around. All that way to the top, all three hundred and eighty-seven steps UP. It does not sound very much but when you try to look out to the world of Paris below, you simply cannot stand vertical to view!

And yes … there is no elevator!

And yes … we had to go down again! Back the other way! Just to unwind our spinning brains!

Indubitably, we tackled the trek to the gardens of the Palace of Versailles. There was a certain magic that fizzed through the air there. Hidden away from the modern world, for the tourism side, this majestic European castle on the outskirts of Paris was a perfectly preserved example of the reckless extravagance of the French monarchy depicting Parisian life at its most luxurious. It was complete with gold-brushed furniture, quilted four-poster beds and lush rolling lawns that stretched as far as the eye can see. It was one of the most beautiful castles in the world with an astonishing seven hundred rooms. Also complete with Marie Antoinette's 'play hamlet' where she could play at being a peasant without getting her hands dirty. No wonder there was Le Revolution! And yes, we walked it all!

We combined our love of chocolate and cakes with our passion for Paris on our walking way to the Arc de Triomphe , indulging in hot chocolates and pastries for our early breakfasts. We meandered west of the city, quite off the tourist track and further than we intended to go We were rescued by a lady who saw us deciphering a map and pointed our tired feet and bodies off in the right direction. More steps!

A definite must was seeing the Louvre. This is the world's largest museum with well over 30,000 works of art on display. Both of us immediately thought about 'The Da Vinci Code movie (and for me, Tom Hanks) and imagined the footsteps of the heroes of this novel/movie as we explored the Louvre, its places, works, and themes at the heart of the story. Believe me, it was such an amazing place, but bearing so much opulence and age. The pyramid of diamond-shaped and triangular panes of glass is where you began! I walked down numerous steps underneath Paris into a different world!

And of course, speaking of down, you cannot see Paris without visiting the catacombs.

The City of Lights lured us into this darker reality which lurked in these infamous catacombs of Paris. A sign near the entrance of the catacomb's famously reads, "Arrête! C'est ici l'empire de la Mort" ("Stop! This is the Empire of Death"). Historically, the caverns and tunnels that had been the remains of Paris's stone mines had been repurposed in the late 18th century as the repository for the bones from the over-crowded cemeteries throughout Paris. Tasked with relocating the bones of over 2 million corpses, an inspired Director of Mine Inspections had the bones stacked in 'artistic' patterns of skulls and long bones. These were nothing short of amazing as they ghoulishly captivated you in their silent underground world. We crept quietly through since my vivid imagination had quickly transformed the scene into heaped gruesome piles of bodies and carcasses. I could feel their fleshless hands grasping, their skinless bony skulls and shapes reaching, reaching, reaching, so depressing, so gruesome, so grisly, so shocking, so claustrophobic, so dark, so wet, and SO MORBID.

The catacombs had been Marc's idea. Such a perfect place for our honeymoon filled with so much enchanting romance ... don't you think?

Obviously, we had to walk down one hundred and thirty stairs into the foundations of Paris to get there! Oh, did I mention it was the same number of stairs at the other end to arise back into the sunlight? Ah, as an Australian advertisement says, "but wait, there's more!

After initially following more cobblestone streets we found ourselves at the base of the Basilique du Sacré-Coeur. This is a 19th century church that sits atop the only perceptible hill in the city. You can see it from every viewpoint! The Basilique is located at the summit of the Butte Montmartre, Hill of Martyrs with the surrounding area renowned for the artists that used to frequent it, Claude Monet, Pablo Picasso, and Vincent van Gogh. The area is also the home of the Moulin Rouge and the red-light district of Paris.

As an aside here - do you know that the "Basilique of the Sacred Heart of Paris" is made of stone that reacts to rainwater and secretes calcite. This acts like bleach so the church remains beaming white even in the polluted air of a big city like Paris. As I looked up at it from the bottom of the hill, I thought how white it was. I would definitely describe the Sacre Coeur as a vision of white crowning Paris.

Of course, Montmartre is a hill with an elevation of one hundred thirty metres.

Of course, Montmartre is the highest point in the city.

Of course, the Basilque Sacré-Coeur is perched on this, the highest hill of the city!

Of course, my husband wished to visit it in person.

Known as the Hill of Martyrs. after all the steps I had already done that day, I definitely thought I was a martyr! Testing out my health, my weight, my thighs, my equilibrium, not to mention my age, this middle-aged, tired honeymooner slogged up the five hundred and ninety-six stairs straight up to what was considered by many, the second most beautiful view over Paris. But on that particular day, God must have been generously looking down at me in my dishevelled state, inhaling any air that came my way, gasping heavily as those seemingly endless steps taunted me, because, when we arrived at the entrance to the dome of the Basilque, there was no queue. We were able to effortlessly enter the peaceful and beautiful sanctuary of the Basilque to recover, to rest and to breathe in the reverence of this building.

But wait ... there was another tower to the dome. My husband looked at me with those beautiful blue eyes and commented, "... *Shall we?*" Tell me, what could I say with what little breath was left in me? My chest heaved as I gazed blurrily into those adoring eyes. I did acquiesce and climbed up the tight spiral staircase of three hundred MORE steps. Finally, we looked out over the city of Paris!

Now this was romance at last!

I stood there enfolded and embraced in my husband's arms as together, we were engulfed in a truly magnificent view. As my breathing and racing heart calmed, I finally stopped and enjoyed this part of the honeymoon. I could now say that all my climbing up all those stairs was worth it. I enjoyed his human embrace, enfolding me in his arms, treasuring these special moments for just us. Enjoying just being together.

But what do I see below? Standing at the top looking down, I could see the shape of a tram full with people disembarking at the entrance of the Basilque! Did you hear me correctly? Yes, there was a tram … with people … sitting … riding … breathing normally … no stairs! I turned to my husband with eyes wide as I pointed down to the felonious vehicle gesturing widely! He simply smiled and gave me another huge hug. I think he was 'saying', would the moment had been as special if we hadn't walked and climbed all the way to the top together?

Perceptibly, we left the best to last!

As a tourist you cannot go to Paris and not see the Eiffel Tower. You can see it from all over the city. You even see it when you are flying over Paris. And the Eiffel Tower definitely gesticulated to us, speaking very loudly with its metallic voice and laced metal attire …. "*Come to me, climb me … Come and rise within me!* "

As it was our last day, with every inch of my aching body, I argued hard with that metal voice hammering, clanging inside my head, but I listened. Irrefutably listened! I mean I had to! And there we were! You stop and admire this huge, wonderful structure that is so revered. A structure that has a total of eighty-one stories and stands three hundred and twenty-four metres tall. You look up. Do you know that it is only when you are actually standing directly under the Eiffel Tower that you truly can understand the sheer magnitude of it? (Oh, It is so high!) As you stand there, looking up the giant arms lean inward, beckoning, offering to embrace you, to lead you up to the pinnacle above. No mention of the steps involved, just the glittering of the lights beckoning you. Your stubborn, throbbing, oh so very tired feet silenced by the siren of the call to rise to the summit.

Do you know there are actually elevators that can take you up all three levels of the Eiffel Tower?

Did we go up the Eiffel Tower using the lifts? No. Of course not! We used our feet and climbed. So many stairs that culminated in one long enduring rise. Neither was this journey for the faint of heart when it came to heights. Oh, did I forget to mention that I do not like heights! Just a minor reference! My husband simply grinned at me, *"Who needs coffee to get you going when you can hike up one thousand and twenty-one stairs?"*

Actually, I have to tell you, there are a total of one thousand *six hundred and sixty-five* stairs in the East pillar to the top, but you can only walk one thousand and twenty-one of them! Reason being is that the public can only climb as far as the second level via the stairways and then public access to the summit is by lift only. Oh, what a shame! I was of course devastated! The smile on my face told me so!

And you climbed.

And you kept climbing.

From the very moment you climb the stairs to the first floor, you feel as if you've embarked on a fantastical journey. As you clambered up that beautiful monstrosity, not only can you see between all the supports around you, but you can also see through the stairs below you. With each new staircase the view grows more magical (and of course higher).

I continued my climb back and forth, traversing metal staircases and wire cages, every now and then taking a moment to gaze out but not over! (I really could not look over). My legs were not only throbbing intensely but felt like quivering sloppy jelly. I did take a moment every now and then to stop at every other platform to read the informative signs that the Parisians have placed at each stage to inform the climber of the history of the tower. (Personally, I think it was more to give the climber an excuse to catch their breath. I used both excuses).

By the time I reached the top of the stairs, I was sure my camera had gained ten kilograms, not to mention my small backpack. Someone must have secretly placed a brick in it while we were climbing up! Eventually we arrived at the second level and looked for the lifts. You could not hike any higher due to safety reasons, so our ascent in the lift took us to the very top observation deck.

At this point, even if you don't have a fear of heights; this final part of the ascending journey can make any person feel uneasy. Imagine crowding into a tiny glass elevator and the operator hits the button and immediately it starts to ascend. Then, quite suddenly the lift begins to go faster as if some kind of turbo had kicked in. This increase in speed was so noticeable that everyone on the elevator with us gasped aloud and looked at each other with wide eyes. Not helping the matter was the mysterious clicking noise every few hundred feet, but other than that, the elevator was a relatively smooth ride. Not great for my fear of heights but thinking positively, I was grateful for the number of stairs I did not now physically have to climb! (Without the lift, Knowing Marc, I am quite sure he would have walked up all the stairs to the very top!)

Finally, we disembarked at the highest part of the Eiffel Tower! It may have taken me some time, breathing heavily from panic, and clutching my husband's arms, I slowly ventured to the edge of the panoramic precipice, to appreciate the surroundings. But when I finally was able to stand at the rail and look around, I was stunned at the beauty and culture that filled every centimetre of the panoramic view. The Eiffel Tower is undeniably the most famous symbol of Paris and there I was standing at the very heart of it. Yes, this now was romance! Yes, this now was my honeymoon! Yes, this now was the City of Love.

Do you know there is also direct lift connection for all three levels for the way down?

Do you know that the journey to ground can be completed in a delightfully rapid twenty minutes and sixteen seconds?

Did we use the lift to go down? What do you think? I won that decision!

It was such a wonderful honeymoon and there were so many places that we went to in Paris, but all the tourist sights had stairs that went up! Come to think of it, even the non-tourist areas had stairs. I thought I was so clever in preparing myself for a lot of walking by attending exercise step classes for a few months prior to our trip planning on being trim, taut, and terrific - well maybe not so trim, nor taut, but somewhat still terrific! I honestly thought I was adequately equipped for my honeymoon excursions, but nothing quite armed me for what we really did do. Love really does makes us do things we never thought we were capable of! But every romantic story has an ending.

Tired, worn out, we left the dominating tower of lights, the interweaving steps of the Louvre, the low tunnels of the catacombs, the high stature of the Notre Dame, the opulence and vastness of the Palace of Versailles, the tall straight curves of the Arc de Triumph, the cobbled streets of Moulin Rouge and the rising hills of the Basilque at Montmartre. Winding our way through small exclusive shops to intimate cafés and bars, we stumbled blindly along beautifully coiffured garden pathways, past all those ten-hectare large gardens laid out around that huge rectangular pond, back up all those steps to the foot of the terrace of the Palais de Chaillot and weaved our way slowly, romantically, hand in hand, to our accommodation.

Leaning heavily on my husband's arm, I was tottering and staggering through the eternally romantic City of Lights, Paris. In my drunken state, not from steps or stairs but filled most comfortingly and consolingly with hot chocolate, copious amount of red wine, and exhaustion, we meandered back to our hotel of love in that wonderful city of romance, happily swaying at all intersections, even those that were not there.

Winding, swaying, bumbling our way up around that green circular staircase to our petite hotel room, my so romantic, so chivalrous, so kind and considerate, so handsome, always the gentleman, husband, on our last night of Paris, … looked at me and said,

"*You know, a gentleman does not take advantage of a drunken lady.*"

I stopped, gazed unclearly into those dazzling, daring, blue eyes of my silver-streaked dashing, debonair, delicious, doctor husband that I so loved …

Do you know what my response was to those chivalrous words on that last night of our romantic journey into Paris … in that beautiful City of Love … on my honeymoon?

"*You are so going to take advantage of THIS lady!*"

Oh, he definitely did!

That was not a challenge at all!

That was an adventure!!!!!

Chapter Seven

Can I Take a Rain Check?

"Okay?" asks a gentle familiar voice beside me. I look up into this face as I wipe away the running water from my own dripping eyes. Who is this man I was prepared to not only go right outside of my comfort zone with, but willing to sidestep completely what I considered to be rational logical behaviour? I stare at him intently as I speak, "I love you my darling, but right now I do not like you very much!"

I was told once by a friend that each day you should experience something that challenges or even frightens you. Do you think that this statement is true? I am not sure that it happened on a daily basis, but since meeting Marc, I certainly braved more challenges than I ever would have faced in my prior life. Meeting Marc and learning more about him, how I did things myself, categorically changed. No, I am not complaining. They were fun. But there were tough times too. One of those challenges and at times I will admit, was quite a frightening experience for me was the Routeburn Track on the Southern Island of New Zealand.

The Routeburn Track is a world-renowned, tramping track found in the more rugged part of the South Island of New Zealand. The tourism office officially informs you: "*With soaring mountain peaks, huge valleys, waterfalls, and jewel-like lakes, … the highest point of the track is 1,255 metres above sea level, so the views are simply spectacular.* The Track itself winds through a landscape that has been shaped by continuous glaciations into fiords, rocky coasts, towering cliffs, lakes, and waterfalls". Being informed that this walk was world-famous for its spectacular scenery and accessibility made it sound Beautiful, Calm, Relaxing, exhilarating to see. Having already experienced Cradle Mountain, the fact that it was designed to suit all fitness levels made it doable for me!

And this is where my story begins.

The bus groaned slightly as the wheels rolled upwards towards the mountains. The road curled around and around as the peaks came more dramatically into view. I stared pensively out the window. "*Please God,*" I prayed, *"Please let it stay fine. It was raining last night, but now it looks 'okay'. Please let it stay that way."*

Last night was an awful night. Not just from the rain pouring down but from panic. Me 'panic'? I will admit it is an unusual phenomenon, but I experienced an anxiety attack like I had never before! This attack was a previously unknown condition to me, and it basically quite scared me because I saw myself change from a calm, loving, easy-going person into a rampant hysterical lunatic!

But what caused this panic attack?

On the previous evening, we attended a pre-hike 'chat' about this '*beautiful, exhilarating, nature loving, inspiring*' Routeburn Track that we were going to walk over the next few days. I was already nervous since I had never before attempted a 'through-hike' but anticipated the rundown on what would be expected of me. I continued to constantly think positive thoughts to ease my anxiety. But in contrast, all I received from this presenter was negativity. Instead of providing our small group with a 'pep' positive uplifting chat, all she talked about was the rain, the cold, the water we would walk through, the physical steepness, and the clothing that we should have bought to do such a hike and therefore would suffer if we did not have the 'right' gear. Understandably, already anxious, by the end of the 'talk,' I was in such a state of panic thinking I was not ready for this! I was not fit enough for this! I did not have the right gear and what had I got myself into, thinking "I can't' do this!!" Well, wouldn't you had thought that way too?

Of course, straight after such a 'positive pep' talk, I rushed out to buy quick-dry walking pants but the only ones available were way too big for me! I tried to remain calm and rational, but it was all in vain because as the night progressed, sleep eluded me. I waited for dawn to break much as a person on death row must wait on the eve of their day of execution. I tossed, turned, sweated, ranted, raved, cried, and panicked vocally as my fear and angst of this new 'travel adventure challenge with my husband' rose and rose even higher, eventually exploding into a full-blown panic attack! (I had never in my life been like this before. I must admit I quite surprised myself in how I was feeling and definitely stunned Marc).

Poor darling Marc. In good faith, he had tried to reassure me that this hike was designed for 'retirees' with usually much poorer fitness than what we had so we should be fine! And we were not even at retirement age yet! Did I believe him? In my stress, NO. But as the morning sun broke, I finally reflected upon his positivity and ended up with my psychological state agreeing with him. I thought to myself, I was not a retiree yet and I could do this. So, putting on my brave face, I decided to look upon this walk as a new challenge to undertake! Onward. Forward. Good positive thoughts. YES?

But on that bus, as I glanced out through the condensation beginning to build on the window, the sky did not respond to my prayers for continual blue heavens and bright beaming sunlight. Instead, it became increasingly threatening and even more dark. The vegetation became thicker as our four-and-half hour bus trip wound its way higher. I scanned around at the other fellow hikers who all appeared oblivious to the changing weather as their vibrant chatter and laughter echoed through the bus. But I was quiet. I couldn't converse. I couldn't chat. What I had to do was to concentrate inwardly and prepare myself mentally for this new *adventure* I really did NOT want to do but was prepared to embark upon.

As the bus crawled slowly to a stop, I espied the green Department of Forestry sign just visible through the rain that proudly '*Welcomed*' us to the beginning of our 'walk'. Swirls of grey mist floated in front of my eyes. Was my panic returning? No! The weather had deteriorated even further. The grey mist was not panic, but believe me, that 'Panic' feeling was once more rising. The once welcoming sapphire-blue heavens at the beginning of that bus trip had definitely transformed to ominous black and rain slowly, heavily, began to fall. I stared steadily out the window. My eyes not moving away from the now driving rain slicing in deluges across the glass panes. Fear and dread accompanied the brick in my throat as the weather worsened. No, I was not going to back out, but neither was I happy to go!

Excited, cheerful voices attached to nameless bodies, nonchalantly grabbed their backpacks, their raincoats, their walking sticks, and clamoured excitedly in their apparent eagerness to begin their walk. I gazed out the window at the pouring, drenching rain, my insides now matching the outside. A familiar calm male voice asked, "*Ready?*" I nodded, and hesitantly followed the others off the bus, to roll out the door, a new version of the Michelin man in so many layers.

Freezing air slashed at me.

My raincoat with its view-obscuring hood, far too big over-pants, gloves, and walking shoes (already drenched) comprised my 'wet weather gear'. Underneath, every piece of warm clothing once in my pack now being worn, valiantly strived but lost in its battle to keep some heat in my body. Tendrils of hair escaped from my hood-covered head and a familiar male hand tucked them gently back into place. My fingers were frozen as I hoisted the unfamiliar heavy haversack almost half my size onto my small back. This backpack was not what I had quite envisioned. What I thought I would be carrying was a small backpack - you know, the kind kids take to school every day … the kind of day pack you take a small, packed lunch and a thermos of hot drink with you on a lovely day stroll in the mountains. The type we had previously used in our walks. Oh, how wrong I was - this was so much bigger than a day pack! Feeling the weight on my body, how was I going to carry it uphill for three days?

"Hey, you two, smile!" drifted a happy voice towards me.

I turned to the source of the voice and forced through gritted teeth an obligatory smile as our guide for this three-day-through-walk took the customary photo of the two of us at the start. Then, without any of the eagerness displayed by the others before me, we began the eight hours of ascent.

Grey wet skies soaked the grass and moss before me and made slippery the rocks protruding from the path. White mist puffed from my mouth as I breathed, and the mountain rises seemed to get steeper with every step. This is November in the Southern Hemisphere, and I was cold! This is absolutely crazy!

So why am I doing this?

Yes, I had agreed to do the challenge. No-one had forced me, but really, it was truly not what I wanted to do. It was probably the last thing on my mind as I now thought about my warm cosy hotel room, I had left a few hours ago where outside the sun was shining brightly. But I had to force myself to accept that was not where I was now. I was there on that wet freezing mountainside wanting to prove to myself, to Marc, and to my grownup family that I was still 'young' enough to do this hike! Oh, what a silly woman I was to even think that!

The track was overshadowed by silver beech trees festooned with 'Old Man's Beard' moss. It created what would be, in other circumstances, either a romantic pathway or a scary movie set. Fellow walkers passed me by, laughing, happy, enjoying their rambling chatter as they meandered up the wet track. Furtively watching my feet, encompassed in thick hiking shoes, trying to mimic the others' walking confidence. I nervously smiled a greeting to them but followed silently. Lifting each leg gingerly and tentatively, I precariously balanced on the uneven ground, weighing the outcome of where to place my foot with each hesitant tread. With each muddy footprint I entrusted the so-called safety of the wet terra firma underneath.

Many kilometres now below us, six more kilometres of uphill climbing still ahead.

Wet.

Cold.

Unhappy.

And adding to that was the voice of my beloved talking about landscapes, the green moss, the ambling ever-rising pathway, the mountain scenery before us, the people we were meeting and of course the weather. All I could really say, most horribly, at that point was, 'Who cared!'

I watched others boldly walk through the water that cascaded across the path before me. To my eyes, what was a gentle stream was now a flooded torrent. When I discovered there were 'no stepping-stones', the terror of falling in, of being soaked in that swirling water, embodied my thoughts. Did they really expect me to wade through this 'raging river' in my shoes? I already had endured freezing rain, a wet slippery track, I was already wet and cold and now this stream of water! I stopped dead! So, what does my gallant husband do? Such a knight in shining armour, he picked me up and carried me over the stream. I was in his arms clinging tightly only to realise that it wasn't that deep at all, because as I looked down, the water was only covering the edge of his boots. I could have walked through. Not quite the raging torrent my tired self-had made it out to be. Not quite the romantic vision of being a damsel in 'real' distress either, because I felt like an idiot! Chagrined, I walked on, but little did I know that ahead was a more *real* danger to emotionally threaten this little damsel. It was called - THE WATERFALL.

In my already water-soaked brain, the sound of crashing water gradually grew louder, like a train charging at great speed towards me.

Deluges of water crashed onto the rocks that was the 'track'. This can't be right. There had to be a mistake. The track must go behind the waterfall. I looked around to reassure myself, but the torrential cascade of water before me went through the entire width of the waterfall! You are joking! Really! Wasn't I wet and cold enough already?

Swirls of a red jacket bounced into my vision and the warm hand of one of our guides enfolded my icy one and led me gently through the pouring rivulets. I clung tightly to this human buttress as I navigated through the combined downpour of rain and falling deluge of water and spray from the waterfall that was hitting me from above. I discovered (after the fact,) that I had my wet weather gear on inside out which allowed some of this cold water to seep into all sorts of places that should have stayed warm and dry. My mood of course matched my clothes, now quite soggy and waterlogged. But then what did our cheerful guide do? Had the 'little bit of water' dampened his mood? No, because after walking through the waterfall, it was time for another photo opportunity! Another obligatory photograph was taken of a soaked, drenched, dripping body that grimaced into the camera!

He told me to 'Smile!'

After hours of walking for what seemed like forever up, the track eventually turned downhill as a gentle slope but with a series of uneven giant's rock stairs. And what a sight for sore eyes as our 'lodge' for the night finally appeared. I could see the walkers who had arrived earlier already sitting there with drinks in hand. They greeted us with friendly exclamations of, *"Hi, you made it. Oh, you must go down and see the lake, it is so beautiful!"*

Standing in front of them, in my wet bedraggled clothes, my hair stuck to my face, my blistered foot distressing me immensely, any semblance of a professional woman well and truly washed away, I replied politely but very quickly to my new-found friends, *"No thank you. I am not going anywhere except to the HOT shower!"*

I do wonder why everybody laughed. I have no idea!!!

The next day was blue and beautiful, and my spirits lifted. This was a new day, with a new challenge and I was determined to attack this in a better frame of mood. It is amazing how sunshine and blue skies can so change your outlook perspective and reinforce your thinking to 'I <u>can</u> do this!' I was determined to follow through!

Our first part of the walk on the second day was a steep uphill route. Two hours of continuous vertical uphill climbing was endured with very little to see until we broke through the tree level at 1000 metres above sea level. Sadly, no rest here because the zig zagging switchbacks of the trail had begun. Four more kilometres of uphill climbing conquered and then finally around the Ocean Peak Corner were beautiful views into the Hollyford valley 1000 metres below backed by snow -capped mountains on the other side! A most picturesque, scenic view. It was stunning and yes, definitely worth the climb. A challenge accomplished, (but I dared not look down).

As we rested, I looked at our guide talking to us, readying us for the next section of track that just happened to be avalanche prone and I thought of the words from the travel companion I had been reading prior to this trip that had said, *"Travelling improves your productivity, problem-solving skills and creativity in how to deal with situations"*. So, being positive, I followed the others in a single line all spaced out at 10 metres intervals and reflected on how I could do this. (The guide had reassuringly told us this 10metres-apart-rule was to minimise losses in the event of an avalanche. I found this not very 'reassuring' at all!)

Walking on this part of the track, of course, what did I hear? An almighty **crack**!

I froze.

Where were my problem-solving skills then?

Where was my newfound hiker's self-confidence?

Daring not to move any part of my body for fear of thundering snow falling from above, tumbling me shattering to the valley far below. Marc from his 10 metres distance behind me called out, *"It's ok … it was just the ice melting. KEEP walking!* Ice melting? Really?

The track ahead was covered in deep snow.

Actually, hiking through snow was a new experience to me. I had seen snow before but never had to hike through it, let alone with a pack on my back and so I was not sure where to place my feet on this precipitous, uphill track, for fear of sinking into the snow up to my waist. That was not a good thought, believe me. My hesitation encouraged my husband to walk beside me, holding my hand, as I placed my foot into an already planted 'footprint' in front of me. Yes, that was passable. I was doing fine! Did I tell you that Marc was the one who went up to his waist in snow?? His path beside me, holding my hand was not quite as good! Ooops!

However, informed by our guides that the weather was closing in, we were forced into a quicker march to meet the helicopter that would take us over the 400 metres section that was too snow-bound to trek. We had to rush our hiking to ensure we would meet the helicopter before the weather changed. Definitely a quick hard trek uphill on ice and snow! But the prize of being surrounded by the safety of steel, Perspex and rotor blades, viewing the panorama over the mountains and the partially frozen Lake Harris, all combined to a simply indescribable recompense for the previous several hours of hard work and nerves. Words cannot do justice to the beauty of what we saw so I am not even going to try! Of course, the delight of not having to walk at least those 400 metres of the trail was an added bonus. I certainly did not have any trouble declaring loudly to my fellow walkers that night at dinner," *I could undoubtedly do more of that kind of helicopter hiking any day!!*

I wonder why they all laughed.

Our third day dawned beautiful, and we were on the downhill run through temperate rainforest. In retrospect, the last day was also the most humorous part of our trek. The track was fairly wide, and the last part was easier walking. A much simpler journey than the past two days, but it was here that I actually fell!

Tripping and losing my footing I tumbled, rotated lengthways 180 degrees due to the keel-like weight of my backpack and I simply slid along the ground flat on my back with the pack beneath me. Having seen me trip in front of him, Marc actually thought I had deliberately flipped mid-air to save myself an injury and was quite impressed at my quick thinking and athleticism. But then, my subsequent stranded state belied the truth. Basically, if you think of a turtle caught on their back, that was me. I was lying there, arms out in front, flat on my back with the shell (that large onerous backpack) underneath me. I was stuck! On the easiest downhill straightforward stretch and I had to fall here! How embarrassing! But we laughed and laughed!

* * *

I must admit, on that trip, I learnt that it was always good to laugh at yourself! I also learnt not to let go of my husband's hand on a swing bridge as we had to cross one on the same trail and he obviously could not resist seeing how high the bridge could swing while I was on it!

Routeburn was definitely a new travel experience for me. Many kilometres trekked, and amazing views as we climbed up and down. It was a challenge that was both exhilarating and frightening at the same time. This was the city girl right out of her comfort zone. She had panicked. But had also discovered new friends and her own self-humour, and Marc's understanding ability to deal with irrational fears and at times tears. This was all synchronised with our great guides on this three-day-through trek whose sense of comedy, antics, mental support, and positivity, balanced my fear and apprehension as I hiked defiantly – yes *defiantly* which contributed significantly to my personal sense of achievement. When handing me my certificate of accomplishment my guide articulated the simple words, "*Yes, she got there in the end. She-did-it!*"

I did!

Would I do it again?

No!

Never!

Not for all the money in the world!

Life has a way of moving you to the next level……
whatever mode of 'transport 'you may use…
It does not matter what you use as long as you get there.

Lyndell Heyning

Chapter Eight

If The Shoe Fits

If the shoe fits wear it, if not then wear thicker socks!

Marc's philosophy towards life of challenging yourself and experience new things … at least once a day… certainly stands. The more time spent together in our new life, showed me exactly that. I know he is a risk taker, so much more than me but generally speaking, we are quite balanced in our outlook towards life. This being, that while he takes both feet off the floor and jumps, I stay with both my feet on the floor or perhaps lift only one foot, the other one hanging on and calculating! But it works for us both.

Part of travelling is having to think about when things can go wrong.

In your planning, you have to calculate the risk and think about major things that could occur. Such as Being robbed; Being scammed; Losing or forgetting your passport; Hearing that line, *'We don't have your reservation'*; Missing a flight; Losing something really important and irreplaceable; Getting sick or having an accident, you know, those main incidents that could happen at any part of your journey. All those substantial issues ensure you really must have a risk management strategy in place before you leave your home. Obviously, after trying as much as possible in your planning to minimise things going wrong, once you are in the midst of the excitement of travel, you tend to push those unpleasant thoughts aside until they actually happen!

But have you thought about some of those simple challenges that occur when travelling? I mean the uncomplicated tasks, the straightforward things. Like thinking about how you will get from one point to the other. Those questions that involve mobility, movement, and transport whether on foot or by vehicle!

Take crampons for example.

If you do not know what a crampon is, it is a traction device attached to footwear to improve your mobility on snow and ice during ice climbing. It is also known as a cleat. Besides ice climbing, they are also used for secure travel on snow and ice, such as crossing glaciers, snowfields, icefields, ascending snow slopes, and scaling ice-covered rock. They are a 'foolproof' way to traverse ice or hard, slippery snow - provided, that is, if you know how to use them.

My first experience with Crampons was on Franz Josef Glacier in New Zealand.

Fitted out with appropriate over clothes and heavy boots, we took an exceptionally long white-knuckle ten-minute Helicopter journey through the glacial valley, flying awfully close to the valley walls complete with several steep turns over the glacier face before finally landing on the top. Giddy after that 'air raising' experience, I had the task of having to work out how to put the crampons on my boots! That was a feat all in itself! Walking with them turned out to be another one!

All aspects of using crampons depends upon your balance, confidence, and commitment to trusting them when you use them. You are supposed to think of your crampon or cleats as your claws, rooted deep on your feet where the technique of you walking, depends on trusting each foot placement. Once mastered, they apparently are a safe, quick, and efficient method of movement over easy-angled snow and ice and provides a convenient way to rest on steeper slopes without sliding. It is important to believe in the holding power of your crampons!

That was my first task.

Can you imagine me doing that? The one who has both feet firmly on the ground? Not just trusting but believing, as I stepped out onto the icy terrain with its ridges and crevasses, that those small ice picks on the bottom of my heavily clad boots were going to hold my big female body up, even bigger now, enveloped heavily in snow gear. There I was, fearing to slip and slide all over the blue and white landscape but our guide said, *"Keep moving." Keep walking on the ice!"* Really? *"Confidence is gained through experience,"* he declared. The problem is that slow movement allows time for fear to happen.

I picked my way hesitantly, gingerly on the ice. Seeing a fellow hiker accidently step on some blue ice to fall through the crust ending up knee deep in icy water only added to those frightened inner thoughts! I think the guide felt the groups uneasiness, as it was at this point that he offered for those who did not feel confident to come towards the front near him. Without any hesitation, I pushed myself past my fellow passengers to be the first one to hold his hand. No, CLENCH his hand tightly!

* * *

Then we have Jasper, Canada.

We arrived early at this beautiful scenic town and our room was not quite ready yet. That was quite okay. After a night on the train, thoughts of wandering around, stretching our legs, seeing the delightful snow-covered postcard picture type town filled my head. I thought that was a good idea. You thought so too? On that one we can agree. But no! Instead, Marc quickly organised for us to do an Ice Canyon Walk at Maligne Canyon and somehow, I quickly found myself VERY hurriedly outfitted in snow gear, helmet, ice walking boots. I had no time to breathe, no time to soak up the local scenery. No time to think. No time to *assess the risks!* No time to cogitate about where I was going or to consider what I was about to do! Reflecting now, I do believe *that* was his plan!

Our continuous walking trek took us past a total of 5 bridges, each with a story told by our wonderful guide, Pal, from Pursuit Tours (I know why they are called that now!) Down, down, down, through snow into the depths of the canyon we went. For those music buffs reading this, it reminded me of the Phantom of the Opera musical song that goes ... *"Down once more to the dungeon of my black despair ... Down that path into darkness deep as hell!"*

As we headed down the valley, I was physically trying to master the actual 'walk' of using crampon cleats into my own natural walking stride, definitely a little slower than the others in front of me. Learning to place my toe first, I listened to the voice of my, at that moment, very-not-much liked husband ... *"Toes first, toes first"*.

Right then, I knew where I would have liked to put my spiked toe!

Amazing frozen waterfalls and beautiful ice scenery summoned us further into the canyon. "*The rocks are your friends*", calls our guide as you grab onto something solid to stop your fall. (Now where have I heard a similar phrase before!). Two hours later, we could actually climb down onto the slippery blue and white ice floor of the canyon. The highlight of this tour!

Four people in our group. Three sure footed, walking gracefully over the ice. Their steps confidently followed the tracks roughened by our guide's ice pick. Taking photos, smiling, laughing, a lovely happy picture. The fourth traveller, me if you didn't guess, timidly placing her one foot in front of the other, not seeing the 'safe' roughened tracks. No graceful stride for me. No pretty mental imagery as I erringly and naively perched my foot with its supposedly *safe* cleat onto a rock covered in ice. That was never going to end well as I felt both my feet slip from under me, only to be heroically saved by fiercely clenching Pal (the guide's hand) until he had no circulation left! Breathing heavily, trembling hard, placing my cleat slowly onto the slippery ice, I was so unsure of what I was doing, of where my foot was going, thinking wildly, would this cleat stop me sliding onto my bum?

* * *

Another day in Banff, during an afternoon walk, we were faced with an impromptu climb up a series of stairs that had suffered sequential freeze/thaw cycles resulting in a virtual ice slide. The end result did not resemble anything that a reasonable person would actually walk up.

Marc did his usual 'glass half full' risk assessment. He was so positive and smiling as he informed me that '*of course we could get up those stairs.*' He then proceeded to show me the way to do it. His method being to walk up the slope *outside* the handrail. He advised me to walk outside the safety of those rails despite the long drop into the frozen river below. The grooves in the snow and ice showed that many other people apparently had come to the same conclusion. But the slope outside the handrail was only marginally less icy and slippery than the stairs within and we both had to grip the handrail firmly and pull ourselves up the icy slope. Yes, I had my cleats on, but they gave me little reassurance – or grip!

Believe me, it was not a pleasant afternoon walk in the park. Particularly as the path followed the riverbank and there were more than one flights of steps to be negotiated, both up and down! In fact, if I were truthful, I would tell you that I actually had another mild panic attack climbing up those very first ice-covered steps. You know that side of me that does not happen very often!

The first ice covered steps, with an equally icy handrail, went up steep and high, and quite a long way at a 45-degree angle with an ominous edge either side that beckoned to me like a siren. I climbed up slowly. Pulling myself up. The cleats still on my boots failing miserably to dig into the ice as I was in fact, still sliding. Right then I was not at all thinking of the cleats as claws, rooted deep on my feet. Nor was I trusting each foot placement or thinking about the holding power of those cleats as I struggled on that steep ice staircase! Instead, sliding backwards and sideways, fear had now overtaken any semblance of calmness and rationale and my calculated risk assessment informed me, "I cannot do this!" More importantly, I did not want to do this! What was even worse was I could not go back down as I had to keep going up, my panic attack became more acute. I could not breathe, and all I could do was cling to that icy handrail, on the outside of those steps, above that frozen river below me, breathing heavily, too frightened to lift my legs up at all. My feet stubbornly refused to move as my arms clung tightly to that rail. There I was, frozen on the spot on the wrong side of the steps, looking at that dizzy drop below beckoning me to fall. I could not move up or down.

To my embarrassment, two strong, good-looking males were making their way up the same ice stairs by clinging and sliding so gracefully on the other side of this same flight of steps! As I hung over that rail, they appeared to make their way up easily! In response to their looks of concern, to my own surprise, I actually stopped, took a breath, and calmly stated to them … *"Its ok - I'm just having a panic attack".*

Can you believe that?

Can you believe I calmly told them I was ok and just having a panic attack!!

However, once spoken, they had moved on ahead of me. My 'calm' response must have triggered a mental change in me. I started to shift my feet once more and climbed back over the rail. In hindsight, perhaps I should have crumpled, played the helpless female, and become wrapped in those young men's strong arms instead to assist me up the frozen slide! That would have been a much better ploy to get me off that icy staircase as I was definitely NOT talking to my husband at that moment in time.

* * *

Also, I must not forget the venture in Iceland.

To set the scene, we were entering the world of the movie, "The Secret Life of Walter Mitty" where, if you know the movie, Walter skateboarded down a road into a fishing village called Stykkisholmur. Like us, most visitors to Grundarfjörður arrive by road, but there were also thousands that come by sea. The Harbour hosts 30 cruise ships each year - and that is a lot for this small village conveniently located in the middle of Snæfellsnes National Park. A cute village but not that big. However, it does have one of the most famous photographed mountains in Iceland.

The peninsula was majestic as we explored beautiful scenery with snow covered mountains so high and huge. We climbed up a volcanic crater called *Saxholl* and were almost frozen to death as howling winds brought the wind chill to -20 degrees and found any gaps in our clothing. Even when there were no gaps the wind meandered around corners and down necks to chill places that should have been warm. Marc's fingers went numb, and my face was wind-burnt from the howling gale. Returning to the warm and safe haven of our car, we set off to find a welcoming tourist venue where we could thaw, to cajole feeling and warmth back into our frozen bodies. I guess it is not called 'Iceland' for nothing!

Now what do you think Marc observes!

A Lava Tube Cave Tour with a small group of tourists coming out indicating it was actually open. Of course, Marc stopped, looked, asked, and was informed the next tour began in five minutes. Not given any time to think about it, not enough time to come up with a non-wimpish reason why we shouldn't do it, I unofficially *consented* to the smiling guide and went on this 'special' tour since there were only the two of us taking part. (We were in Iceland in the off-season). I mean, after-all, although I knew it was a 'cave tour', in my minds eyes, I had picturesque visions of Jenolan Caves where these particular caves are the largest, most spectacular, most famous caves in Australia which has some of the most outstanding cave systems in the world. That meant I had images of huge caverns, lighted walkways, and easy meandering along well-lit paths to see the flood-lit stalactites etc. I am not sure I was at all impressed as I was firstly instructed to place a helmet on my head and then handed a small pocket-sized black torch in order to 'see' in front of me. Once more, with very little time to think about where I was going or consider what I was about to do, looking at the small hole literally in the ground in front of me, my confidence did a huge plummet as I was asked to descend! Marc smiled at me.

Have I mentioned I am claustrophobic?

Down we went!

Down a spiral steel staircase into the depths of the lava tube!

Down into this hole in the ground.

What was I thinking?? It was so dark, it was scary … no well-lit cave … just following that little spotlight of my torch into the depths of lava blackness. Again, those same words from the Phantom of the Opera floated through my mind *"Down that path into darkness deep as hell!"* Yes, that was where I now going! Hell! Believe me, if we were not going into Hell, Marc was surely going to be in it well and truly on our return to the top!

The last level was thirty-five metres down. Thirty-five metres straight down.

My heart was thumping apprehensively as we descended vertically via a single steel spiral staircase. All through the descent, water on my Helmet dripped intermittently in front of me. My whole body began to shake as I glanced (most stupidly I might add) below me to the cavernous mouth of darkness that leered up ready to swallow me within its huge black jaws. All pitifully lit only by the small beam of light of the guide's torch below me. Claustrophobia and fear of heights blended together as my shaking legs trembled all the way down this staircase to the black underworld. At that point, I was not sure I was going to make it back up to heaven! But once standing firmly on the solid floor of the cave, normally breathing, feeling more serene and listened to our guide explain the surrounding lava formations, I did begin to relax. I must admit here, the personal tour guide was interesting with his explanations of various aspects related to the lava tube as he took us to three different levels below the surface. As my racing heart slowly calmed down and serenity returned, I enjoyed the visual picture in front of me. Then, he asked us to turn off our torches.

What?

Turn off the only torch light we had? That miniscule, microscopic beam of light we had to use.

Was he mad? Was he joking??

No. He was not joking.

The lights went out.

Oh my ... oh my ... if I swore, I would have done it there and then.

It was so dark. I truly could not see a thing. I could not even see one finger in front of me. I was deep in the fathoms of this cave, completely consumed by blackness. Then in this darkness, he asked us to stop and listen to the sounds of the cave around us in silence. Yes, I could hear 'sounds' but not quite what I think he wanted me to hear. All I could hear was the sound of my hastening breathing, the noise of my heart pumping the blood through my veins as adrenaline soared, and my brain said loudly, "What are you doing, what are you doing?"

A gentle voice beside me whispered; *"Did you like what you hear?"*

The torch flicked back on.

I smiled lethally at my guide.

Up and back out of the yawning mouth of that lava lion ready to consume me into its hungering blackness, we went. Out of the depths of obscurity and dark. I am sure I climbed up faster than I moved down. Marc took the tourist photo of me to say, "I was here". A beautiful picture in my lava tube helmet and gear where I was smiling and laughing outwards while inwardly, I could have killed Marc ! No doubt about it, he does have that positive outlook of doing one thing a day that challenges you. I was quite sure, there, and then, I could have thought of something entirely different!

* * *

Of course, we must not forget the helicopter rides.

Arriving at a Helipad in the Canadian Rocky Mountains, we donned our snow gear and continued on to meet our pilot and guide. Well, that was the start of a beautiful friendship! His name was Ralph. He was about sixty-five plus in years, very confident, very chatty, very funny. We hit it off immediately particularly when he found out I was my husband's practice manager and did he use that relationship as a basis of humour many times on our trip!!

Squashed into the helicopter where Marc and I sat together with Ralph in the front, me squeezed in the middle, my right knee hard against Ralph's left. Something he, nor I for that fact, did not feel uncomfortable about, but a fact that would be important later in the flight. There was the late arrival of the other two passengers. They climbed into the back without even time to get their snow gear on – a feature that would again become significant later in the trip. The helicopter ride began, and Ralph was full of lots of quirks, witty humour, and smiles, as we rose up above the world.

A grand sight floated in front of us of snow-covered mountains surrounded by beautiful scenery as the helicopter climbed into the cold air. I reflected and thought what is it about mountains that incite some of the greatest adventures and triumphs? Is it their unpredictable force and unmerciful weather? Their towering, grandiose heights? Their demanding presence? The way they beckon some primitive instinct in us "the mountains are calling, and I must see, I must go?" (Well, that would be Marc anyway!). This time, we had the nice scenic version without any of the exertion and I could handle that! We flew closer and closer to a set of mountains and then, when being dashed against their rocky sides and dying a cold and miserable death seemed inevitable, Ralph showed his expertise by allowing an air current to just gently lift our aircraft higher and higher over a rocky ridge. As Ralph took us higher, the air became bumpier and rougher, and the helicopter buffeted its way.

Now, buffeting' according to one source "is an irregular motion of a structure in a flow apparently excited by turbulence in the flow." Well, this helicopter was definitely excited by turbulences as it elevated itself trying to peek over the summit of one of these mountains into the valley below. So high, so beautiful, so bumpy, and so, so, so rough! But a warm male hand, (not Marc's,) rested on my knee, together with a little pressure from the adjacent knee, and comforting words through the headset from Ralph encouraged me that, *"It's okay. You can breathe. Actually, it's probably good to breathe!"* I did not realise that I had been holding my breath. I had tensed and stiffened up; my knee jammed into his, in that small seat, seated between two males, to stop me falling. I exhaled. If his hand on my knee was my payment for being safe in that small helicopter as we inched over the top of that thin saddle between two formidable rocky spires and then plunged down into the valley below, ready to land. that was quite 'ok'.

But where was the helipad? All I could see were trees! Amazingly, Ralph landed this bird on an empty snow-covered patch of land adjacent to a partially frozen river – just the right size for this helicopter. A remarkable feat! Another challenge! (But this time, not for me!).

However, the real reason for this helicopter ride was the experience that followed!

I have read a quote that states, *"A determined woman can conquer anything, simply with one foot in front of the other"*. I do agree. Particularly when you have been dropped off in an isolated heavily snow-bound wooded area high in the Rockies, given a pair of snowshoes and told, *"Right. Let's go"!* No training, no basic instructions of 'how to do it', including how to put these contraptions on, no 'nothing', but merely standing in snow, the devices in your hand with absolutely no idea what to do. Then told, "Ready, let's move"! But please, allow me to immerse you in my whole experience.

The whole challenge of Snow Shoeing!

You have probably gathered by now that I do a lot of research prior to travels.

One of the tourism pages I had read suggested that there was no better way to attempt snowshoeing than by just doing it. The web page recommended you, *'Take a risk, dress for the elements, and enjoy'*, adding encouraging words like *'start your trek on a flat trail, where the snow is packed to get used to how your snowshoes feel on your feet.'* They also recommended, *'that it will take a little while to find a good pace, so start the walk-off slowly and you will find your groove in no time.'* Well, as the written authority, I had to trust the guidebook.

Right?

Wrong!

Jumping out of the helicopter we initially all plunged into snow up to our thighs. Marc went first and I followed but such a shock to my system. No gracious established pose in this beautiful snow that kissed the land so gently and then covered it snug with a white quilt that gave off the impression of a smooth and likely solid surface. Beautiful imagery! This snow was quite different from the snow we have in Australia. Instead, I was stumbling around, falling sideways, stuck deep. This was snow that did not provide any support for either your feet or your hands, and I struggled to stand up again after having fallen. Nothing to push against! Do you know that snow does not care whom it touches as I was ultimately covered in a soft white 'fluff' after dropping back heavily, after many attempts, into that soft powdery snow!

I floundered around in the snow feeling like a fish on a hook flapping widely, while all the time laughing at my antics of trying to get back up on my two feet. Ralph, our helicopter pilot, come snow-shoe guide, the gentlemen, relented and also laughing, came over to assist me to stand upright in the snow, to try and stay upright that is! This would not be the last time he had to render that service

Ralph then handed us all snowshoes and told us to put them on.

Simple, right?

Now, have you ever worn snowshoes?

They are not a normal shoe. To describe, a snowshoe is oval, about three times the size of your normal adult foot. It has open footing with clips and buckles and bent in a ski type shape from front to back. Very different to anything I had ever worn on my foot before! In fact, I had not actually ever seen a snowshoe in real life before that experience that day! Living in Australia where I reside, with its humidity, heat, our beautiful beaches and bushfire conditions, there was not much chance of a snowshoe being in my shoe rack in the cupboard at home. I had absolutely no idea what to do!

I was told to place them on my feet. Easy!

I could not even see my feet.

They were buried deep in that powdery snow. Let alone could I conceive lifting one foot up, balancing precariously on the other, and then trying to strap my boot into a contraption that I had no idea how to actually fit onto my boot! But learning very fast with some very basic instructions from Ralph to slide my foot into the snowshoe, to allow my foot to flex when I walk, to allow the "tail" to drop snow that will collect on the back (and don't forget the front and the side and all over). Later, with copious amounts of laughter, we were off!

Apparently, snowshoes work by distributing your weight over a larger area so that your foot does not sink completely into the snow. However, my own visual imagery and understanding of snowshoeing had been the image that you perched 'on top' of the snow and floated along the surface. With that picture in my mind, I proceeded to lift my foot and follow the small group (yes, I was last!)

Floatation?

What was I thinking?

You do not float.

Neither do you walk on top of the snow either.

This was not effortlessly walking along on top! This was working hard to make it easier for those following behind. Curiously, this turned out to include Ralph who wisely was quite happy for everyone in the party to take turns to 'break the virgin trail' while he 'gallantly' followed to 'help' if someone fell. He was no fool.

Surrounded by pristine alpine national park, each lungful of crisp, icy air enhancing that invigorating experience, I had to literally carve a path through the snow. I had to lift one leg as high as I could, before pressing my snowshoe forward and downwards to 'compress' as much snow as possible under me, before again repeating the process all over again with the other foot.

Do you know it was such a strenuous effort to lift your foot and walk?

And you sink!

Maybe not as far as you would have without snowshoes, but you DO sink and there is no semblance of floating at all!

My imagery of gliding effortlessly and gracefully over the surface of the snow held up by snowshoes had been totally WRONG! My hope of 'taking a little while to find a good pace and start off slowly finding my own groove' did not happen either! Instead, I carved a trail most ungraciously in those huge contraptions attached to my feet through the forest. This was definitely a challenge! Definitely an experience! There was certainly nothing glamorous or graceful about it at all as my balance was so off! Under ordinary normal walking conditions, I do not have the best balance in normal shoes. So, imagine what my balance, or rather my lack of balance was like, 'walking' in snowshoes was!

I do not think I have laughed so much!

'Walking' through the snow on those contraptions for me meant I was often on my backside. 'Walking' for me meant falling sideways and backwards as I tried to move those gigantic monstrosities' underneath me. More accurately, it could be described as "Walk, Fall, Laugh, Walk, Fall, Laugh! Repeat! Add to that, consider me trying to learn the somewhat supposedly *simple* manoeuvre of turning around?

Pirouetting around turned out to not be one of the popular options as I overbalanced yet once again. So, my solution was to try to walk backwards ever so slowly, raise one leg in that tennis racket, turn slightly, raise the other leg, turn a bit more, while always remembering to not step on your own snowshoe in that 'delicate' process of your feet crisscrossing or over you go again! It truly was such a great balancing act! Complete with abundant amounts of laughter! So much laughter!

Do you know, falling into that powdery snow, so deep beside you, was actually the easiest part? It felt great to fall! It was luxuriously soft! However, getting up and out of it was nigh impossible. As described earlier, there was no substance to it. Nothing to push against to help you up! Your snowshoes could not help you either, particularly if you had one snowshoe on top of the other one (remember, that was why you fell in the first place!)

Or if your foot went under a tree root, log, or rock, that snowshoe was effectively in some vice-grip, held deep under the snow pinning you to one spot. In those picturesque scenic white virginal conditions, you could not see those unseen obstacles until you were tripped or rather, I should say trapped by one. That was because you were walking, supposedly on top in thigh to waist-deep snow, so you had absolutely no idea what was underfoot. You walked a little faster, gaining confidence, gaining a good pace, following the others, and then once again your foot in this huge snowshoe was caught by a branch or a rock. You cannot move. You are Stuck! Laughter again!

Marc plunged on, taking the lead. Walking in the snow and confidently striding out. But that is Marc. Taking the snowshoe walk lead for the first time was an undertaking for me but I did not last in that position for very long. Probably due to the fact that I was moving – dragging- sliding- whatever you want to call this feat – my huge floppy tennis racket size feet upwards over a small hill of snow in front, creating the 'trail' for the others behind me. Feeling confident, I began to move somewhat self-assuredly up that mound, but this trek was followed by a face-first tumble into a deep trough of snow where now I was properly jammed. That was a little scary. My left knee was twisted behind. My other leg bent in the other direction. Again, Ralph tried to come to the rescue but this time, I simply could not move without twisting my knee in a bad way! I felt like one of those twisted cheese sticks! All knotted up! However, with two males to the rescue, to unlock the old knotted-up cheese stick, vertical stance was regained once more (well at least for about 5 more minutes). However, I went to the back of the very small group following them, as I had finally worked out Ralph's wisdom from the start. I was no fool either!

Now, two in our party had not had time to change into their heavy snow gear before jumping into the helicopter. One did not even have gloves, but Marc lent him a spare set he had brought. (Marc sometimes astounded me with what he has in his pocket, his backpack, and more scarily, what is in his car – but that is another story). So, please feel for those two as you continue in this story since everything we did, they did in normal clothing, not designed for deep snow.

Something about hiking, whether it is bushland or ice, there always seems to be rocks and water. But have you ever tried balancing on wet rocks on an icy plateau whilst wearing oversized tennis rackets on your feet? Well, that was how we crossed a creek with running ice-cold water, the water calling to those humans above to just have a little slip and check out the temperature of the water for themselves. I tried to keep that thought well down in my consciousness in case it triggered a fall. That event would not be laughable I might add!

Marc in his much-admired confident form stepped from rock to rock, sure-footed enough to help those following across, before taking the lead to blaze a trail through waist-deep virgin snow. Eventually he tired and passed the lead off to the other male member of our team whose job was to navigate a safe passageway along a frozen riverbank. Our small group had separated at this point and this young man (without the snow jackets etc) chose the flatter easier route across the ice. All good until there was a loud crack caused by a large sheet of snow-covered ice dropping a few centimetres with him in the middle of the sheet. Our wonderful guide Ralph, ever the optimist said, "*Just keep going. You'll be right*!" Marc, considering himself to be the heaviest in the group, had already set off cross-country away from the rocks making his own path across more difficult undulating but 'proper firm' ground. Of course, I followed him! Plunging and floundering my way back to the helicopter in those snowshoes eventually, my experience ended on a high note! In more ways than one!

* * *

On that trip, so many times, I was hauled up by sixty-five years plus Ralph as I was simply wedged. At times I thought I was jammed there forever. But it was so funny! All I could do was laugh! I definitely provided much amusement for the others as I continuously fell again, laughed at myself again, assisted to my feet by Ralph again and then did it all over again. (If you were observing the antics, you would probably assume I was drunk, but all those falls, were without the effects of alcohol!) Reality, I could not even imagine doing it inebriated! The best part for everyone, was we all had a great time laughing at my antics. For me, it was laughing at myself trying to walk in those things! Personally, I think my 'snowshoe walk' should properly be addressed as a 'snowshoe tumble'!

On that day, I did take a risk and accepted the challenge.

I was determined to do it and to achieve, albeit with much laughter, many tumbles and falls and I truly did enjoy it. (I also think our pilot/guide Ralph did too!)

Hard work? Yes.

Exhausting? Yes.

Confronting? Yes.

Would I do it again? Maybe. Probably. Yes!

So, if the shoe does not quite fit, then you need to grab a thicker sock! Because a determined woman can conquer anything by placing one foot in front of the other.

That was what I did.

Even if I could not see the other foot!

I do believe that Cinderella was right in her proof that "A new pair of shoes can change, shape, or adjust your life!"

Even when it fell off!

Chapter Nine

Why Walk When You Can Slide ... or Glide ... but with Style?

When you travel in Winter, you do need different types of shoes! Without a doubt, walking in a Northern Hemisphere winter environment and climate, calls for appropriate shoes, as I certainly found out! Being on snow and ice is a place your feet and at times your body, must be crammed into different apparel, to allow you to move gracefully across this unstable terrain in apparent style. Sometimes gracefully! Sometimes you roll along! Sometimes you fall! As I certainly found out!

It was the middle of January in Banff, Canada.

I was in the most beautiful hotel I had ever been in in terms of 'historic' and 'aristocratic manor-like' surrounded by a snow-filled background. Outside the winter sky was blue and clear. Inside the fire was glowing in the huge grate. People around me were chatting with each other. Sharing coffee, sharing conversation, exchanging ideas and comments. The friendly service people were walking backwards and forwards performing their routines admirably. The whole effect was of a wonderful winter dreamy setting. The kind of thing you see on a Disney or a Hallmark Movie at Christmas. So romantic!

One thing missing. Marc had gone skiing. Me? Well bluntly put, I am not ever putting skis on my feet!

I once read somewhere that skis are not just pieces of wood, steel, and fiberglass. They are instead tools for escape, a way to challenge fears, push your limits and share incredible experiences with your friends. A very good description and Marc would agree, but skis for me evoke quite a different image!

The thought of my feet being locked into heavy boots which in turn are attached to two unsteady panels of wood of an unusual shape, designed to apparently slide effortlessly *out* from under me when least expected, does not impress me. Add to that a couple of sticks called 'poles' in my hands to assist me staying upright? An uncomfortable helmet being crammed on over a beanie on my head (those who know me understand that I detest things covering my head with tinted goggles of assorted colours shielding my eyes and face .To complete the picture, a bright scarf draped around my neck, intended apparently to dramatically fly gracefully behind me; now attired properly to 'sail' down the mountain, does not conjure for me at all, a comfortable contented image.

Then, after all the above clothing assembled in place, the next step would be to propel myself actually physically off the edge of the mountain. That would mean actually letting go of whatever was holding me upright. I would be ready to ski down that mountain, when I eventually had my hands pried from that supporting figure's hands, arm, or whatever object I was clinging to with an iron-vice like grip; my arms would be wobbling, my teeth and face would be chattering. My body would be most definitely straining hard to hold those poles straight (if I hadn't lost them by then that is) as my booted feet were being pulled by gravity, irreversibly downwards. My skis would be moving, individually making their own autonomous way, to trees or rocks in my path, as they bounced over, or preferentially crashed with delighted mirth into objects in the way. All with their purposeful intent to dramatically sprawl me, breathing heavy and winded, face down in the uncaring and icy hard snow. My voice box would be screaming in terror, but no one would know of my fate because my scream, howling off the edge of the mountain, would have been lost in the wind, chasing that brightly coloured scarf! No, nothing elegant or likeable about that at all!

Skiing actually scares me because I prefer control.

There is a quote, "Skiing is a dance; the mountain always leads and is the next best thing to having wings". To me the whole concept of those two slippery boards supporting your body is terrifying! Tell me honestly, how could those two narrow boards on an icy uneven surface be able to counter the inexorable effects of gravity? I am aware that falling is a normal part of skiing as Marc has showed me many falls on his 'GoPro' on ski slopes (which in response to I laughed,) but that does not help me at all. All I can visualise was myself contorted in agony with one knee bent one way and the other one, in a twisted fashion, squashed underneath me. My skis sliding off somewhere else with their own conversation of, "*take me away from that unsafe person*". I would rather dance around the mountain in my own time, with my own comfortable surefooted boots on! As far as having wings … no thank you. The only wings I need are the solid metal wings of an airplane flown by an aviation pilot with many, many, many years of experience.

The thought of me skiing with style on those two slippery fibreglass boards was just laughable! Marc can perform that one, all on his own. I am more than happy to let him fly like the wind all by himself! I preferred the glow of the warm fireplace! Mulled wine in hand!

* * *

When the Olympics are underway, people who never think about ice skating, all of a sudden, are giant fans of this sport. They watch that person jump in the air, twirl around and land flawlessly and gracefully on teeny tiny blades on the ice. Amazing stuff! I love watching them and I too take the time to observe from the comfort of my armchair. However, how on earth do they not fall flat down on their face?

You do know that when you ice skate, you are standing on thin metal blades attached underfoot?

You do know it is those thin blades that propel you across a sheet of ice?

How on earth, on those contraptions called ice skates/boots, are you supposed to stay on your feet the whole time and apparently slide with elegance across that delicate sheet of ice? When I look at someone who does this so effortlessly, I think, how wonderful, to be full of unwarranted confidence like that skater I am watching. But look closely, if you see that person in the back, standing very still with the 'granny-walker' on the ice? That would be me!

Having ice skated in his childhood, Marc was confident and competent. In a previous travel, when we visited his family, he skated then too. Doesn't he look clever in this picture? (Preferentially, I sat on the adjacent comfortable park bench in the sun and read my book! I thought that was a much better choice).

In Jasper, we did not have an ice rink, but rather a real Christmas Card image frozen pond at the bottom of the hill. Off Marc went, stylishly pushing his ice skates' outwards. Beautiful cadence and rhythm as he handsomely raced around that frozen lake. Following him were other younger skilled skaters, who were laughing, chatting, effortlessly gracefully gliding, and sliding along on their skates. He was a magical picture in motion.

Now, we know that Cinderella's life was changed when she put on those glass slippers! But apart from the transformation it gave her, she must have found that dancing with her Prince quite uncomfortable. Those glass slippers would have been so hard to not only wear but to dance in, not to mention the run down the stairs at midnight. I mean after all; she did lose one shoe! Nonetheless, like Cinderella at the palace, in my own 'palatial ice arena', wearing my uncomfortable 'new glass slippers', I 'had a go'.

Skating can make you feel graceful, athletic, beautiful. You move free as a bird as you propel your feet with forward, skates parallel to one another, pointing the same angle, urging you to go further and faster down the pond. You glide across the ice like a graceful swan moving naturally. One glide. Two glides. Three glides like a graceful pendulum, a beautiful ice dance. Such an effortless image! Did I really believe those two steel knives would safely stay under me as I gripped Marc's arm tightly just to stay upright, (even before I was actually on the frozen pond itself,) attempting to traverse the pathway to actually get onto the ice! Just like those Christmas movies, on one of the most slippery natural surfaces on a true frozen pond with NO 'comforting' rails around the edge to cling to, having knives on the bottom of your feet, where would your feet automatically go? What do you think happened to mine?

Perhaps you may think 'how hard can it be?' I am just exaggerating!

Once on the pond, I did not slide with flair or elegance. Instead, I staggered, wobbled, toppled, and lurched sideways, all with extremely loud sound effects. No three clicks and I was back in Kansas (or Australia for that matter). No, not even three clicks before my feet were no longer below me and I was on my bum. Ouch! My husband to the rescue again as he bought me a folding chair. This apparently was as a semblance of support designed to give me confidence.

With that four-legged encouragement, gripping the chair back firmly and bravely, I actually skated around that pond in my own *controlled* style and my *own* way (I have video footage to prove it). I called it my own Granny Ice Walker!

This time I had control, even if it didn't look pretty! There was nothing at all attractive about my 'ice skate ', hunched over, firmly attached to that sliding chair. However, my Grammy Ice walker meant I could actually skate on the ice, although not sure that skating was the correct term. Rather, my style was to slip along ever so clumsily, awkwardly, and inelegantly. No gracefulness seen anywhere as my legs glided out behind me, not at all parallel at the same time. Neither were they pointing in the same direction. We did not have a very good relationship as each of my skates wanted to individually go in a completely different direction away from me! But miraculously, the ungainly, ugly duckling manoeuvred herself around on the ice. Like Cinderella in her glass slippers, dancing at the ball for the first time, I was actually ICE SKATING! Successfully circumnavigating this large frozen pond, not once but twice!

Once again on terra firma, a happy, tired smile on my face, we walked in normal boots back towards our room. I was feeling extremely proud of myself for this new accomplishment. Then it happened. My feet slipped and OVER I WENT! Skidding and plummeting to the ground onto my hip and knees and bum in a most un-lady like fashion.

Do you know the most embarrassing part about that?

This was on a normal footpath!

Tell me, where was the challenge in that?

* * *

Oh, what fun it was to ride in a five-dog open sleigh!

I can hear you say that rhyme sounds familiar, but aren't I singing the wrong words? Well for us, they were definitely the right ones! After all, what else do you do when you are in in Lapland, Finland, covered from head to foot to keep the warmth inside, experiencing temperatures between minus fifteen and minus twenty degrees outside and snow is everywhere? Should we stay in our nice cosy room and read a book? No, we went for a Husky Sleigh ride! Why not!

Dog sledding dates as far back as 6000 BC, when the practice of dog sledding was used as a means of transport. While some northern populations still use dog sledding as a means to travel across icy tundra, today it is primarily used for entertainment and competitive sport. Of course, it is now also offered as a tourist attraction for people like us!

Nervously I faced the prospect of being in an open sleigh. I truly wanted to go but my dilemma was about how many layers to wear on each body part – top, bottom and feet – including how many extra layers of socks I would need. Just thinking of those outside temperatures that we were going to be exposed to, made me ponder that aspect quite seriously. Even though we were to be given a full thermal body suit, I knew from our previous day's experience of a reindeer ride I had not been warm enough, as my feet and hands were frozen on our return at the end of that journey. So, I stressed myself just a little, before this trip, wondering if I was going to be warm enough for this much colder and much longer ride ahead.

Have you ever wondered why astronauts always had someone help them place their suit on? Well now I know why. Getting into a Thermal suit, you cannot move! On our husky sled ride day, I felt like an astronaut attempting to get into my 'thermal space suit'. Marc had to assist me as I could not even lift one foot up and into the one-piece padded suit, but we worked together as a team, trying to adjust my own three layers underneath the suit to make it comfortable. At one point of the robing, I could not breathe and thought perhaps I may return a slimmer person as my fat in all those layers, would have been squashed out of me! But once checked that all tiers were in place and tucked in under the suit, I stood up.

I looked like Michelin woman.

I have used this term before but for those readers who are not sure what I am talking about - a Michelin man is small, fat man made out of tyres used in advertisements by the French tyre company Michelin. Get the picture? In that suit I was the female version! In that 'appropriate' gear, I walked like Michelin woman, bowlegged, like I had been miles on a horse, my feet stomping in heavy boots, complete with thick mittens and hood!

But there I was.
Ready.
Eager but Nervous.
Oh dear - I wanted to pee.
Forget that one!
Far too many layers to take off!

Thirty minutes later we were greeted by howling dogs. Touching their fur with my bare hands was quite a mistake, as the hair on those huskies was quite cold on the surface being full of ice. Mittens on and able to resume the stroking and the caressing of the dogs ... whispering rather loudly in their ears that, *"you are taking me out today and please be nice to me" ... stroke, stroke, caress, caress."* I am not sure whether they were listening or not, because as various huskies were bought forward to be harnessed to the two sleighs, intense howling of all dogs began. Apparently all thirty-three dogs on this farm loved to work and ALL wanted to pull the sleighs. When one dog starts to be harnessed, all become excited and howl. What in incredible sound! The excitement in those dogs in wanting to go to work. We should really inject that enthusiasm into some humans!!!

Our dogs harnessed; instructions given how to drive the sled with the dogs, and we were ready. Did I tell you that we were not going to be driven, but we ourselves, had to drive the sled across the ice and snow. Yes, We, two novices, had to drive the sled!

Marc listened to the instructions from our guide *(who was French mind you with limited English)* and he had to take in what to do. Driving the sled was not a matter of just standing on the back of the sled, and following the guide, you had to manoeuvre the thing too! You needed to give the dogs a helping hand on the steep up-hill bits. You must hold on, steer, and to make sure the sled didn't go out of control on the downhill bits. And don't forget, if you fall off, the dogs will go faster, and you will be left behind. In those temperatures - Survival unlikely!

"Dashing through the snow" ... our dogs took off.

Sled dogs travel at an average of 25 to 30 km/h on journeys of around 40 km long. On longer trips, the average speed drops to 16 to 22 km/h. Even in bad conditions, however, sled dogs could still maintain an impressive average speed of 10 km/h. Our experience on that day was not just for a fifteen-minute ride either. We were to be in those elements for almost three hours!! We had five huskies pulling us, each capable of pulling its own weight – about 25kg – each. (*A bit flattering that the guides thought that the two of us, plus all our warm clothes and the sleigh only added up to 125kg. I think they got their measurements wrong there.*) The two guides on their sleigh in front of us had eight dogs which meant they kept getting much further out in front. On several occasions, as we were the only tourists with them, they were totally out of sight. Hopefully' we were following their tracks.

Driving the sled, at first Marc was going well until his hands began to burn as frostbite commenced to attack his fingers. Amazingly, how quickly that happened. A change of gloves and back in business, his fingers thawing with the warmth of his new mittens emanating through the cold. That was a little scary! A doctor who could not use his hands! Black frost-bitten fingers!

The dogs ran along the track set by the lead sleigh. Minor corners happened by just leaning the sleigh and pivoting the sledge on the inside runner. On tight corners, the sleigh behaved like any other child's toy pulled along by a string, bouncing off whatever obstacle it hit, as the dogs pulled it around the corner. Cornering between trees was hair-raising as you needed to 'catch-up' to the dogs before they turned around that tree. Basically, when they jerked the front of the sleigh into the corner, Marc, as the driver, had to be already lined up with the direction we (actually the dogs) wanted to go.

Any uphill run required Marc to assist by using one of his legs like being on a scooter, or, if the hill was steeper, jumping off and running along, pushing the sled from behind (and oh yes there were some steep hills). Of course, the latter manoeuvre required him to jump back on before the sled gathered too much speed on the downside part of the hill. Failing to make the jump led to falling off the back of the sled. That meant no one would be in control as Marc would be up to his hips in deep soft powdery snow unable to catch up. The dogs freed of the extra weight would then I imagine, simply take off with Lyndell helplessly tied in! (Not quite what I wanted to happen!)

Up and down the hills … *(poor dogs had to pull me up the hill)*, with Marc driving them, we glided, crunched, and slid over the snow between trees, around trees, as those beautiful huskies sped us across the virgin snow! Far too regularly, when what Marc was doing was obviously, at least to the lead dog if not to Marc, not 'right', that lead dog would look back at Marc with a stare from her intense, ice blue, intelligent eyes that said, "What *the h*** are you trying to do back there?" (But of course, the look was in French since she was a French husky)*. Oh, so glad I was not driving! But Marc did a fantastic job. I could clearly hear him grunting and puffing behind me.

What's that? Did I have a go?? No way! I had absolutely no intention of driving the sled. I could see myself driving and something would happen. Or I would slip and take my hands off and the dogs would simply keep going without me. Plonk - into snow. End of ride … no Lyndell. Instead, for me, my part of that glide-slide-ride was being tucked up in the sleigh itself, complete with reindeer skin/fur covering (which didn't do much I might add at minus twenty degrees) and tied in with a tarp to cover me.

Two scary experiences do come to mind.

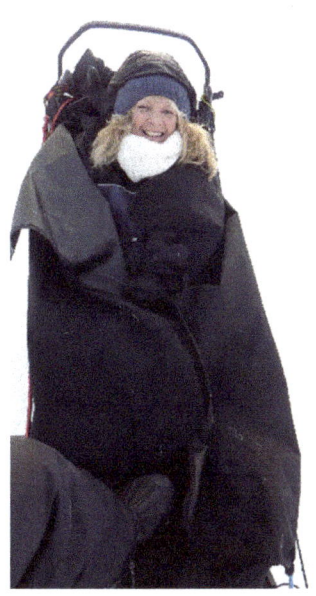

One being a corner with soft snow on the downside. The sled wanted to roll over, but Marc pulled it around the corner to keep the sled, and its important cargo – 'Me' - upright. The other being when the dogs in a U-turn manoeuvre decided to do 'their own thing'. Instead of following our human guide in the snow (walking hip deep mind you) to perform the U turn, the dog leader instead decided to fold back exactly where she had come from, causing the sleigh to pivot 180 degrees on the spot. When all thirteen dogs (two sleds) had the same mindset, there was nothing we could do, and Marc had no time to react. He himself sunk hip deep into the soft powdery snow and could only use his thigh as a pivot point for the runners. He watched the sled start to topple towards him. Remember, I was in that sled bundled up like a Christmas present.

I felt like it was part of a slow dream as I sensed the sled tip sideways and over, capsizing, me tied in with nowhere to go except down and into the snow headfirst with that sled on top of me. Luckily one of the guides at that particular time was close enough to jump on the opposite runner, stop mid-air, the topple of the sled holding tied in 'Michelin Lyndell' and assisted Marc with completing the U-turn. Our guide was then left with the task of untangling the mess the dogs had made with the traces. But even with those incidents occurring, the combination of the exquisite scenery, the white silence of just the runners gliding on the snow, the majestic indescribable exhilaration of that day, the unqualified thrill of the husky sled, even at absolutely freezing temperatures, we decided that dog-sledding excursion was the highlight of our trip to Finland. One we still talk about!

It may appear for you reading this, that I was just sitting in the sleigh *"watching the scenery go by, watching the sun reach its zenith all of one hand breadth above the horizon, admiring the view, leisurely taking photos ...* "but I did not do that.

It was also such a strange, entirely different experience being on that snow sled wrapped up. You know how I like to be in control. There I had no control of anything. I just had to trust those dogs and hope Marc actually knew what he was doing. I had to trust that we would not fall off, extremely importantly trust the guide in front on his sleigh would not leave us too far behind!

It was also quite one thing being physically active and manoeuvring that sleigh on the beautiful snowscape. It was quite another to be completely still for almost three hours, scrunching your toes and fingers to keep the frostbite out as your extremities were freezing. Neither could I take too many photos with my phone because my fingers would freeze so quickly and burn with the cold. Inside that sleigh, I was too busy trying to stop my teeth from chattering, my toes from freezing and the rest of my knees and upper body from not going stiff by sitting in one position for so long. By the end of that three hours, I was extremely cold and worn out from having been inactive, for being far too long in arctic temperatures. I felt that despite the thermal suit and my own layers of clothing, the severe coldness of minus twenty-degree Celsius temperatures had won! Although Marc had been physically active running with the dogs, his eyebrows and eyelashes and hair were all iced over, so can you imagine what my hair looked like after all that inactivity of sitting! Completely frosted with ice. All White! I had aged 20 years in three hours. I was just sitting down! Of course, my bladder was definitely singing, "Need to pee, need to pee … NEED TO PEE NOW!!

Returning to home base, you could imagine the relief of the 40-degree shift from -20 to +20 deg Celsius as my bladder began to once more relax and thaw with the heat from the room. Mind you I frantically had to get Marc's help to get the clothes off me before I could attend to Nature … and fast!

Through coffee and a chat with our lovely French hosts, we discovered that even the professionals suffer frostbite. Our guide and the owner both had frost bitten fingers and toes from the previous week temperatures of minus 45 degrees. They had not lost digits but definitely skin, and both had the green colouring of frost bite. So glad I was not sitting in the sleigh then!

Would I do it again? Yes!

I might even try driving it. But a word of advice. If you ever have a go at sliding a sleigh on the snow, don't forget the six rules of dog sledding …

DO WATCH THE MAGNIFICENT SNOWSCAPES PASS BY - as you realise that the undulating white pathway that you are travelling slowly changes as you ventured deeper and deeper into the backcountry of Lapland.

DON'T USE YOUR MOBILE PHONE OR CAMERA TOO MUCH unless you're willing to experience frost bite quickly!

LEARN HOW TO 'SPEAK DOG to try and communicate with that lead dog who truly looks at you and thinks you are stupid and definitely knows more than you do!

DON'T GET IN THE WAY OF THE FLYING POO. Remember when learning to run in teams, the sled dogs very quickly learn how to use the bathroom on the run so as not to reduce the tempo of the sleigh slide. Ducking a few times was a rather unattractive part of the adventure!

DO KEEP RUNNING: No matter how many layers of clothing you have on, if you are sitting idly for many hours in minus 20 degrees Celsius, you will start to feel the cold. Running with the sleigh will warm up in no time, and your dog team might even appreciate the extra help i.e., that lighter weight going uphill. I did feel sorry for the dogs!

And the most important one:

DON'T FALL OFF THE SLED! And if you do, it was nice knowing you.

(Oh - I think that one definitely speaks all for itself!)

CHAPTER TEN

Why Walk When You Can Ride?

Many of my experiences or challenges were not always Marc's fault or arose from his lack of risk assessment. Challenges', 'encounters', 'experiences', whatever the word, or definition gleamed from those words, sometimes simply just happen because they happen! They just appear and we fall headlong into them!

Our trip to Fiji held a few such 'challenges'!

There was the experience of visiting Nadi township itself.

We asked some locals whether we were standing in the right place for the bus to take us into town. These same lovely locals then flagged down a non-descript aged rattling minivan and we all literally piled in. Not quite a traditional bus but we were in a different country so, when in Rome (Nadi), do as the locals do. But I became increasingly uncomfortable, not only because we were in an ancient vehicle loaded with more people than the manufacturers ever safely planned for, but also because I was seated in a position immediately behind the driver and could observe the nonchalant way, he was prepared to just risk the lives of his passengers. From my observation point, I was able to monitor him as he continuously texted on his mobile with one hand, changed gears using a huge highly decorated padded gear stick with the other hand and, with no third hand available to actually steer the vehicle, use his knee to manoeuvre the wheel in and out of traffic whilst apparently expending only an infinitesimal amount of time actually looking at the road! I cannot say I am an excellent driver, but maybe he was relying on ESP or divine providence to guide us into town. It was interesting that no-one else in the crowded van seemed to have a problem with what I was seeing, nor did they seem to place as much value on their own lives as I placed on Marc's and mine.

Marc was apparently oblivious to the danger we were all in, as he was wedged further back in the van and could see very little of the potential catastrophes that literally might be just around the next corner. The van, the bus, whatever you wish to call this vehicle, with each stop became crammed even further with more locals and became even cosier and smellier. Loud blazing reggae music added to the atmosphere. The sights, the close company, the music, the odours, and most importantly to me, those quite legitimate nagging concerns about whether we would survive the journey and if we did, where were we actually going to end up and how would we ever get back to the hotel, all added to my/our initial local Fijian cultural experience for one day. And all that local cultural immersion for a total and very realistic price of $1.10.AUD! Imagine that! What a bargain! But not for the fainthearted.

Flying to Savusavu from the main island was another unplanned challenge!

At the airport we boarded an aged Twin Otter plane that looked like it could have been a relic from the second War World judging by the state of its worn and tired appearance. For readers who do not know, a Twin Otter is a small island-hopping sized plane that seats a maximum of 16 passengers. Yes, I like flying but preferably in big luxurious stretched out aeroplanes. This was not quite my kind of plane but seeing this was how we were going to get from one place to another, always positive and ever smiling, I boarded and sat in my designated seat immediately next to the window, ready to be impressed by the island views below me. However, my vision was instead of the large propeller that would soon be spinning at just short of the speed of sound just next to my face. That is, I certainly hoped it would keep on spinning AND remain attached to the engine AND continue to remain outside my window for the entire duration of our flight. We noted the latch on the door that separated the cabin and cockpit was broken, resulting in the door just sliding randomly open and closed. Together with the age of the aircraft, any assumptions on that propeller staying attached could definitely not be taken as a given. By the way, there were 6 passengers, including us, and, occupying ½ the seats, one long surfboard, that were embarking on this flight. The surfboard seemed to be the calmest!

It must be exciting for the pilots to feel the power from twin turboprops push them back in the seats as they accelerate down the airstrip ready to lift off and fly up into the sky. But, for a passenger, in a small airplane like this one, only an arm's length away the pilots' cockpit, with views of both the ancient and worn flight controls and the ever-looming larger view of the end of the runway and the trees, my anxiety level amplified. Eventually we took off to rise laboriously against the force of gravity, much as a struggling albatross finally pulls itself off the surface of the water before gradually, ever so gradually, climbing away. But I was in the plane! I was flying!

This elastic-band powered plane begrudgingly, surged and lurched us first into the air and then after a short trip again, carried us to a dubious landing strip on the island where we were going to stay. Since the intervening cockpit door was being held from opening and closing by the careful application of Marc's foot for the entire duration of the flight, and since we sat immediately behind the pilots at the front of the cabin, we were able to peer through the pilots' window as we approached a strip of lawn that was apparently our landing strip. We were perturbed but not surprised given our experiences so far this flight. But on this postage stamp bit of grass, we did land safely, disembarked and walked to the tin lawn mower storage shed that doubled as a terminal before waiting for our ride to the 'Pearl Shack' where we would spend our stay, both of us looking forward very much to our island get away! And like the travel research said, it lived up to being a wonderful time, of reading, swimming, and exploring.

Of course, during our lovely stay on this island, Marc had one of his hairbrained ideas.

A family member of the owners of the Pearl shack where we were staying, mentioned there was a waterfall nearby. Already having seen many waterfalls in our exploration of this rainforest island, one waterfall began to look like the other. Naturally, I was not really that keen to walk to another waterfall, but as it was a beautiful day, and near the end of our time away, I caved. With directions sought, we set off.

Under hot and humid tropical island conditions, we walked the track. At least the track we thought we were meant to walk. This was not a constructed, organised track. As we progressed, it became a trifle muddy and slippery, and then, deteriorated to the point it started to resemble images from World War One trenches. The quagmire of mud winding through the trees to an unseen and unfathomable distant end did not make me happy at all. Neither in our messy walking, did this 'must-see' waterfall appear. Refusing to be daunted (at least at this stage), a hot, sweat-soaked couple in steamy, tropical conditions, continued onwards, forwards, searching for that cascade that was supposed to be 'jumping out soon'. We reached a decision point, both physically and mentally, at a creek, where it meant, I would have to do some delicately balancing on some small stones to cross without falling into the thick oozing mud. Not the kind you had for a spa kind mud bath either! This was deep brown and heavy layers of sludge!

Not Happy Jan!

Oh, forget about 'Jan', Not Happy Lyndell!!

I know I sound like such a complainer but with my feet rooted in thick mud I had to choose what action I was going to take. I had to decide to either walk on the slippery stones and kill Marc if I fell in, or, to stay firmly where I was, determined I was not going to move on, turn around, and then kill Marc!

Right at that moment, (most fortunately for Marc since his longevity at that point seemed unlikely no matter what my decision was going to be), a young Fijian man came along the trail on a quad bike. He must have thought us quite mentally unhinged as he looked at us strangely, wondering what these two white Europeans were doing out alone in the middle of someone's private property, in the middle of the day, on this extremely muddy track, and apparently, lost. We discovered through broken English communication we were on the Wrong Track! Once that was determined, this lovely, bronzed Fijian man took pity on us and offered a lift on his bike, to the base of the falls. The falls were rather unimpressive, but I was happy and more than grateful to my Fijian saviour in not only rescuing me from the endless mud-filled track and driving us to the waterfall base, but then taking us all the way back out along the 'correct' track to the road! Two bonuses. No more mud to endure, and that was my very first ride ever on a quadbike!

As I sat behind this Fijian young man on his quad bike holding his waist for stability, I discovered the 'payment' for this ride. He many times nonchalantly seemed to snuggle back into my perspiration-soaked T-shirt clad breasts. I could have objected but realistically, it seemed to me an acceptably small price to pay for not having to walk back through the mud. I could definitely handle it and I did.

Oh, you ask where was Marc all this time? He was on the quadbike too - but on the carry rack at the back. His cost was being splattered and splashed in brown oozy sludge all over his body by the thick oozing mud from the tyres. We so laughed about that one!

* * *

There are other ways that are not as conventional or traditional of getting from one place to another. Like inner tubes.

When I first met Marc, before we were married, he was involved in scouts as a group leader in the local area. We went on a scouting weekend camp together and his role that particular weekend was to teach the scouts about white-water canoeing. The venue was the Nymboida Canoe Centre. I was nervous, firstly of meeting his scout troop as the 'girlfriend' of the leader and secondly, exploring new recreational activities I was not at all familiar with. That weekend involved many physical activities, some of which I partook and others that I totally refused, choosing to be an observer only. But it was an enjoyable weekend, and many entertaining hours spent watching those young people canoe, climb and create and experience exciting entertainment in a 'safe' environment.

One of those activities was this *'tubing'*.

Tubing as it is called, is a recreational activity where an individual rides on top of a tractor tyre inner tube, either on water or snow, and is definitely a fun but non-conventional way to get from point A to Point B. River tubing involves free floating down the river on an inner tube. All you have to do is sit in your tube and go with the flow. To some it might look a bit tame compared to white water canoeing, but I could see it was ideal for this weekend, for the scouts and for their families. I watched people come down the rapids on those inner tubes, hearing their screams of delights, the sun on their faces, hands trailing in the water and bobbing along to the river's song, propelled only by the current. So, after the troop had left on the Sunday afternoon, the weekend activities completed, and being a bit daring for a city girl, I suggested to Marc, that I would like to have a go!

Climbing up the valley to the beginning of the river, we pushed our tubes into the water and started with some very gentle rapids. Realise this was not a waterpark ride but a real flowing river. Neither am I in swimmers but dressed in t-shirt, black tights, and boots. However, I was soon drifting gently along, being carried by the current, thoroughly enjoying the peaceful natural water ride. But someone forgot to tell me about *Eddies*!

Eddies are where the water, instead of continuing downstream, strikes some obstacle and starts to turn on the spot. Anything, or anyone who might be drifting downstream in an un-propelled inner tube, that gets caught in an eddy, stops flowing downstream and just spins continuously slowly on the spot. In order to break out of an eddy, you require some form of propulsion applied in the right manner at the right time. But remember this is me, naïve 'never before done this' person, we are talking about! I had neither the knowledge of *how* nor *when* to do this, so for me, the result when I got caught in the eddy was that I stopped moving forward and started turning helplessly in circles. Yes, round, and round and round and round in one place!

Then there are '*Stoppers.*' That is when the water strikes a rock or other obstacle under water and 'folds back' on itself, creating an endless recycling wall of water that keeps you from moving forward. On my stomach, in my very first ride down the river on this inner tube, the water coursing down the river, I became stuck in one. Flat on my face lying on the tube, unable to move forward, water continuing to flow hard up against my legs still poking upstream. Nothing lady like at all here in my wet day clothes! To my chagrin, the force of that water was forcing my legs apart, wide, wide apart. As much as I tried, I could not close my legs at all. There I was face down, on an inner tube, unable to move forward and my legs were being held outspread! Of course, I said the first thing that came to my mind. Speaking loudly to the cascading water I shouted out, "... *Here I am ... come on boys*". I definitely did not feel like the lady my mother brought me up to be.

Thank goodness no one was listening! What would they have thought!!!!!!!!

* * *

If you are religious, you know that Jesus walked on the water.
So did I.
I walked on water.

No, I am not intoxicated or letting my imagination run loose, in fact, I honestly walked on an ocean. In fact, I walked on the Bothnian Sea.

Can you picture the world of an ocean? The shore? Can you see people cheerfully playing in the water, cavorting on the sands, enjoying the sunshine and the glorious blue ocean stretched before you? That blue extending so far that it mingles with the blue horizon in a far-off world 'to infinity and beyond' (as my grandsons would say!) Visualize now the same world of water but in white. That once blue ocean turned into a creation of arctic white. Your eye travels towards the horizon where it meets the blue grey of infinity and beyond, and as far as your eye can see, all there is, is white. The air is clean, crisp, laden with ice. It tingles your face, filling your eyelashes with tiny icicles.

Frozen. Solid. White. Water, ice, air, snow. The sea became ice. Ice became land.

In Kemi, Finland, you did not know where the land finished, and the frozen sea began. The boundaries between elements were blurred in this coastal Lapland. The ice on the frozen sea was so thick that the sea had become land, or our interpretation anyway. Snow was everywhere, covering land, sea, and ice with a soft, fluffy curtain as if it were concealing what lay below, keeping it hidden until the thaw of spring arrived. On that sea, you could walk on it, ski, ride a kick-sled all the way west, until you reached Sweden.

On arrival, at Kemi, Marc suggested that we 'view the sea'. I looked at Marc in disbelief. What sea? Naturally, I was expecting the normal blue water and white sands like home, but instead, in front of me was a frozen solid view stretching out ahead. A white world where you could not see the difference between land, water, or sky. Endless white.

"Come on…lets walk on it", came the words from my beloved, as we watched others using cross country skis skimming their way across the ice. I glanced down to my heavy warm thick winter boots and back out to this frozen sea.

Marc wanted me to do what?? Really? Was he mad?

My imagination as it does, went to catastrophic viewing (from movies) of images of bodies that had plunged through the cracking ice into freezing deathly waters below. Tentatively I tapped one heavily booted clad toe from the safe land to the sea … not that I could really see the difference between either. Stepping fearfully along the shoreline beside him, I began to walk. Slowly … fearfully …, timidly, staying close to where I thought the edge was, gaining a little more confidence, and then great trepidation rushed through me as I heard ice cracking below me. Keep walking I told myself, just keep walking … breathe … breathe …

as I clung tightly to Marc's hand. I was not going to let go of him in this instance. I thought, well if we were going to die today, we were going to die and sink down together!

But we didn't die!

In fact, I followed the track across the ocean and walked far out to sea, (so much better than swimming the same distance, believe me). I walked stronger, more confident, and then turning around, began to slowly laugh as I saw the distance between myself and the tiny houses on the shore, whose windows now reflected brilliantly, the sun rays that had just struggled to make it above the winter horizon.). We were so far away from the 'real' land. Being in the middle of an ocean, still standing upright and actually walking on water!

I could not believe it.

Snuggling into my husband in our warm safe hotel room that night, both of us laughing and reminiscing about the new experience of ocean walking antics (and faces) of the day, – what does he then suggest, but to go back and do it all again tomorrow, but this time to glide instead? My firm answer to him as I rolled away to contented sleep was 'we will see!'

The next morning, we drove back to the same Bothnian Sea. Marc gave me 'that look'. Of which I returned to him that look that women give their 'biggest male child', their husbands, when they suggest something totally insane, (you all know *that* look I am talking about?). Marc then provided me 'that' shrug men give their partners that indicates they are going to do whatever 'it' is anyway, and he left me standing there on the white ground, to hire a 'kick ski'. A 'Kick-Ski' is a device that looks like a child's scooter but has two ski-runners instead of wheels and designed to allow you to 'glide' on the ice. The kick sled is driven forward by the driver standing on one runner, kicking backwards on the ground with the other foot, hence the name. It glides over the ice as you kick!

Like hell, I thought, was I going to be 'sucked' into this antic, even if Marc did bat his beautiful baby-blues at me and smile his innocent alluring grin? Onto the ice, he went, upon the kick sled, skating and gliding his way out towards the horizon we could not see.

He was happy, calm, serene, enjoying every moment of gliding on the ice! Like some form of courtship ritual, he returned to me with that inquiring smile on his face. Back out to sea again. Once more back again, tempting me to respond.

No. It was not working.

Not at all.

Well, maybe it was working! Just a tiny bit.

I looked at the kick ski.

I looked at my boots.

"Come on, just have a little go", he says.

Then a slightly 'bigger go'. Then a much bigger one. And then I was off! Gliding alone on the ice! Gliding on the ocean!

But the task of using a kick ski, is not that simple.

Between trying to keep the kick ski gliding forward and not toppling over, plus, trying to steer something that does not have any means of steering, it is quite difficult. While my legs and knees worked hard to keep some speed up gliding along on the sea of ice, I was feeling the burn of gasping down that freezing cold air into my lungs. I have to admit, even though it was hard work, I was actually laughing and starting to forget that I was only just suspended above metres of deep-freezing water by a layer of ice of indeterminate thickness. My feet happily sliding and gliding gracefully (well I imagined they were) and I sincerely enjoyed the feeling of being on the frozen sea! Enjoying every laughable motion. Nothing like the ungraceful motion of the ice-skating chair. Nothing at all like the floatation of snowshoe walking! Quite different! Ralph where are you now?

Contrary to my original vivid imagination, I did not fall through the ice to suffer a hypothermic death .Not only could I walk on water, but I could also glide on water, on a different type of transport I never before knew about! This was fun! Immense fun!

So, whether the challenges, encounters or experiences in our travels have been foreseen, planned for, or have just arisen, I look back and realise that no matter what the risk was, when I took it, I had to have enough courage and a lot of faith to continue to propel myself forward with whatever form of 'transport', body, or vehicle, was at hand. The most important ingredient, lots and lots of laughter. That part I do so well! You know what, I have actually come through those mostly unscathed.

Would I repeat all of them? Probably not.
Have I enjoyed most of these challenges conversed above?
YES, but please, keep it a secret and don't tell Marc!

Chapter Eleven

The Call of The Ride

*"I don't ride a bike to add days to my life,
I ride a bike to add life to my days"*

Do you know that riding a pushbike can be a task? You know, the type of bike that only works and moves if you sit on it and pedal! Keeping your balance on a small bike frame, using the momentum of the wheels and the pedals to counteract that inevitable pull of gravity trying to tumble you to the ground can be quite complicated.

Riding can be a great experience. I really like riding a bicycle! We do it frequently and the first task is to physically learn how to ride that bike. Once you are moving, you grapple to learn to not only balance but to also control your speed, direction, cornering, all without crashing and losing skin from knees and hands. But once mastered, those two wheeled metal machines have all sorts of uses!

When I ride it is relaxing and can really set my soul, heart, and mind free. It can place a whole different perspective on travels. I mean, think about it, you are riding for pleasure, being in the sun, feeling the wind in your face, cruising down the road and simply because you are not whizzing by at sixty kilometres per hour, you see so many things for the first time. For one of our holidays, that is the type of touring we did!

Our travel explorations together this time took us to the Coromandel Peninsula on the North Island of New Zealand. Geographically, the Coromandel Peninsula is located on the Pacific Coast Highway - on the east coast of New Zealand's North Island and is within an hour and a half drive of the major centres of Auckland, Rotorua, and their international airports. The NZ tourism bureau touts this area as renowned for its natural beauty, green pastures, misty rainforests, and pristine golden beaches.

Once we had arrived, instead of driving the peninsula as the normal tourist does, Marc had earlier suggested we do something different by doing a bicycle ride along the 'Hauraki Rail Trail'. According to the cycling brochure, this trail was where you *'cycle between heritage towns and through the Karangahake Gorge, pausing to sample organic cheese and ice cream, wood fired pizza and boutique wine'*. It sounded delightful and when Marc recommended that we change our plans for the Mother's Day long weekend to attempt this three-day-through-bike ride, I agreed happily. I was foreseeing visions of scenic countryside, sunshine, and romantic picnics as we chatted and leisurely, side by side, pedalled along. No challenge at all, just a fun, relaxing journey. With that in mind, I begin our story.

* * *

Day One.

The day dawned with the light peeking itself around the corner of the blind at the local pub where we were staying. Gone were the horrendous tones from the ground floor below from the night before of off-key karaoke we had had to endure. Gone also was the hassle and frustration of travel. Gone was the concept of 'work tomorrow'. I smiled, feeling relaxed as I woke, rolled over ... listened ... and then heard ... Rain! Yes, Rain.

And what was wrong with that you say? Rain is wonderful. The gentle sound of rain rapping on your roof as you enjoyed a nice 'sleep in', snuggled under the covers curled up like a cat, or just to enjoy a pleasant rainy day to chill out inside doing nothing is always a luxurious sound. But No. Not today. Being day one of our bike ride, this weather was not quite what I had in mind for romantically riding through the New

Zealand countryside! Rain was not part of the plan! Remember I had already had the 'wet travel' experience when we had done the Routeburn Track in New Zealand. It had rained continuously throughout the first day of that trek and I had not been a happy Lyndell that day. Gone were my visions of us weaving gently along bike tracks, enjoying the fresh air, the countryside, AND the SUNSHINE! Instead, dressed in wet-weather gear, layers of clothes underneath, helmets on, paniers packed, before starting I was already feeling the cold and the damp seeping through our protective gear. On the bikes we went!

Reality, I guess I should have known! The heavens had simply laughed at my romantic images. As the first spoke of my bicycle wheel turned, down it really poured. Two people, travelling gently in the wet weather. *"Riding along on a pushbike honey…"* as the song goes. Raincoats, scarves, and rain hoods on with only eyes peeping out, balancing delicately on our bikes venturing "into the unknown." (There is a song like that!) Me, getting to know this strange bike, gaining awareness of the trail, riding on gravel tracks, moving up and over many cattle grids. The bike was also getting to know me!

Now I must mention those cattle grids. These were actually horizontally aligned concrete blocks designed to rattle your whole body as you traversed them, and, in the process, bounce your underside against the bicycle seat. Definitely not pleasurable believe me! The 1950's song, 'All shook up', certainly took on a different meaning. But this rail track meant that we travelled through cow paddocks and dairy land. Farmland usually meant cattle or sheep and we regularly had to negotiate with cow or sheep dung and mud-filled farm tracks that crossed the trail. Not places you would want to fall over in let alone deal with the spray from your tyres. But the track itself was actually quite good. It was clear, yes bumpy, but an easy ride, as me and my friendly-getting-to-know-you bike, climbed up and over significantly raised bridges that had replaced the old level railway ones. Those replacement structures required a little bit of a run up and much oomph for the bike to go up and over. (Many times, my oomph ran out!) However, the soaring aspect down the other side was most enjoyable as I did not have to peddle!

Journeying along together side by side. The pouring rain now easing to showers, the showers reducing to drizzle and the drizzle eventually fading to nothing. I was beginning to relax, my 'pleasure-metre' starting to rise. Then, that unexpected event occurred, because without warning, over I went sideways into a fence! Nothing major but caused by something so simple as a bug that had flown into my eye and stung so bad that I could not see, and I fell. Trying to remove said sting, had me cavorting and wobbling sideways on that unsteady metal machine resulting in me upending into a fence. It all happened quite quickly. My body ended up contorted into an uncomfortable position. My arms were caught in the fence wire and the bike stuck on top of me. Not a good picture! I was not able to extricate myself.

At that point, my darling 'ever-caring' man stops, and being the medical man he is, thinks of the first rule of Basic Life Skills and First Aid Training ... whilst I lay entangled in the wire fence and unable to extricate myself, he asks, *"Is the fence electric? Is it turned on?"* How considerate of him! I guess there was no use both of us getting shocked!

Right at that moment, I was not feeling any significant jolt of electricity, but a burning sensation in my arm where the wire was caught and, on my cheeks, where redness from humiliation flamed! After first checking the fence was not electrified, ever the gentleman, my gallant husband lifted the bike off me, raised me up, seated me back on the bike to start us once more on our bicycle journey. This time though, I wore sunglasses! I chose to ignore the fact that I could not see from the fogged-up sweat being raised on my glasses but was not going to let a bug zap my eye again! Onward, forward we rode, resembling once again, a happy bicycle trail riding pair, and I began to take pleasure in the track, the feel of the bike and the small pleasurable conversation between us.

Of course, it was not for long, before down came the rain. Again.

Two wet riders, now navigating along the rail trail bedraggled with water that definitely exceeded my Gortex jacket's ability keep me dry! As we rode the final fifteen kilometres to our destination for the night at Paeroa, my man says to me:

"You know, we have all the time in the world to get to where we are going!"

I looked at him.

"Marc - you do know it's raining!"

* * *

Day Two.

A new dawn.

Unfortunately, poor sleep due to Marc's snores. Was this not the trip that was supposed to recharge us? I was not quite sure anymore as I crawled most unwillingly, already exhausted, out of bed as the morning was moving on and we resumed our seats on the bikes again. But the best gift provided was that the weather today was fine. The sun shone brightly as we made our leave from the lovely motel. Luxuriating in this warmth with the sun on my back, I climbed upon the saddle of my bike and reflected that sunshine does make the world a different place. A much-preferred start to my day!

Walkers and other bike riders were also on the path today and we smiled at each other as we passed by. I was slowly weaving my way along the track, happy.

My tired knees however were complaining. My knees and quads really didn't want to move, talking firmly at me in their grinding and groaning mode ... "*Hey you ... why are we back on this bike ... hey, didn't we do this yesterday ... no, I don't want to push the pedal anymore ... hey, are you hearing any of this ...?* I tried to ignore them! I did my best anyway! What made it worse was that in our morning travels, I espied a rather large woman and her partner come up from behind and overtake us. Compared to me, this person was quite big and to my horror, she easily passed me. I felt terrible because I was moving moderately due to my noisy knees complaining. I also felt rather mortified as I was not that old, nor that unfit, but watched this person pass me by. However, my ever-vigilant husband says ... *"Look - she's not carrying anything, and she has an electric bike".* I guess that made my knees feel a little vindicated! At least I could say bravely to my complaining knees, ..." Hey we did this yesterday with full panniers and it was all just you and me – no electric assist!"

On this second day I was not sure where we were going as there were no obvious signs to say, 'This Way' or 'That Way', but I slowly followed behind, trusting that my husband was heading us in the right direction on the bike track. The scenery was different from yesterday. It was almost tropical. Today, there were no dairy farms but a temperate rainforest appearance as we weaved and wove along the gravel track gradually climbing to meet the gorge's old rail tunnel. We stopped at the entrance to take those photographs of '*smile ... we are here and really doing this ...*' However, the 'smile' was a little forced as I have to admit the tunnel looked dark and extremely long! The video mode on the camera goes 'on'. Our bikes were ready, poised at the entrance, bursting at their metal bits, charged eager to go ... and we entered the long ominous gaping hole that opened its mouth to engulf us in its darkness.

Wow - what a ride that was.

We entered one very, very, very, very long kilometre of wet, gravel, dripping water, dark and ever rising up trail. Being so dim it deceived us into believing that the track in the tunnel was not rising at all. On the contrary, it certainly was! At first, Marc was behind me on his bike, taking the video of his brave wife weaving her way through the darkness. He then decided to pass me (probably because I was going too slow) and continued to video all the way to the end of the tunnel. *"And here she comes,"* says the bright male voice on the video as a red-faced, heavy-breathing, knees-screaming, tired pedal-rider eventually appeared with a grimace and words of, *"That tunnel definitely got higher!"* My husband laughingly agreed! (See ... I told you knees ... I was right ... we were rising, you were not complaining for nothing!)

The scenery continued with more kilometres of pedalling along on the trail as we visited the derelict Victoria Battery left over from historic gold mining. We passed beautiful waterfalls and stopped at the much desired and needed railway station café for coffee, cake and 'Lemon and Paeroa'. After all, we were in the area that made it, so of course there is the obligatory one glass ... or two ... or maybe three! That part of the track, although still hard travelling, was worth it for the views and ambience. Perhaps the travel research was right this time. It was worth the ride.

"Worth it?" Did I really have those words utter from my mouth? I think I jinxed myself by saying it. because the last nine kilometres of Day Two definitely came at a price.

To find the words to accurately describe that section is quite difficult.

The railway track was no longer abandoned, a real train still travelled on it, so we left those gentle gradients dictated by the needs of the old steam engines and embarked on following the banks of the adjacent river, with topographical contours that nature created over the eons. In simple terms, it went up ... down ... up ... up ... down ... round, bend, twist, round, up ... more ups ... more downs. My husband humorously calling out a verbal dialogue of, "We're going down again", "Here's another hill," as he bravely rode out in front.

Now riding on heavy gravel, I was swaying, and sashaying through underground passes, on steep tracks still wet from yesterday's rain, on undulating tracks that steeply bent and twisted without much break between the rises and the falls. Sweat was pouring off me, running down parts of my body I don't wish to discuss with you! What happened to my romantic images of riding for pleasure? Of enjoying being in the sun, of feeling the wind in my face, of sensing the breeze rushing through my hair as I cruised down the road setting my soul, heart, and mind free! It had all gone. In its place, my knees fought me and refusing to work saying, "NO!" My oomph and puff had fizzled and simply sputtered out.

After reaching the top of one of those never-ending rises, I found myself stopping at a bridge and could not breathe. We know that breathing is a wonderful thing as we unconsciously inhale and exhale air to assist in our daily activities. But struggling to get that breath of air into your lungs and it is definitely not happening, you wonder if you are ever going to breathe again at all and you panic! My regular breathing rhythm of 'in and out' had become confused, out of normal rhythm, and left me gulping for air. Leaning over and hanging onto the rail, constricted in my chest I thought I was heading for a heart attack. Such a scary feeling as I struggled to desperately suck in oxygen. Trying to regain my ordinary breathing pattern. Eventually my breathing settled. My life no longer in imminent danger, my colour again restored, and my ever-happy, positive husband says, "*Look, only five kilometres to go!*".

Albert Einstein states that life is like riding a bicycle. To keep your balance, you must keep moving. To that I must agree! But it all depends on the type of balancing you do! With only the last five kilometres of this treacherous track and the end almost in sight, I felt rather elated, riding with delighted thoughts of finally leaving the track and heading for comfort! But I spoke too soon.

Almost at the end of the track, final township in sight, we were moving down another descent, gaining speed, when all of a sudden, the gravel trail turned to a concrete track, then, without any prior warning, it also introduced a severe right 90 degrees turn and an upward 33 degrees incline. To the rider, there was no runoff, no warning, no informative sign to say, "Severe Turn, Be Careful" or "Slow Down, Sharp Turn Ahead". So, you can guess what happened.

That demon bike of mine kicked, turned 90 degrees, and reared its way sideways into the wire fence and adjacent gully, bucking off its rider. I went sliding along on my already bruised exterior and hit an unexpected concrete edge rather abruptly! On impact, the air was sucked out of me. The bruises on my arm from yesterday were joined by bruises to the torso, the left bum cheek and thigh plus the addition of a twisted right ankle. I was tangled again and entwined within a wire fence! My bicycle again lying on top of me, in a fence and I could not move.

Again, my hero, came rushing to my assistance and lifted the bike off me. No electric fence to worry about this time but a very hurt, bruised, upset, angry, woman with freely flowing tears coursing down her tired face who was spitting out a few choice phrases and words to deal with! Words and phrases I do not wish to share with you!

But what did I do?

When offered assistance, that very determined middle-aged woman took the bike from her sweet tender husband and limped angrily up the rest of the hill, only reining in and mounting that demon bike when she could see the smooth tarmac of a gentle country road that would take her into the town and to her accommodation for that night. Later I did so enjoy severely chaining up that fearsome wheeled creature at the motel so it could do no further harm to this sore and bruised damsel. With a tremulous smile to the owner of the motel, I placed the key in the door and entered my safe refuge for the night. A hot shower then a fall into bed with its warm embracing eiderdown that beckoned me. Head under the covers, I was hiding. I was not moving!

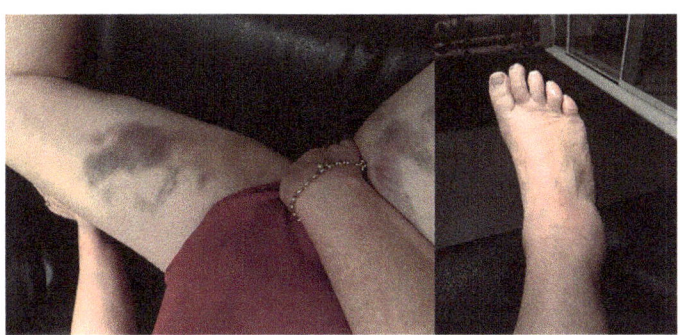

And my darling husband says to me, "*You know this is our holiday … it is such fun resting and enjoying ourselves…*

I think I would have kicked him if my ankle had not been so sore!

* * *

Day Three begins.

How do I describe day three on our pushbike ride! Truth be known, it was not all that bad. I do exaggerate somewhat. A good night's sleep, a positive outlook returned and the trip from Waihi back down to Peroa was quite a thrill. On the third day, the pair of happy bikers in wet weather gear (yes, it was raining again) actually sailed down most of the track, although I did get off a few times and walked that demon bike down the steep sections. I was not going to let him buck me off in the downhill run again. Today I was severely keeping him on a tight rein as I had no intention of being up-ended again by anything! I was determined to enjoy myself and win, namely, to have the upper hand. Today was going to be a great day!

In my exhaustion yesterday, I certainly did not believe Marc, when he informed me it would be better when we retraced part of this journey. In my weariness and tears, I had lost faith in myself. After that final fall, nothing was going to convince me it was going to be an improved ride back because I was too tired and cross to believe he was right. However, heading *down* the rail track was indisputably so much easier! I admit, the long uphill gorge tunnel we came through the day before was so much more fun going back *down*.

On our previous days ride, we did not realise how much uphill there was in that tunnel, constantly grunting and grinding the gears, teeth, and jaws to match! You just kept going. Whereas, on this final day, on the downhill run, I had to keep putting my brakes on. Even though I was holding the reins tight, as my bike felt the descent of going down in that deep wet dark tunnel, it kept wanting to accelerate and plunge faster into the darkness! It was a little scary, but rather exciting! What was even more curiouser (as Alice would have put it), the lighted hole at the other end of the tunnel was definitely lower visually heading west, and maddening deceiving, because on the day before when a red-faced lady rider, peered through the dark hole towards the east, puffing and panting, the track did not look uphill at all!! But true to his word, as Marc predicted, it was easier. But alas, as the story goes, it was not all plain sailing after riding down the hill.

Let me enlighten you.

The motel in Waihi where we had stayed the night before was not only on the outskirts of town, it also did not include breakfast. That was quite okay, as the cafes were all in the centre of town but up a significant hill from our motel. However, there was no way I was going to add extra kilometres and ANOTHER hill to my already tired bruised legs, bum, arms, and sore ankle, before we had even commenced the proper track. So that morning, in our bright wisdom we decided we would head back to Peroa but stop at the train station café at Waikino for breakfast, which according to the map and travel guide was only about nine kilometres ride. After yesterday's travels, deemed easy!

Unfortunately, on arrival nine kilometres later, the café was not opened.

Sunshine on our shoulders, smiles still on our faces we made the resolution according to the trail map, we would continue along the track and stop at the winery estate for coffee. You know John Denver's song, "Sunshine on my shoulders makes me happy," …well it does certainly enhance mood! Ten kilometres later, Winery Coffee shop also not opened. So, two hours later, a little 'hungry', we ended back in Peroa with the first twenty-five kilometres ridden, but our trouser belts tightened.

The rail trails met at the edge of town and questions were posed of, "Do we travel the extra distance into Peroa for a meal and then have to ride out again?" or "Do we skip riding the extra distance and head on towards Te Aroha?". (Te Aroha was the next destination that was another twenty-three kilometres plus. We deliberated over this as the trail guidebook said, *"roughly 10 kilometres into the ride, there was a Café with scones and cream and jam to 'die for."* Decision made as the delicious sunshine streamed encouragingly on our backs, and this supposedly 'café to die for', sounded tempting and would be our next stop. We would ride on, stop there, and consume a brunch! (Remember, we already had missed breakfast!) Onward, forward. Yes, let's go! Andiamo!!

Now let me tell you about this part of the ride.

Imagine a railway track and parallel sleepers. Imagine the gravel underneath it. Remove the sleepers and what do you have left??? Gravel … thick gravel. That gravel is what we ploughed through. Add to that impression, the gravel track slowly climbed, climbed, and climbed some more! Even so, the sun was still shining, and we could endure this easily. We could both hear the scintillating coffee being made and taste the amazing scones that beckoned us to come closer. I could already smell their savouring aroma. I could taste their cream and jam. I could feel my fingers wrapped around that mug of hot cappuccino coffee. Knowing that delectable vision was waiting for us, we felt, it would make this part of the track bearable.

WRONG.
WRONG.
More WRONG
IT WAS NOT OPEN!
Really?
REALLY??
REALLY?????

It was now about three and a half hours or so into our peddling journey without anything in our stomachs since the one small hamburger of last night. This little black duck was not feeling very pleased at all. In fact, her emotions were rather stronger than 'not pleased'. After my positive thoughts of day three, that new part of the track was so boring, no views, only more chunky grit, corrugated fencing at times and now NO FOOD! As the shut gate of the café displaying the "Closed" sign laughed at me, my feelings plummeted ankle deep around my feet, my tired legs moaned, my stomach growled and groaned from hunger and the small dark cloud of hunger unhappiness quivered tremulously above my head.

We pulled up at a small bus like shelter, drank some water whilst inhaling the 'lovely aroma' coming from an adjacent silage pit that was being dug up. (For those who do not know what a silage pit smells of – it is the 'sweet smell of semi-decomposed vegetable matter', so use your imagination). Although I was trying so hard to still be positive and not a spoilt brat, in my defence, I was upset as this was not what our guidebook had indicated when we had embarked on this adventure. That research that had advertised what we would see, what we would eat along the way! This was not what the last part of the rail trail was supposed to be like. I was now quite 'hangry' as my daughter says (hungry and angry). I was supposed to have food! I was hugely disappointed since everything promised in the brochure was closed. Those 'had to have scones and cream' were categorically dead!

The sun now rode high above us in the sky. My darling husband was singing and talking about the book he was reading. I knew what he was doing in trying to improve my mood. But it was doing the opposite as I could have thrown that book at him, he was talking about. Especially when a sign indicated we still had fifteen kilometres to go! Marc tried to entice a smile from me and attempted to lift my spirits by bringing out the chocolate bar he had conveniently bought the previous evening. *Chocolate*, I will admit, has an amazing medicinal effect - physically and psychologically … more the latter for me! Breaking each piece of that one small chocolate bar, the feeling of that chocolate sliding into our empty stomachs, savouring its flavour, licking the lips, we moved on, we rode … or should I say, ploughed on! My stomach now laced with that morsel of chocolate which encouraged me to reinvest some energy, knowing that there had to be something opened along this track.

Buildings began to appear in front of me. Our destination. The end of the three-day bike ride.

I think …
There will be Shops.
There will be Food.
There will be COFFEE!!!!!!
And I lifted up my head.

With one final blow, the shops, their food, and their coffee are all situated at the top on one last STEEP hill. Hungry, exhausted, I was not defeated. I dismounted., I PUSHED that bicycle vertically up that last hill to get to a café at the top. I was determined I would FINISH this journey.

Three days of push bike riding mounted upon a single small bike saddle was accomplished.

Three days of travelling one hundred and twenty kilometres from beginning to end on a small bicycle frame, with filled panniers, using only the momentum of my legs and wheels was achieved.

Three days later, I was sitting in a café with a much-needed coffee in hand, happily crying into my mug knowing,

I DID IT!!

Trials make life interesting.

Overcoming them makes them meaningful! For me, challenging myself and doing something entirely different, involved finishing three days of riding under various conditions. Different weather settings, viewing scenery not seen before, negotiating rail bridges, exploring rising tunnels, finding unexpected concrete edged tracks and ninety degree turns, surviving gravel and numerous uphills, encountering wire fences 'up close and personal', recovering from many falls and rear-ended bucks, of black and yellow bruises in unmentionable places, enduring hunger pains from lack of food and overcoming frustration and tears, all made quite an interesting time. Magically completed with the romantic part of sharing, chatting, laughing and significant time with my husband.

Ernest Hemingway suggests that it is by riding a bicycle that you learn the contours of a country best, since you have to sweat up the hills and coast down them. After this trip, I can now say that is quite true. I have now completed in New Zealand, a three day through walk and a first ever experienced three-day through bike ride.

I still do ride my bike over many tough hills with Marc. Interestingly, I am the one who generally suggests we go for a ride but love and hate him at the same time, for the sweat running down my face and the pain of my knees, but also for the challenge it gives me.

Would I do a trip like this again?
Surprisingly, yes! I most likely would.
In fact, I will say a decisive yes.
But the next time, I think I will achieve it on an e-bike!

"Happy Mother's Day!"

Chapter Twelve

On the Flip Side of It All

If time permits, I have discovered, that I need to research *before* I venture into something new with my husband. Perhaps, because it is we are that much older? Perhaps, I am not as trusting of his *little* walks or his cheeky lovable smile anymore, or maybe, (and more likely the reason,) I am just using my research not to go or do one of his suggestions made, as an excuse! Whatever my reason might have been, I was so glad that, yes, this trip, I did take the time to investigate and research!

Lord Howe Island is a quick one and half hour's flight from Brisbane, off Australia's east coast, and has World Heritage listing for its natural surroundings. The island is described as a remnant of an extinct shield volcano dating back 7 million years but now eroded to one fortieth of its original size. It has a population of only 350 people and will allow only 400 visitors to be 'on island' at any one time. On this Island, you can experience some of the world's best day hikes, snorkel the world's southernmost coral reef, hand-feed the fish and relax as you wander along white-sand beaches, The travel guide sounded appealing and being a place we had never been to, plus the fact it was so close to where we lived, we decided we would take our one week off from work, visit and explore a venue close to home! So, there I was, sitting there, on Lord Howe Island, looking at Mt Gower, one of its mountains.

My husband had gone to climb that mountain. Needing a challenge each holiday, he wanted to climb Mt Gower! Fair enough. That is Marc. No, I did not go with him, and I can hear you ask me, why not? I mean this would have been another challenge to conquer! Actually, I was going to go with him … until I did my research.

My investigation informed me that the Mt Gower walk was described as 'not for the faint hearted'. It was the highest *easily* (really?) accessible rainforest in the world. At the top of the mountain, you could stand upon its iconic peak, its misty forest, and experience breathtaking 360° views of the island and its crystal blue waters. The mountain is only 875m tall or so, about as high as Mt Warning (which is the highest mountain near where we lived), but that is where the similarity stops. Climbing Mt Warning (which I have completed approximately thirteen times with our visitors) is mainly just a steady climb on well-maintained paths with many switch backs that allow you to meander, wind and zigzag your way up the mountain until the last chain assisted scramble to the top. But Mt Gower is rated as one of Australia's challenging hikes.

Why?

It is an eight to ten hours return trek, complete with rope-assisted, cliff hugging adjacent to vertigo-inducing drops into the sea below, and that is even before the vertical-rope-assisted-climb up the mountain itself. The tourist information site actually states, "*Despite there being ropes to steady yourself on, it is quite an unnerving experience walking along the slope with cliffs rising straight up to your left and dropping over 100m straight down to the ocean to your right. The track starts to climb steeply – about 200m up in less than a kilometre…and there is still another 450m to go up, … .. there is a lot of rock climbing in that last kilometre. Again, there are ropes to aid you, …*"

It seemed, in order to climb Mt Gower, you had to use ropes at the edge of a cliff to wind your way around from the first climb off the beach. To start climbing almost vertically up, on and over rocks, while at the same time hanging onto another rope to assist me from falling and then to climb even higher, was not quite my idea of a relaxing holiday. Not to mention, to walk extremely close to the side of the mountain edge, hanging onto, what seemed to me, quite an inadequate lifeline, while overlooking the precipice just waiting for you to slip and you to plunge down … down … down into the water and onto rocks below, was not quite my cup of tea as the English say.

From my previous chapters, I have happily undertaken numerous challenges presented to me by Marc, but I knew I didn't need that *particular* kind. If I had gone with him, I know I would have simply frozen. I would be clinging motionless to the rope unable to move one foot in front of the other. Going up would have been very hard but coming down would have been even more terrifying! As I viewed pictures from other tourists and read feedback from those who had been enticed/conned to take this 'walk', what I saw definitely made me refuse to go. Even the official island tourist site said, "*if you have a fear of heights* (definitely me) *or bad knees or back* (me) *then think twice.*" Oh, I didn't have to think twice at all. I simply said, "NO THANK YOU!"

So, armed with my research, I sent Marc off that morning with my blessing to 'enjoy himself'.

I laid on my nice white crisp sheets on my delightfully cool bed under the fan, to then later, sit in the shade of the Norfolk Pines alongside the lagoon gazing across at Mt Gower. Knowing, in the distance, somewhere in between all that rainforest and those ropes, Marc would have climbed to the top. Thank you, research, I am more than content being here!

* * *

How easily we get used to our comforts! Like everyone else, on this island, you hired a bike for a week and made your way around on that two-wheel transport. Easy you say? Well, both yes and no. In the car, there is no effort as you glide along, the air conditioner on, conversations happening as you look at things and gently meander your way around the island soaking in the scenery and the palm trees ... lovely ... beautiful ... ideal, pleasant, to arrive at your venue glowing from the scenery and coolness. On a push bike you meander the same way around the island, on those exact same roads but there is no air conditioner. Instead, your exercise is accompanied by the sun beaming upon you the sweat drips heavily from your brow fogging up the much-needed sunglasses sitting in turn underneath the baseball cap, that is positioned underneath the bicycle helmet (as the law of the island instigated). Any chance of a conversation between you is stilted as you ride along, breathing with the exertion of a hill ... and yet another hill ... and even yet another hill!

Of course, we mustn't forget the road near the small airport aptly called 'Windy Point! I found out why it had that particular name because at that point, as you continually ride into a headstrong wind, your little legs peddling and peddling and peddling as you creep along the road, the strong gusts of wind on 'windy point' push you straight backwards!! Yes, definitely windy and it had nothing to do with bodily gas propulsion either!

However, the rides were doable as they say, and we did them. (Do remember the island is of volcanic origin!)

But we mustn't overlook that where we were staying was at the top of a steep hill. That meant that every time we returned to our accommodation, the same steep hill presented itself to be. Do you know, no matter how hard I tried, how much I turned my little legs and pedalled and pedalled and pedalled, I could not make it all the way up to our cabin. Every time I had to get off, and physically push the bike up that hill, weaving my way - puffing and wheezing. Marc rode up in front of me so easily. All I can say … it must be nice to have leg muscles!!

Now those that know me well understand Boats and Lyndell do not mix. Sitting in rocking, swaying water always made whatever was in my stomach want to come up, say 'hi' to everyone and land outside. 'Happiness comes in waves' they say, so, here on this island, a challenge for me was being part of a snorkelling tour for a few hours. Armed with pressure point wrist bands strapped tightly (which I was told were supposed to be great for motion sickness), dressed in swimmers and towel and after a few momentous nervous trips to the toilet prior, we entered the boat. We travelled over the so-called calm lagoon waters into deeper rockier ones, and then told to look down through the glass at the bottom of the boat. This was where we were to gaze upon beautiful colours of coral and the colourful fish following us, that belonged to this island hideaway.

I was truly engrossed in our wonderful guide's information about the coral and sea life but then he wanted us to look down. Me? Sitting on rocking, swaying, 'here comes my food up again' waters, REALLY???? Don't think so! Instead, I told Marc, "*When there was something worthwhile to see … then I'll look down!*"

Arriving at the further end of the lagoon, the boat stopped, and we were invited to jump into the water. Unlike being *in a boat*, I am okay *in the water*. Swimming is fine. But Snorkelling was another challenge (see later).

But once 'mastered, while snorkelling under the water, when I did look down, I was presented with the most glorious sight of coral, of shapes and colours in and under the water. Such beauty of underwater scenery in this glorious world of hues and bright iridescent fish, was absolutely amazing. Mind you, I held Marc's hand the whole way! I was not letting go! No way!

After leisurely gliding in open sea under water, I had to re-enter the human world of *the boat* and endure the choppy journey back to shore. My wrists were adorned with dents from pressing so hard on the motion sickness bands. Oh well, the good with the bad I guess!

Back to snorkelling. Snorkelling can be a very rewarding activity. It benefits from its simplicity, where you can easily grab a mask, some fins and off you go. Fun time! But there are various components of snorkelling.

I have to ask, have you ever tried to stand up or walk with flippers on?

Me, before this trip, I had never had flippers on. This was my very first time and now I know why they are called flippers. That is because they flip you right up, over, sideways, and flat on your bottom! It was like someone took my own feet and gave me theirs. I simply had no control over my tiny twinkling toes in these bright orange long rubber things on the end of my feet. On that beach, they kept flipping me over and under! Not to mention the extra drag and weight of the fins that put additional toll on my muscles - an unknown mode of transport experienced for the first time. It did take me quite a while to find out how to use them effectively, particularly once we left the rough waves and windy swirling waters of the famous Ned's beach and headed to the tranquil calm of the flat main lagoon! There, after few more feet-flipper wrestles, my feet finally became mine again!! Yes, memories are made in flip flops but not the normal land type!

There is a saying that says, 'life looks better underwater;' and 'all you need is a good dose of Vitamin Sea', 'That is of course when the underwater breathing concept of snorkelling appeared to be easy. Let me explain.

The Snorkel is the apparatus that allows you to breathe easily under the water … except when you have a face mask, an air piece and a claustrophobic female attached to them. With that snorkel in my mouth, I had to learn to breathe quite differently! That scuba face mask outer seal covered only your nose, while the inner seal covered every other place on the face except your nose. Basically, you sucked in the mask, so it was attached to your face (because you had to see where you are going); you breathed through your mouth in and out … (just forget the nose … it's attached to that face mask …) and under the water you go. All I had to do was breathe deep and slowly to fully fill and empty my lungs and kick gently through the water with those flippers! To those watching, I would then present a beautiful vision beneath the surface, gracefully gliding, my long hair floating out behind, as I swirled about in the underwater world never generally visited.

So Serene.

So Peaceful.

But it is not a good look when your face mask becomes foggy, half filled with water and that extremely important thing keeping you alive, the snorkel fills with water. Meanwhile your flippers, winning again, flick you over and tumble you about in your huge uncontrolled feet. You rise frantically and ungracefully to the surface. Choking, coughing, and spluttering up salt water. A totally different picture! What was even worse was not laughing! Have you ever tried to breathe underwater through a snorkel, and you start laughing? I did! Hmmm … gliding beautifully … me thinks not. However, snorkelling was a successful challenge I really enjoyed! That was once I got used to the silence of that underwater world where all you heard in your ears was the ominous deep breathing of DARTH VADER from Star Wars movies, hearing that 'deep menacing gasping sound and then realising it was only you!

So, on this trip away …

Shall I tell you that our long awaited short few days away from work on that island was worthwhile …?

Shall I tell you that the weather was glorious? Hot but glorious?

Shall I tell you that the water was so green, clear, and delightful to swim in?

Shall I tell you that the cabin was sweet and cute and easy to live in where we read books, played games, and rested as we should?

Shall I tell you about the meals we ate each night of fresh fish, meat, and vegetables with tantalising tempting tastes?

Oh, I can tell you about all those wonderful things experienced.

I can also tell you I sat relaxing on that small, intriguing Island, so close to my own hometown only a few hours away over the water, and I looked at Mount Gower. As I viewed its tall rocky peaks resting alongside that landscape of water palms and sand, I pondered where my husband was, in his descent within that tangle of ropes and rocks, returning to me hopefully from the dizzy mountain heights.

What I know I can definitely tell you is, I was extremely glad to be exactly where I was.

Right there!
Where I chose to be.
A challenge all in itself!

We can only know how strong we are when we strive and thrive beyond the challenges we face.

Kemi Sogunle

Chapter Thirteen

Something In The Air ...

I can feel it coming in the air tonight ...
Christmas is a succession of magical moments that brings us closer to our families and loved ones. It is a time for relatives and friends to make new memories together.

Growing up, as a child, I looked forward to Christmas all year. I loved the food. I loved the decorations. I loved watching the Christmas shows on television. I loved the anticipation of opening gifts. I loved the music - I could go on and on. And while I thoroughly enjoyed pretty much every aspect of the season, my all-time favourite, as a child, was waking up in the morning and racing out to find what Santa had bought me! What else!

Families have, over the years, developed many traditions just for Christmas. As a child, on Christmas Day, after the traditional church service, I would be surrounded by my extended family, generally from my mother's side and in particular by my two cousins, Narelle and Glenda (the three of us would often get into so much mischief). We would share a magnificent meal and then we would gather around what I would think was the most beautifully decorated tree in town and open gifts one by one. We were connected together understanding the significance of the day. For me, this was the most wonderful time of the year.

Christmas Celebrations have certainly changed over the years, As an adult, things obviously were altered. I grew up. I married a man whose idea of getting the Christmas spirit was to become Scrooge and he thought Santa Claus had the right idea in visiting people only once a year! But although not a favourite of the Christmas season, he did enjoy many years of cherishing and valuing the time and pleasure we, as parents, received from watching our two young children open their gifts. Sharing that special day as a family. Our family. While the rest of my family slept, it would also allow my daughter and I to sneak out late on Christmas Eve to attend Midnight Church in my own local town, something which was sacred and special to me.

However, Christmas time also allowed me to make and keep one tradition that we still uphold today: the viewing of "Carols by Candlelight" on national television. From her teenage years, every Christmas Eve my daughter and I would sit in front of the television and watch the Carols together. Now, she is married with her own family, in a different home, in a different state, but we are both still 'together', watching the show at the same time and use the media of SMS to comment to each other on the acts. This tradition has been going for many years.

As my family grew up and conditions (and husbands) changed, needless to say, my Christmas Eve setting no longer includes the most beautifully decorated tree in town, nor a Christmas Day shared with grandparents, aunts, and uncles, nor my cousins as I did as a child. Though, as much as I would love to be together with my family and grandchildren concurrently, it does not always happen. But Christmas, no matter what transpires, is still an exceptional time of year to me in many ways.

Therefore, being away from family at Christmas time is extremely hard for me. Being away from each other in Australia is usually doable as we are usually in the same (or close) time and weather zones. Being overseas can be an entirely different matter.

Marc and I have shared one such Christmas on the other side of the world - just the two of us - in Salzburg, Austria. When originally suggested, I was not sure I was going to like it at all! Being used to having some, if not all, of my family gather around me on Christmas Day, I was quite worried about not being home and how much I would miss them! Being on the other side of the world on Christmas Eve/Day without family, was an entirely different challenge all in itself!

Austria has various Christmas traditions.

In Salzburg, we attended the "Christkindlmarkt". This term is what Austrians call their Christmas markets. The markets were amazing to see and were nothing like I had seen before. These huge markets offered regional specialities, homemade delicacies, and handmade Christmas tree decorations and gifts. There was something to please every taste including an alcoholic drink or two … hot cider, punch, or mulled wine. (I love mulled wine!)

In Europe, Christmas Eve is the more "Christmas" part of this festive time. It is when families meet together, share dinners, decorate the tree, and open the gifts.

Austrian children do not generally believe in Santa Claus, but that the so-called Christkindl or Christ Child brings the presents. The Christ Child is usually depicted as an angel-like child with blond curls and wings. We were informed that on 24 December, the Christ child flies from house to house, sometimes bringing a completely decorated Christmas tree in addition to the presents. If the Christ Child himself does not bring the Christmas tree, it is then traditionally set up by the family, decorated on Christmas Eve, and remains standing in the Austrian houses until Candlemas on 2 February. (Hence why the wealth of Christmas tree decorations in the Christkindlmarkts on December 24!! We certainly bought a few ourselves from the markets to bring home.)

On our Christmas Eve in Salzburg, we went to an early Vespers in St. Peter's where the whole service was sung in Latin as a Gregorian chant. Interesting to listen but not comprehensible at all. No wonder Martin Luther found such fertile soil preaching that religion should be available directly to the people without priests having to be the intercessors. In that service, we felt totally disconnected as the music was ritualistic and chanting. Probably significant of the age and time of those Gregorian chants, but I do not feel a strong need to experience that kind of service again unless it is just for the musical experience of a chant alone. Definitely not for Christmas and will not be a tradition I would follow!

Christmas Eve midnight service though was quite extraordinary! We attended the Dom in the middle of Salzburg and lined up with everyone else! The service itself was very ritualistic and full of ceremony, with incense and bells tingling, right down to the little Red Cap being taken off the bishop and being replaced with his mitre before he spoke. Although we had lined up for an hour, the seats we had were quite a long way back from the front of the cathedral. However, I had an unobstructed view of the ceremonial part of the Service performed by the bishop and his cardinals. The mass was long. We entered the cathedral at 11pm and did not finish until 1am. I had never attended a midnight catholic mass in a huge cathedral before and it was quite a learning experience for me. The monotonous chanting of the priest as he told his sermon in German did not help us from switching off a little bit … or perhaps, if we were being honest – from closing our eyes and even falling asleep at times. I am sure God would have understood! I must add though, the sombre mood of this religious experience, was lightened a little by either a drunk or a mentally disturbed person coming in, walking right down the enormous cathedral centre aisle talking to himself and to the many people there quite loudly and, from the tone, abusively. He was eventually escorted outside. A little unexpected entertainment. (Perhaps intentional to keep you awake?)

But the music was spectacular. I mean spectacular! It was the music I had waited for and had sacrificed much needed sleep. I certainly was not disappointed. The music in the cathedral, consisted of a full orchestra, full choir complete with soloists – tenor, bass alto and soprano - singing Mozart's music. It was absolutely beautiful. As it turned out, our seats, being right on the central aisle and halfway between the entrance and the central dome, were perfect for the music. We were basically in the middle of the 'sound stage' as the choir, orchestra, and organ delivered their musical renderings.

When the three huge gates opened at 11pm, the choir was situated at the front of the cathedral and sang acappella for about 20 minutes, mostly in German, without microphones. Being a huge cathedral, the acoustics were brilliant and there was definitely no need for amplification. As the bishop's party entered, a separate choir at the back and high up in the mezzanine section, with full pipe organ playing, introduced the whole service. Throughout the service, diverse types of music were played and sung, but mostly Mozart since Salzburg was his birthplace.

The highlight at 1am was the dimming of the lights and the candelabra. The dark cathedral was lit by just a few candles and the whole mood changed. You could have heard a pin drop! High above us, perched in the dark shadows of the gallery, three gentlemen with one guitar, sang Stille Nacht (Silent Night) in German. (I did not realise Silent Night had so many verses!) After the previous full orchestral singing, in contrast, this quiet harmonious piece was so reverent and peaceful. The song was then passed on to two female singers and then to the full choir, but it concluded once again, with the same three men singing quietly, as the final strums of the acoustic guitar faded away. It went for almost 8 minutes. Absolutely breathtakingly magnificent!

The service over and Marc and I, along with the thousands of other people, exited the Dom. As an encore … the huge cathedral bells began to chime. They were thunderous in nature, and I mean loud literally booming their sound above us. Huge bells. So big and so deafening. So many of them all resounding at the same time for about 15 minutes heralding Christmas Day into Salzburg. An amazing experience. I was completely taken with them as I stood there and listened to their peals die away. I realised then that even though I missed them immensely, Christmas Eve away from my family had given me two new experiences. I had certainly had never been in a huge immense cathedral overflowing with people with standing room only, and I personally had never heard anything like the music including the pealing of the bells, and probably never will again! The whole experience musically for me was sacred.

The early hours of Christmas day in Salzburg found us skyping the children 'Merry Christmas'. Not quite what I was used to, as we were standing outside in the dark and the wind. The hotel was old, built solely of stone and sound resonated quite loudly. I missed my family greatly, and desired so much to chat with them on their own summer-heat-saturated Australian Christmas Day, all the way, on the other side of the world. But to skype, the only place we could get internet and yet not disturb the other guests with our voices, was to stand outside our hotel's front door in the freezing cold. Such a contrast! Finally, at 2:30am, on Christmas Day in Salzburg, we crashed into bed.

However, I must share with you a most embarrassing moment!

We had prebooked a Christmas Eve dinner. Apparently, there are not many places open that you can just walk into and eat at on Christmas Eve in Salzburg, so we had been advised to pre-book. So, we had booked at the Sheridan across the river from where we were staying. Oh yes, a luxurious hotel! Where else for Christmas Eve dinner so far away from home?

The dinner was scrumptious with a lovely accompanying brass band and then later, a piano. The food was available as a buffet so you could try as many dishes as you wished. The wine also was a lovely soft red that was easy to drink. Our butler was responsible for pouring the wine. As your glass emptied, it was filled. That was the problem, not only was the food too easy to eat, but the red wine was also even easier to drink. After five courses of this special dinner, and copious amounts of wine, we were quite replete as they politely say, or in Aussie terms … totally stuffed! More so, because up to that point, in our travels, we had only been eating two small meals a day and many times, one of those was only soup. Our stomachs had shrunk a little and after that enormous dinner, I could not put my coat on without feeling my waist had gained a few centimetres in one single sitting!!! In the end we waddled outside with all our layers on, and I mean waddle.

Now it is normally presumed, in the essence to the fully human spectrum of perceived male humanity, that boys/men are allowed, in polite terms, expel gas into the air in a public place - or in colloquial terms - to 'fart'. Typically, from childhood, girls receive the message that their bodily functions have to be confined and controlled. Although this attitude is now changing, the norm out there is you find yourself laughing at a young boy that 'let one rip', but there is a different reaction to a girl doing the same? We shouldn't do it, but think, have you ever looked disapprovingly at a young girl who had passed gas and wondered how such a girl could have slipped out such a noxious and loud fart? Burping, farting, and the rest are considered 'laddish' behaviours and women/girls being 'laddish' are not considered desirable. We tend to keep it in! Tightly Contained.

Well after this Christmas Eve dinner, somewhat intoxicated with the wine flowing freely through my veins, the food swishing in my stomach, I definitely waddled, gurgled, and belched all the way back to the hotel. I felt so lightheaded and so full, and it was on the way there, I embarrassed myself quite badly.

Prior to the beautiful service described above, with all that food in my stomach, we walked in the dark silent night, and apart from a few other walkers, we were to some extent quite alone. Feeling uncomfortable, I needed to 'let off some gas'. It was quite necessary as I knew I was not going to make it back to the amenities without doing so, so I had to do it under controlled conditions. Sometimes when in a small or large crowd, the techniques of passing gas silently, works most effectively. Hence, thinking I was safe, I expelled into the air. In colloquial terms, I "fluffed".

I was quite wrong.

Walking in a walled cobblestoned, otherwise deserted, square in the old part of Salzburg, not only did the noise I made emanate loudly, but also bounced off the walls of the square to reverberate loudly and continually from one side to the other. I was shocked! Marc too was shocked. I could not believe what had happened. Horror and mortification consumed me. But oh, how we laughed. Although I was rather embarrassed, I can quite assure you, after hearing the not at all silent 'explosion' and its many echoes bouncing and reverberating around the square, our continuous eruptions of laughter accompanied our remaining waddle back to our hotel for that much-needed anti-reflux medication for our over full stomachs. Very necessary prior to us later attending the cathedral for midnight mass.

I can say wholeheartedly, there was definitely 'something in the air' that night!

And it wasn't a Christmas Star!

Missing loved ones at Christmas wherever you are in the world, can be incredibly gut-wrenching and emotionally hard. Missing someone during Christmas can be tough and quite a challenge! You can feel isolated by the festive cheer and celebration around you. My family fills my life with love, and our own Christmas traditions embrace that ideal, so for me, it was absolutely quite a test to be away from my children and grandchildren on that special day, in that particular time of year.

With the beautiful scenery of the Austrian alps and snow-covered villages welcoming us, we shared a quiet Christmas Day reading books, writing diaries, and sorting our photos, but I felt the lack of my family. I truly missed them. It was strange and different. However, sharing iced Christmas cake my best friend Margaret had given to Marc, to carry in his luggage, together with a card to celebrate 'some Australia away from home' helped. Some special highly treasured memories were made that year! Some that should not have been mentioned (but I did anyway) and others truly magnificent.

What better way to remember the Christmas of 2013?

To finish this chapter, I also must say, that as women, we should not let the men have all the benefits attributed to allowing 'gas' to pass. Women too, should also be allowed to feel like, if they have to expel something into the air, it should be acceptable to happen when and whenever. Although, I have to admit, on a personal note, I would rather not do what I did where I did again! In hindsight, it probably would have been more preferable to have kept my air expelling for during the thunderous pealing of the bells. Then I could have simply let my gas go, or in feminine terms … "fluff" … and no one would have noticed a thing except perhaps an unusual smell! That, I could have blamed on someone else!

I will leave that for next time!

Chapter Fourteen

Celebrate Good Times but ...

"Sometimes the greatest challenge in life is doing what people say you cannot do!"

New Year's Eve.

New Year's Eve is one of the largest global celebrations because, before the new year commences. it marks the last day of the year in the Gregorian calendar, December 31.

Celebrating New Year's Eve is all about fresh starts and looking towards the future with optimism. New Year's Eve can signal the end of a chapter and the beginnings of a new different period, along with all those resolutions that we make and never keep! Conventionally, there is the singing of *Auld Lang Syne* at midnight, which hits you just at the right moment of tipsiness and you cannot help feeling all warm and fuzzy, thinking about your loved ones. Traditionally we celebrate this occasion with friends, family, parties, champagne, well, you know how it goes! New Year's Eve brings everyone together. No matter what we are like most of the year, everyone attempts to put in effort to have fun to mark the special occasion with lots of fireworks – and lots of fizz! Being away on New Year's Eve does not worry me as much as being away at Christmas. So, in our travels we have spent a few New Year's Eves away from family, from home.

We were in Vienna, Austria, for New Year's. Imagine 1.5 million people in crammed into the city centre, in freezing temperatures, gathered at various music stages all enjoying themselves, drinking and eating, and everyone behaving. Even when someone let off a firework early, it was always done in a safe manner in a space with no-one at risk. It was actually such a wonderful environment.

As midnight approached, I remember we tried to make our way to the large open area outside the Hofburg Palace where the fireworks were due to go off. That was quite a scary experience, as trying to get through the crowds was like salmon trying to swim upstream against the force of the flow. Often, we were at a standstill unable to move forward at all, jammed against people. If you lifted your legs up, you would simply get carried along with the crowd, turning where they turned, going where they went without your feet touching the ground at all. I know that New Year's Eve is a party time, but that was quite not the partying scene I actually wanted.

Everyone celebrates this special occasion in different ways, but tell me, what stupid people would stand in one spot in the cold for four and half hours to celebrate New Year's Eve? I mean literally stand in one place, in one spot, on a cold winter's night in a temperature of about 2 degrees. What two idiots would stand there, in this one position to eventually become encircled and smothered by a large crowd cheering. Yes, you guess right - Marc and me. Who else?

We were in London on a different New Year's Eve. We were away from the heat, the flies, our usual hot humid sweaty weather of Australia, where you partied in beautiful floating dresses, or shorts and tops, or sarongs, where you viewed the fireworks either on the television, or from your own place of celebration, or with friends or from the vantage point in your capital city. But because we were in London, on New Year's Eve, the expectation was to do something different. I guess we were on the other side of the world, in a different country, and just like the Brits, we had to spend this auspicious occasion traditionally! So, we did!

We learnt that Londoners like to queue. They are quite happy to wait in lines, to simply wait for things to happen, even young children. I was quite impressed by their patience and their ability to line up for hours and not complain. You have probably gathered by now that patience is not my virtue, and on New Year's Eve in London I certainly gave it a workout. Both my feet and my patience!

New Year's Eve in London meant a huge exhibition of fireworks displayed from the London Eye and from along the river Thames. We understood this was the 'place to be 'and needed pre-purchased tickets to see it. As the time approached and the gates opened on the bridges, people ran to vantage points and stood. Marc and I had chosen the Westminster Bridge, where we would be looking sideways at the London Eye, purely because it was away from the enormous crowds who would be looking forward. A much more preferable vantage point as I could not imagine being closeted in within those immense crowds in the park area facing the London Eye!

Arriving at 7.30pm, already the best vantage points were taken, but this was not a problem. We took up a stance in the second row, behind other people leaning on the bridge and we waited.

And waited …

And waited …

And waited …

The clock face of Big Ben ticked slowly by as the hands moved sluggishly towards midnight.

Did I mention we waited?

As the cold seeped in through the clothing hugged to our bodies, we both thought what on earth were we doing? Were we mad?

But, when in London do what the Londoners do?? We had been doing that, but this was absolutely ridiculous!

Did I mention anywhere in my writing it was freezing?

As we were close to the bridges edge (they closed the bridge and major roads) the icy winds from the water below, whipped, whirled, and swirled around our faces as we stood waiting for midnight, balancing on one foot, then on the other foot and then on both feet. The icy weather continued to spin its cold cloak around us both, as we remained waiting for this New Year's Eve festivity of fireworks to begin.

The music began. LOUD music. Loud blaring upbeat not quite our usual music scene … but we listened. Curiously, like the rest of the crowd, we began to move our bodies to this 'not usually our scene' music probably because it was the only way to keep warm but oh, it was really loud!!!!!

More Clock watching of BIG BEN - one hour, two hours, three hours. We were still standing in exactly the same spot. As it was a public place, we were not allowed to bring chairs or rugs to sit on, you had to stand upright. As we were positioned near the bridges edge, the crowds were getting noisier and closing in on us! As time ventured closer to midnight, the crowds began to intensify and move further inwards. People jostled and elbowed, attempting to gain a place nearer. They kept pushing gently to succinctly achieve a spot adjacent to the 'better viewing areas" by gradually moving you out! This basically meant if you moved from your spot, someone took it! So, no we did not dare move. We didn't dare!

But we were already tired and worn out from previously endured hours of walking, prior to standing on this bridge that New Year's Eve! You have to remember in London that nothing was nearby. From our accommodation, it was about forty minutes or so walking to get to most places, which meant the same time home again afterwards. To then stand more hours brazenly in the crisp clear cold night in one spot on stiff hard concrete to welcome the new year in of 2017! Thinking longingly of the heat of Australia, I pondered what were we doing here? Were we mad?? I was beginning to think so!

But what does Marc do?

As the crowd moved in, the noise and music got louder, he stood in his spot, scarf tucked tightly around his neck, his jacket done up snug, beanie on his head with a book in hand, under the lamplight reading! He was reading! To top that off, while continuing to stand upright in his designated specified spot, closing the book, he shut his eyes and simply chilled out from the noise and the cold and dozed. Amazing! Trained from years of catching sleep when he could, being a medical resident and then in the Emergency Department, I guess!

As for me, I stood there and tried to read my book, but the same paragraph kept jumping out at me. With the beat of the loud music, the same words on the same page kept vibrating its letters in time with the music. After reading the same page about 10 times, I gave up! Instead, I moved my legs to stop them going stiff from the cold. I flexed my fingers. I leaned over the side of the bridge and gazed at the water below me. I talked to different people around me who were really very nice and chatty, while gently prodding back those annoying people who were sneakily attempting to take my vantage spot - ('how dare they, go and find your own …') As my bladder contracted, I admit, I also looked longingly at the 'porta loos' which were just on the other side of the bridge but knowing if I took my much-needed pee, I would never return to 'my spot'. I doubt very much I would even find my spot again beside Marc in that thick suffocating crowd. As the hours continually ticked by with watching BIG BEN's hands move so slowly, I kept thinking this was crazy! But we did it.

The hands of BIG BEN chimed and as the last stroke of midnight resonated through the air, the huge fireworks of London display began.

Was it impressive? Yes!

And exciting? Oh yes!

But even more remarkable, was the use of everyone's mobile phone at the end of the fireworks display, when the co-ordinator of that loud music, asked everyone to turn their light on their mobile phone and wave it in the air, as 'Auld Lang Syne' was sung in one unified immense crowd voice!

What an absolutely amazing incredible sight.

Picture before you, the bright white light of thousands and thousands and thousands of mobile phones beaming through the midnight darkness, travelling for kilometres and kilometres around the river Thames till your eye could not see any more.

I stood there (yes in exactly my same spot from four and half hours previously) and watched in awestruck amazement. So amazed at how wonderful this display of harmony looked and sounded as countless thousands of people cheered, sang Auld Lang Syne and waved their phone/lights to welcome in the new year! I can honestly say I personally preferred that sight, to the fireworks! It is a memory etched inside my mind forever.

Was it all worth it?

Was the cold, holding my bladder tight and not using the toilet, the intensified crowds, the enduring torture of standing still on one spot for four and half hours all worth it?

One simple word - Yes. Most definitely yes!

Oh, by the way, Marc did wake up to view the same spectacular.

Of course, as midnight faded away and 1st January 2017 began, I rushed back to our accommodation to pee!

I have never walked so fast in my life!

Worrying is a waste of time.
Good and bad things happen, and you just have to not stress over what you cannot control.

Unknown

Chapter Fifteen

Taste of Family

Home is people. Not a Place!

I love travelling.

I gather by now you have worked that out! That is why I am telling you, my stories!

People travel in different ways but for me, travelling as a couple is unlike anything else. It means, you are not alone, nor just traveling with friends. It is much more than that. As a couple, you get to share all your experiences (including the downsides of travel) with that special person. You see places and sights for the first time and create those 'couple' moments, seeing new things, meeting new people and new memories are made! Together. Generally, in the time Marc and I had been travelling together, it has been just the two of us. Doing our own thing; being where we want to be; at the time where we want to be there; eating the things we want to eat; seeing the things we wanted to see, you know - just us. But of course, it could not always be that way.

One day, because I had married into 'the family', Marc raised the suggestion that perhaps we should be using some of our work holiday travel time to meet family members whom I previously had never met!

Marc is American/Australian. I had met all his Australian Family but not his American one. That was about to all change!!!!!!!!!!

By this time, we had been married for almost four years and had corresponded only through Facebook with this family-from-afar and I guess it was the correct moment in time to 'meet the family' – 'La Famiglia'. Remember Marc is also half Italian, and that half Italian part are all living in America. A trip to the States was planned with the premise of seeing some USA sights and to also meet those unknown American parents, aunts, uncles, cousins … (think of the movie, "My Big Fat Greek Wedding"). I was rather excited at the thought of heading to the United States but extremely nervous, actually, quite apprehensive. Being the second wife (with the first one still very much alive), with contact still in place between first wife and his family; as 'the new wife', I was not sure how I would be welcomed. But … always the optimist, this would be a new adventure and my new challenge began.

A trip to Los Angeles International Airport (LAX) was then about seventeen hours one way. Unfortunately for both of us, my excitement at flying became rather jaded, as for the entire trip, the unknown passengers occupying the seats immediately in front of us both had 'wind'. With low cabin air pressure, we all let the infrequent one slip out, but I have to write about this because those were not the occasional 'oops I am sorry', embarrassed little escapes of gasses, like I did in my previous chapter, but rather 'wind' of the stinking, odiferous, malodorous, fetid kind. This had the type of smell that could wake you from a dead sleep, which I might add, did, to make you not only feel sick, but feel repetitively nauseating enough to even comment OUT LOUD about the smell. This was not something that *'shy-usually does not want to make a fuss-Lyndell'* would usually say! But on that plane trip, I did! I really do not know what those two passengers in front of us had eaten, but even when they were sleeping, the entire journey, was flavoured by recurrent smells from our flatulent neighbors. I sincerely wanted to wake them up and ask them to please use the conveniences! Even the air steward avoided them unless forced. On arrival at LAX, after our recent prolonged exposure to a hydrogen sulphide rich atmosphere, it was most fortunate we were not checked for 'explosive residue' at customs. I am quite sure both of us would have come up positive after our exposure to fertilizer-based explosives from our seventeen hours experience earlier of hazardous gasses! That is a most unpleasant memory of this trip. A windy trip, indeed, and nothing to do with normal outside air turbulence!

At immigration, Marc walked through arrivals easily, holding his American passport. I was happy to tag along and avoid the long queue of 'Aliens'. However, I was still subjected to being fingerprinted and having a full body scan. Looking at my fingerprints on the electronic scanner I remarked, *"I guess I am now on the NCIS data base (TV Show). If something happens to me while I was in the USA, I can see (the character of) McGee looking for my prints on his phone."* I thought it was funny but no, the customs officer was not impressed! Marc had already told me that the officials at Americans airport do not have a sense of humour. Not-at-all! He was right.

'New York New York' as the song goes … and where do I start?

New York is renowned for all its people in such a small geographic place. They were right, there were people. Everywhere.

Through our taxi driver, just like the television shows and movies, we learnt that the vehicle whose driver has the biggest death wish and the least regard for their vehicle was the one to get through the intersections. Bicycle riders and pedestrians both considered traffic lights to be simply advisory. As long as cars were not moving, you crossed the road, which also included stepping out in front of vehicles stopped across the official pedestrian lines.

As a pedestrian, you simply ignored the cars and walked around or in between them, hanging on tight to each other as you strode. At one time, I learnt this the hard way ending up being wedged between two cars as Marc, unaware of my predicament, disappeared into the sea of people ahead. Rather funny and a humorous memory, but at the time of it happening, quite scary. Basically, I was locked in place, my legs wedged between two yellow cabs, surrounded by other honking cars and swarms of anonymous faceless people, watching Marc walk off into the distance. Alone, on a pedestrian crossing. Trapped! And what a huge throng of people it was! Never ending.

There is also a designated 'people lane'. Not a footpath, but a lane on the road allocated for people. It is to cater for all the people in this amazing city all trying to simultaneously move somewhere during peak hours. Solution, permit them their own traffic lane on the road. Open-mouthed and utterly amazed by what we saw, coming as we do from a small fishing town, little did we know that we would soon adopt NYC pedestrian road rules when trying to negotiate our way through the crowds. How quickly we became official New Yorkers by not waiting for the lights but just follow the masses.

There were also queues everywhere. Like the Brits, New Yorkers queued for tickets, desired eateries, ice-skating rinks, and together with the tourists, for sightseeing. It was nothing for an hour to be lost in a queue in a way I cannot see the average Australian putting up with. No, not at all.

I must not forget the yellow cabs! Just like the movies they are all you see. I stopped to laugh at the continuous display of yellow cabs on the four lanes (one way) of Seventh Avenue. They just kept coming and even as people stepped out from the sidewalk calling 'Taxi', they just drove straight past!!!

So, how do I really describe New York?

Like Times Square.

Standing in the middle of a concrete light show jungle in Times Square both thrills and excites you. Everything is lit up brightly, with larger-than-life billboards. Standing there, you absorbed, breathed, and immersed yourself in the vastness and colours of that visual light display.

What about Broadway! Loving musical theatre as I do, it was so inspiring and exhilarating to be in this part of New York, with its endless stage shows on offer to see. I think of how many theatres there must be with all the musical stars and hopefuls. Yet, here I was, little me, actually standing on Broadway in New York!

New York was so busy with sounds, lights, crowds, of smells of food everywhere emanating from the many street vendors plying their wares on EVERY corner. Visual temperature changes were easily observed where the outdoor chill was suddenly broken by the warm updraft from the vents stemming from the subways. Just like Marilyn Monroe in that famous scene in the movie, "Some like it Hot", as her white dress lifted upwards. To be contrasted at night where car headlights lit the plumes of steam from chimney-like tubes in the roadway producing eerie effects.

To the ear, it was also a huge melting pot of humanity with dark skinned people equally, or just exceeding, the number of light skinned people. We overheard so many languages, some of which may once have been English but now spoken with a hip/jive cadence, at times, making it hard to understand. We saw both affluent and non-affluent society, with countless poor people and rubbish bin divers simply hoping someone had thrown a sizable bit of their lunch away uneaten, or the search for cigarette butts collected from the sidewalk for the meagre amounts of non-smoked tobacco in them. Those observed scenes depicted such a huge difference between the rich and the poor. New York also offered somewhat constant musical sounds, of tooting of car horns, any time, any place, their car conversation going on endlessly, mixed with the crying siren of another wailing feline. We heard many caterwauling sirens like a sick cat, pitifully mewling and meowing but in harmony with other cats, all blending together the different sick sounds of siren but not all in the same key. An interesting mixture of sounds, some not so desirable, but one that is New York. A menagerie of sounds we will always remember.

Then there was Central Park.

A huge park roughly one and a quarter square mile, (in American terms), in the middle of New York, with brilliant autumn colours ablaze of fiery reds and yellows and horse drawn carriage rides. The smells of autumn and the swishing of your feet through the fallen leaves bought memories back from Marc's childhood. I could not help grabbing an armful of fallen leaves and tossing them in the air!

Images come to my mind of our exploration of the Ice Skating rink, the central Mall pathway, the famous lake, the fountains, the boatshed, the sites used as film backdrops for countless movies, the multitudes of wedding parties – brides of different ages with their white trains and flowers - being photographed, sharing their nuptials, not only with their families, but with the general public around, including us!

I really loved Central Park. It was so different from the hustle and the bustle of the city. At time of writing, it was Sunday. Everywhere there were runners and walkers and bike riders and families and children. Many happy smiling faces. Many different nationalities. Many New Yorkers! We walked so far in our excursions, but measurably, you do not obtain much distance in one hour and believe me, we walked many, many hours.

Then there was Ellis Island. We learnt about Marc's heritage since his family, arriving from Italy, had come through these immigration gates. We immersed ourselves in the history as we too walked the same great hallway his own relatives had!

Of course, you have to see the amazing Green Woman - the Statue of Liberty. Did you know the face of this 'green lady' is the image of the sculptor's mother!!

How do I describe The Empire State Building, the famous icon used in so many movies, with its breathtaking 360-degree views of New York? What about Grand Central Station where the vast hall is covered and walled in cream coloured marble? Radio City Music Hall with its dazzling Christmas trees, bright lights and their famous dancing Rockettes. The 'Ground Zero' sombre monument to the Twin Towers attack on 9/11?

Imagine the impact that 9/11 disaster must have had on the New Yorkers?

In 2001 from in our home country, as Australians, watching this scene on television, it was not 'real'. We sympathized and said, 'not good' and similar platitudes. But it did not happen to us. We were too far away. Being in New York, having seen the Twin Towers site in person and the Ground Zero monument, to think how it must have been when the planes flew into the towers. The HUGE amount of people who were in those buildings. The numbers of people innocently simply walking in the streets and the malls alongside. It must have been absolutely horrific. To be one of those who looked up and actually saw those planes fly overhead above you, or to be a person inside the towers with nowhere to go, as it flew at you, I shuddered. Simply not a good thought.

In contrast the American Museum of Natural History was definitely a hit. Nothing is 'small' in New York and this museum is no exception. Even the entrance is immense. We found "Rex", the playful dinosaur, and "Dum Dum", that wonderful Easter Island icon, from the Movie, 'Night at The Museum!' (We waited in anticipation to hear that famous phrase, "Dum Dum" … but it did not happen!)

Such amazing edifices in this city. Far too much to write about and each deserves a whole chapter of their own! The people are loud. The traffic is non-stop. The noise and lights continuous. But an extremely exciting place to be in for a few days!!! Just like those famous lyrics, *"... I want to wake up in a city that never sleeps ... to be a part of it ... New York, New York."*. We were there. This is New York!

But it was now 'that time'. The time to venture off to a new untrodden journey of unfamiliar relatives. Meeting your significant other's family for the first time can be a nerve-wracking experience. You are anxious, you want to make a good first impression, and hope they are happy to meet you and see you with their relative ... (even if their relative is over the age of 50!) Well, with the bright lights of New York fading into a distant memory, I was now about to find out!

Watching Marc's face as we arrived at North Elizabeth train station, New Jersey, as he ambled down memory lane through fallen autumn leaves, pointing out to me various aspects he remembered of his past. This was very special. Listening to his chatter and smiling as his recollections were fulfilled. We were then met at the door by two old people who hugged Marc tightly.

Marc's Aunt then was 89 and his uncle was 91. Both have died now but at that age they were becoming frailer, suffering from a combination of hearing and memory loss but still with preserved senses of humour. It was interesting to watch them interact, since each would have memory lapses and turn to the other to fill in the blanks. They still managed though, staying in a house where the main living area was up one extremely narrow flight of stairs, with the laundry down in the cellar two floors below, again accessed by narrow stairs that even a much nimbler younger person would find challenging.

Dinner on our arrival, was served to us on the Best China at 5 o'clock - bringing Sunday Lunch childhood memories back to me of my youth in Sydney. Not the type of food I usually ate but I braved the meal and did not utter a murmur as olives, smoked salmon and extremely spiced curry soup was served. I consumed everything placed in front of me, smiled throughout and left my plate clean, just as my mother would have expected me to do. When normal pleasantries exchanged and after the first shared 'delectable meal', we retired for the night, my stomach less than gracefully flipping around and around. (I thought I did very well!)

Breakfast next morning was at 10am which apparently was the normal time for Marc's Aunt and Uncle. That particular morning, we dined on a wonderful breakfast of potato bread and eggs. Sounds just like your conventional breakfast, right? But this was a different combination. The egg yolks were very white and the egg *whites*, were not at all white. Instead, they were mostly still clear in that 'mucous membrane' style and quite runny – the result of having been incompletely *(or not even cooked at all I think)* in oil. I am quite sure the potatoes used in the potato bread had just been dug out of the ground. This food was so thick and heavy, it would have made a great non-absorbent brick. But thankyou God, the Coffee was ok!

Being polite of course, I said nothing. I smiled to my new relatives and managed to slide down the eggs very quickly, chewed and chomped respectfully on the potato bread, drank the coffee rapidly to help ease the thick 'mucous' breakfast cuisine downwards to my stomach, and politely conversed with his aunt and uncle, while all the time, silently praying furiously the non-appetising consumed sustenance would stay below and intact. Breathing a sigh of relief that the eggs and bread were actually staying down' I became more relaxed.

Until … Marc started talking to his aunt and uncle about his time on the 'tall (sailing) ship' with the Local Australian scouts. He presented such a descriptive and engaging visual images of waves, of the boat, of constant pitching and rolling, tumbling, rocking, and lurching of the ship and swaying of swells, all illustrated with big arm movements and hand gestures. I get motion sickness just watching on television, from the safety of my lounge chair, a boat floating up and down on water, so you can imagine what was about to happen. As his descriptive narrative rendition continued, my breakfast that was courteously staying down inside my stomach, commenced its journey upwards. With a brief apology to his aunt and uncle, I managed to make it to the outside before the heavy contents of my breakfast said a chunderous 'hello' to the floor below. Taking in the cool fresh air, on that front step, I attempted to breathe calmly as my then intact gall bladder, performed its own frivolous jaunts up and down inside of me! So much for trying to be polite and 'good'! I tried that. From then on, I decided I would simply stick with the coffee.

Marc's aunt and uncle's house was typical of this part of New Jersey. This area was very much a working man's suburb with tall narrow houses spaced closely together and split into a downstairs flat to rent out. The upstairs floors were for the owners to live in, plus a cellar underneath as 'shed', laundry and workshop. As Marc relayed in explanation to me, the family would struggle for their entire working life to pay it off. Bought up in Sydney in a conventional one-story suburban home by Sydney standards, it was all so different to me. All available space at his relative's house was taken up with furniture, mementoes, photos, and many religious symbols. The inside of this house was narrow and cramped and included tiny stairwells. The stairs were steep and thin, with doors to be closed at the bottom of each flight, intending to trap the heat downstairs during winter. In our short stay, it was quite exciting to use those internal, almost hidden, flights of stairs. Like the book, 'The Lion the Witch and the Wardrobe', I enjoyed that childlike feeling of exploring the 'backstairs' in an old house with passageways hidden behind closed (secret) doors. Waiting, anticipating, like the character Lucy, for the snow to crunch unexpectedly under foot as I made my way out of each passageway!

On one specific narrow staircase, coming from the flights above, there was an unheralded sudden 90-degree turn at the bottom, followed by a door, usually kept closed. Marc, with his familiar childhood memories in place, made his way down those narrow stairs. I followed him. From a long-embedded childhood habit, at the end of the stairwell, Marc walked out, turned off the light on the stairs, and closed the door.

So where did that leave me? On those narrow steep stairs? In the dark?

Due to that unexpected sudden darkness, and not knowing where these small narrow steps went, a series of continuous thumps was heard as a not so young female body, bounced down the rest of the narrow stairs on her bottom, so much quicker than expected! A voice filtered through the closed door to me, *"Uh Oh … You, ok?"* "*No …*" returned the small pathetic sounding female voice from inside me, as I lay sprawled on those steps, trapped in the dark against the wall on one side, the door on another and the uneven steps beneath me. All in a most unladylike fashion. Marc had simply forgotten I was there and innocently completed what rule had been drummed into him as a young boy, *'Make sure you turn the light off at the end of the stairway and close the door'*. In the now pitch-black narrow stairwell, I missed that entire flight of steps.

Oops … sore derriere!

Oops … not impressed!

Nonetheless New Jersey was a good experience … in more ways than one!

* * *

USA cities after our New Jersey visit were a real delight. We visited Mystic, Stonington, Martha's Vineyard, Edgartown, Plymouth, Boston, and Salem. A country so filled with history and remarkable scenery which we both thoroughly enjoyed. I could write pages and pages about the things we saw. But, as it was a 'meet the relative's holiday', Warner, New Hampshire, beckoned us for the next Taste of Family meeting.

From our previous wet icy day of Salem and its witches' stories, the weather had most definitely turned colder and it had snowed. We entered New Hampshire and arrived at Aunt Sara's place about noon, and it was now thick with virgin-white snow. Sara assured me that this was 'nothing'. But, oh, it was not 'nothing' to me. I was like a little girl as I looked at Christmas card portraits of this winter wonderland I was witnessing. It was all so novel to me!

Snow roofed houses, an amazing sight, and like that innocent girl exploring her surrounds, Marc and I went out and took some picturesque photos including Aunt Sara's place.

New Hampshire, including the town that Marc's aunt lived in, still had many covered bridges. Perceiving one-such bridge capped with snow spanning a snow-lined partially frozen creek with overhanging tree branches laden with their snow ridges, was sensational to see. This was just like the postcards depicting a Christmas we would never experience in Australia.

Aunt Sarah's house was full of character and lots of ambience and to my childlike view, enchanting. Her house was actually two houses pushed together over a century earlier with a series of sections attached sequentially to one end. This was all important given the climate, but quite foreign to my Australian eyes. In her house, you could walk through various connecting doors, never sure where you would end up. Even on the second floor you could go through a door, walk through the attic over the mud room *(which I learnt in my naïve way was the room where you took off your muddy coats and boots),* down some stairs and into the barn, all without leaving the actual house or going outside. That was like being in the movies and totally new to me. I experienced a Real Attic in a Real Red Door Barn. There was the long porch where Marc's aunt told us we could hang up our wet washing. We hung our laundry up and humorously watched our dripping underwear ice up, freeze, crackle, and crunch with stiffness from the ice. A little bit 'hard' to wear and most uncomfortable, but that again, was a whole other story!

Aunt Sara's house was built in 1872 and it was old. The floor was so uneven you became seasick walking across it. The ups and downs were emphasized at the kitchen table. If you sat at one side, you sat so high you stared downwards at your plate. On the other side, the table edge was up to your chest and viewed your plate at nearly eye level. We took turns when we ate, sitting 'up table' or 'down table'.

Being winter, the house itself was heated by the wood stove in the kitchen and one in the lounge room. Our bedroom was positioned above the lounge with a vent in the floor allowing the heat to come up. It was quite the "central ducted heating" of the times. Even though we had this 'heating', I was so cold. By morning, Marc found a huddled mass peeking out from under proper old-fashioned patch-work quilts, with only a blonde tress of hair and just the tip of a nose showing. I now have a much greater understanding of why my cat lies with his paw covering his nose when asleep, it is so much warmer! But it was here, within all the new experiences of weather, snow, barns, and farmhouses, I experienced, my first American Thanksgiving.

Thanksgiving is one of USA's most widely celebrated secular holidays. Traditionally, it is celebrated on the fourth Thursday of November and for people involved, a time to spend with relatives and friends and a moment to give thanks. I learnt that it is a moment steeped in traditions such as where the president of the United States actually pardons one turkey. The lucky bird's life being spared, then spends its final years at Mount Vernon, Virginia, the former estate of the nation's first president, George Washington. (I did not know about that at all! Did you?) Such a weird tradition but important to this festive day! History wise, however, the holiday can be traced back to 1621 when Pilgrims and Native Americans came together in a three-day celebration following a successful harvest. Being a national holiday most offices and schools close that day, so that means an extra-long weekend of happiness and celebrations as people travel from near and far to be with their families. They all do try to go home for Thanksgiving!

It is also a time where people eat enormous amounts of 'turkey and pie'.

First of all, let me tell you what I knew, or thought I knew about American Thanksgiving Day before coming to USA. My knowledge of Thanksgiving from Australia was based on what I had seen on Hallmark movies and television sitcoms. This was that the centrepiece of dinner was The Roasted Turkey. Generally, as dinnertime approaches, families would gather in cosy settings, a room lit with candles and decorated in the season's colours of red, gold, orange, and brown with images of autumn leaves; decorated seasonal napkins, plates and centrepieces that brightened homes and dining tables! No thanksgiving celebration was complete without '*people fighting, getting offended and bringing up the oldest quarrels, but family come home and in the end love wins.*

Although my own perception was from Hallmark movies, and the original meaning of the celebration has changed over the years, Thanksgiving Day was still a time for people to come together and share a meal, which is exactly what I did that weekend. It was here, on that lopsided, skewed, leaning sideways, but beautifully decorated table, I shared my first ever thanksgiving meal with my newfound American relatives.

Thanksgiving dinner at Aunt Sara's proved to be very appetizing and just like my assumption, consisting of turkey, gravy, mashed potatoes, sweet pumpkin, cranberries, brussels sprouts and asparagus, the latter which I actually ate. Those foods, stemming from my childhood, are not high on my palate and generally avoid them. I do not have enjoyable memories of being forced to eat pressure cooked brussels sprouts. But coaxed into attempting those foods by both husband and 'new' aunt, this was in some way, pleasantly, (if I could use that word at all,) 'different'. The meal as a whole was charming followed by pumpkin pie.

I was a little confused with Pumpkin pie for dessert? I only like one kind of pumpkin and that is normally cooked in the oven served with baked potatoes and meat as part of a main course – a typical roast dinner. Therefore, to me, the thought of eating pumpkin for dessert did not really do much for my tastebuds and definitely did not comprehend a pleasurable sensation at all in my brain! In fact, quite the opposite. Lifting my fork tentatively, watching the exchange of looks between newfound aunt and husband as I beheld that slice of Pumpkin Pie placed delicately for me on my plate, I cautiously placed a sliver on my tongue! Expecting something quite different, to my surprise I found it quite sweet! Yes, there was pumpkin, but combined with sugar, condensed milk, and cream. Such a surprise to the tastebuds. A pleasing pumpkin concoction. But one piece was certainly enough!

It was a wonderful dinner!!!

After dinner, in the spirit of 'Thanksgiving', neighbours arrived and joined in the festivities. Card games were played, and politics discussed. After all, what family day, shared together did not have subject matter talked about relating to either religion, sex, or politics, or all three! Marc was able to join in as he has a good knowledge of American politics, but I tuned out as it was not of interest to me at all. I pretended to be paying attention in what they were saying but hoped the conversation would change to something else as I physically tried not to appear to be bored. I think I achieved that! I just kept smiling. (Always a good ploy!) I know every nation has its competitive edge and Americans are well renowned for it as well, but when card games were introduced, I was able to get the assembled parties of friends and families, to agree that scores were not to be kept during the card games. This added to the hilarity since statements would be made, *"Of course, IF we were scoring, this hand would be worth …"* The result was lots of laughter and a night of no winners and no losers.

That weekend, I gained a new experience of a brand-new tradition, distinctive diverse preparation of foods with a new family I had met, all complemented by a sense of intimacy due to the lack of internet and no mobile phone coverage. The hilarious intimate noise of games, chatting and raucous laughter inside, contrasted with the stillness and silence of snow softly falling outside. The outside world was simply locked out.

Today I reflect on that time. I have realized that Thanksgiving Day is a special time to come together and to basically share a meal, but it is more than just about food. It is also about family, friends, and neighbours. A chance to unite together again. In that expression of unity, it is similar to our Christmas here at home but, dissimilar, with no distraction of the exchange of gifts! What I did cherish was the fact that once a year, people at homes like Aunt Sara's, take a moment to stop and think what they are thankful for. In that moment and place, I was extremely thankful for meeting Marc's family who had accepted me most graciously as his new wife! I felt part of this family! I must admit, I was not reflecting exactly on this realisation at that significant moment then, I was more afraid to move for fear of my much-expanded stomach accidentally popping the pants I was wearing!

***

More family visits continued as we roamed from east to west across USA visiting some amazing cities and sights, such as Niagara Falls, Plymouth, Gettysburg, Visiting the Amish, Pittsburgh, Pennsylvania, New Bern, Virginia and into North Carolina, Blue Ridge Mountains, and Washington. I loved Washington and could return! A whole chapter is needed or more for these amazing places themselves and I promise that one day I will write about those experiences!

With arriving at Marc's cousins Lori and Dan's near Princeton, it was a chance to slow down a bit and enjoy some time with this new part of my family. I was extremely anxious again to be meeting *more* relations, particularly since I knew that Marc's ex-wife still maintained direct contact with Lori through a mutual craft interest. But all fears were put aside, (in fact, shoved right away and buried under the table) as I learned more of these new relatives.

Lori and Dan were our age and at once made me feel welcome into their home. Lori is the chattier of the two of them and in a way that made it an easier conversation for me. She was interested in what I did and with each dialogue, I knew I was becoming more relaxed. Lori's home cooking also improved our digestion. A great break from the American diner food we had been eating up to now (barring Aunt Sara's at Thanksgiving of course)! Funny though, the conversations with Lori always seemed to be about seeing art museums. We guessed she considered my work, my master's degree, and PhD in the "creative arts" as *art*. Eventually we clarified that my educational interests were music and drama rather than art, and that created a whole other avenue of conversation. So, a hit here with my new extended family and now feeling more comfortable!

Next family-stop interruption to our USA travels was meeting Marc's father and his Brazilian stepmother. This was probably the most important for me, stress and anxiety wise, as it was *his parents*. With every family visit, whatever the state, whatever the country, the conversation would always drift to talking about religion, sex, or politics! However, the topics of politics and ultra-conservative religion came up extremely early during our stay there in Arizona with Marc's father and stepmother, but Inalda, Marc's stepmother, stated, "*We will not go there, if harmony is to be maintained.*" Inalda continued by commenting that politics or religious discussion would result in no food … then proceeded to actually over feed us!

We did attend Catholic mass with Mum and Dad Saporito. It was a beautiful mass with a full choir blended with exquisitely, glorious music. I genuinely enjoyed listening to the priest, not for his religious lessons, but for his singing voice that he used to chant the mass and then to accompany the choir and congregation singing. Unfortunately, though, through the overfeeding, much of that religious mass was spent by emptying my own build-up of mass in their church toilet!

While at Marc's parents, we were able to visit one of the Seven Natural Wonders of the World.

Arizona's *Grand Canyon* puts the grandiosity of Mother Nature in perspective and serves as a window into the region's geological and cultural past. It really is an excessively big hole in the ground as the result of constant erosion by the Colorado River over millions of years, 446 km long, up to 29 km wide and more than 1,800 metres deep. An amazing vision to behold. Remarkably, the colourful stratified layers of rock composing the sides of the Grand Canyon change over the course of the day, as the sun moves, and light transforms one scene into another. It is so hard to describe those amazing formations and colours of the rocks like you espy in post cards, but there was one huge difference for us. The crisp white snow was falling everywhere. In many ways, I was entranced more with the snow on the side of the Grand Canyon, reflecting and fluctuating in its glorious colours of red, brown, yellow, golden to white, than of the immense deepness of the canyon itself, although that was incredible. It was all so amazing and certainly created a magnificent picture.

We were surrounded by the wonderful Arizona desert with the city of Sedona. Its individual red and yellow rock escarpments interspersed with interestingly shaped rocky spires that silhouetted against the blue sky. There, we visited "Slide Rock", a natural waterpark in Oak Creek Canyon where the Creek flows over grooved red sandstone, creating a natural water slide. This is because the growth of algae on the rock aids in decreasing the friction. That was special for Marc as it bought memories for him, of coming here as a 20-year-old, (just a few years ago, he reflects) and sliding down the rock. Obviously, by the end of those afternoons, lots of fun had, but there would have been very little seat left in the jeans with his underwear remaining as the only layer preserving some decorum! More dignity expressed in this current visit however, by only tempting fate with jumping over the creek, risking a slippery fall into the ice-cold water. Although, I think he would have preferred to slide as he did as a child!

We also had the unique experience of eating at a cattle restaurant that had some 'local' specialities. This was where we tried a 'sampler' including snake balls, buffalo meat and fried cactus. Marc was the only one who tried all three. (I only sampled two of the three. Can you guess which one I refused to eat!)

More relaxed, back at their home, his parents and I talked well into the evenings. I found this refreshing as you can imagine I was more than a little apprehensive meeting this important component of his family.

Within any new relationship, there are at times, quite out of our control, where you are halted by the past. Even though not intentional, there was one major 'past' blot in this visit.

Marc had children from his previous marriage. My newly met in-laws were of course interested in how his ex-wife was. Naturally, driven only by their familial curiosity, they wanted to know how things were going with his children. They were still their grandchildren, and his ex-wife was still their daughter-in-law. After all, his past was still there and had not been obliterated just because I had joined the family. I accepted it and listened with interest to Marc chatting about his family and showed no emotion at all. I think I handled it well. But what was most difficult for me, in this home, were the vast array of family photographs.

There were photos of his 'ex' with Marc in various poses and places.
Photographs of Marcs 'ex' alone with their kids.
Photographs of Marc and his 'ex' on their wedding day.
All understandable of course.

His Ex had been a huge part of his father's and stepmother's lives for many years and brought their first grandchildren into the world. But through all those photographs, it was as if everywhere I turned there was another reminder of his former life, of the woman he previously loved, before me. At times, inescapable, particularly as those photographs were mostly in the room where we were actually sleeping. That was certainly a different challenge. Not one I quite expected to deal with! Sleeping in that room surrounded by photos of the past ghosts while I was living in the present, I truly felt one night, I was suffocating. Being a sensitive matter, it was too hard to really express how I felt to Marc. Neither would I hurt his parents for the world! So, being winter, the central heating kicking in periodically with a loud whirring sound, a clock outside our bedroom door that chimed every hour and all those smothering photographs staring down at me while I lay with Marc in the bed, my mind did not always shut down as it should. Sleep evaded me. A momentous visit and a meet and greet in person to two special people, but a Very Tired Lyndell.

More cities and places across USA explored that ended in Los Angeles.

It was here I met Marc's step sister-in-law, Corrine. Corrine also had two teenage children who were so friendly and part of Marc's family. All of them made me feel very welcome! Another family member but here I found common ground! As conversation transpired, it turned out that both Corinne and I had lost our husbands both aged 49-50 prematurely, through illness. This shared past life experience meant that the two of us spent some short but meaningful conversational time together. Corinne's experience was still relatively new. Mine had been for quite a number of years. But it was mutual ground upon which the two of us could meet, share, and journey through a real understanding type of dialogue together! Emotions, views, apprehensions, questions all culminating in time of common ground discourse. Today she also has married again to a wonderful man and is incredibly happy, just like me! This visit was an unexpected quality of time spent with a new relative.

* * *

Travelling as a couple can either "make or break" relationships and I can see how that could be the case. You are with that other person 24/7, and you really do get to know them on a deeper level and there is no hiding who you really are. On that trip, Marc and I obviously had our share of disagreements, but the thing that made it work for us was compromise. While there had been trying times and some difficult circumstances, we shared that intimacy, friendship, and companionship, and it worked well. I believed this 'Taste of His Family' trip certainly proved that we were that little piece of home to each other, good to have around!

To be honest, I did not have an entirely restive holiday. Meeting new family anywhere can be confronting, and this was no easy feat. It was quite a challenge! We spent in total twenty nights (with intervening days) out of thirty-five with Marc's American family. Each time I met people I did not know and would be quite anxious of being compared and judged. Neither did the Viewing 'Family Photos ' of Marc's former life appearing on household walls assist in reassuring me at all. Although, to their credit, each member of each family group across USA, was warm and positive to me and welcomed me happily. I found out later, they all told Marc that he had made a good choice.

However, I would have been more relaxed if I had known it well beforehand!

Yes, family is a wonderful thing.

My family is now a lot bigger than it was before as his American relations are now also mine.

But we have decided to go back to what we do best – travelling only as a couple.

There is only one caveat. I will have to work out how to discreetly sidestep letting well-meaning family, both here and overseas, know when and where we are travelling!

I will let you know how we go!

Chapter Sixteen

Not all Plane Sailing

*"I cannot change the direction of the wind,
but I can adjust my sail!"*

Travelling with my husband means I never know what is going to happen each day with Marc, what we will find when we get there, or perhaps what manner in how we get there! But that is exactly who Marc is! It has undeniably been a rollercoaster ride but an amusing one and sometimes exciting.

Haven't you had that situation or time where tasks have been discussed and you have calculated and coordinated everything to the tenth degree, but somehow, between your organising and the actual event, the universe chose something entirely different to happen! Despite all best efforts, no matter how much we prepare and organise everything, there are times where it can all go pear shaped. As the good philosophers inform us, we cannot control what happens in life, but we can manage our response to it. Of course, that is their optimistic opinion. In reality, how we react depends on what has actually happened.

Our five-day Easter holiday looms.

The farewells, the race home from work, our travel packing complete, luggage loaded, dogs and cats fed and left for their house sitter, goodbyes texted to family, and we were on our way. Our plane departure for Sydney from Brisbane to connect to our international flight was at 6:05pm. Planned with plenty of time!! Well, that is what we thought!

Even though it was Good Friday and we had two hours to the nearest international airport, the road was relatively easy driving. Combined with our pre-planned extra allowance of time, we knew we would have a comfortable time buffer at the domestic departure lounge. Excitedly, we settled into the business lounge with our books and coffee to wait out the two hours of travel margin that 'disaster planning' had not used up. Contently sitting there, feeling relaxed, we lovingly smiled at each other sharing those unspoken thoughts that are easily shared with your spouse. 'Finally, our Easter Break holiday is imminent and here we come!

First glitch! Flight to Sydney from Brisbane. Delayed.

All good.

Being the positive person that I am, the time delay was only ten minutes and with a two-hour window connection to the international flight, was deemed 'okay' in my books. But then the blue and purple departure screen had other ideas and kept blinking rapidly, updating to indicate a further delay of, fifteen, then twenty-five, then thirty minutes. Our international connection time between domestic and international airports was beginning to silently creep away. Consequently, my feet began to pace around the waiting lounge as my eyes intensely watched the clock on the screen, praying for it not to stretch its digital interval hands any further as we waited for the turn-around plane from Sydney to arrive (delayed of course). With a sigh of relief, the screen flicked to "*Landed*" and we were off. Racing down the stairs to the departure gate … thinking, here we come Sydney, do not fret, do not panic, do not leave us behind, we are on our way!

Second glitch! Transit Bus wait.

Our flight lands, airbridge door opens and walking as fast but as sedately as possible, we rushed to the transfer bus lounge to transfer to our final gate for our international departure. Except for just one solo airline female attendant at the desk, an empty foyer appeared in front of us. This attendant informed us of a twenty-five-minute wait for the next bus. Watches checked. Looks of concerns but still deemed 'do-able' as other passengers entered the room and we once more sat in the chairs provided and waited. Again.

Do you know, the transit bus was actually outside all the time!

It was not until two irate belated passengers with their angry dialogues arrived and headed straight to those transit doors. Who were these people? We did not know their importance until that slow nonchalant airline person suddenly became animated, sprinted up and opened the access doors for those particular passengers. Following their lead, we walked through the same door. As we jumped on the bus, (not that jumping first on the bus was going to make the trip any quicker, but the thought was there anyway), our driver says - "Ticket please?"

"What ticket?"

"The one to get on the bus."

Looks of dismay and frustration shared between us as we bounded back off the bus, espying other passengers lined up behind us each with a glowing hot red ticket in their warm little hands and were now moving unimpeded onto the required means of connecting transport. We hastened back to the transit lounge to the same one transfer lady in red, who, twenty-five minutes ago, had ample time to provide us our tickets but had not deigned to share this wonderful most important piece of information with us! Of course, we were now the last passengers onto the bus, and everyone was waiting for us! How embarrassing but we did not care because now we had those same all-important red-hot tickets in hand. Happily, we settled in our bus seats and handed those prize possessions to the driver.

What did he do? He passed the 'now counted group of red tickets' he had just collected back to the transit lounge lady waiting on the bus step. What? You have got to be joking! He just could have stood up and completed a head count!

Our bus rolled forward. Once more we are on our way.

Positivity returning again as we could now see the international terminal building in the short distance ahead, its lights beaming brightly towards us, warm and welcoming. But do we head directly that way? No. Instead, our transit bus circumnavigates the entire airport before eventually slowing to a ten-kilometre crawl for the last part of the journey. The driver must have thought we needed a tour of the domestic to international roadway! Our connection time was certainly ticking away and undeniably much faster than the ten-kilometre speed limit we were going. I could have walked there quicker!

3rd glitch: Security

Bus parks. We raced up the stairs to pass through immigration as expected. But are the 'open' desks close to us? No, they are at the far end of the immigration hall. Tell me, why did we ever think it would be any other way? Breathing fast, we conceded that was all right as we knew what to do. We knew what the drill was, and it would be easy! Easy? Wrong word unquestionably.

When you head to the USA, you can assume wholeheartedly they do not trust you one bit! This is quite obvious because there are so many different security points and officers to negotiate. I breezed through, which was in contrast to our previous travel logs and quite unusual, but instead of me being chosen for the usual screening, Marc is asked by an officer to actually step into the security screening booth. The kind where you have to spread your legs and place your hands in the air and the X-ray full body sweep is completed. Are we now on our way? Of course not! The X-ray scanning machine did not work which required the computer to be rebooted. Yes, he had to stay even longer because technically, he had to go in and start all over again. And our pre-planned allowance calculated time ticked further away.

The boarding time for our plane had already commenced. But are we cleared of security? Of course not. With absolutely no regard for our plea of, *"Our plane is already boarding"*, Marc is taken to one side, this time for an explosives check. The American security attendant smiles at my worried face and states, *"Oh you'll be fine; they'll board the ones who need help first and then the business-people and will simply take ages to get to you*" Really? Inwardly I screamed, "*Hey lady, we are Business class-that's what we saved and paid our money for - so we did not have to wait*". But, outwardly, of course I am demure. I am sweet. I smile politely all the time at this large USA security person with her explosives swab wand in hand. Not quite the person you really wish to offend.

Finally, we were free to take matters into our hands. We raced to our departure gate. We came around the corner and there it was, through the window, our plane to Hawaii still patiently waiting. Reassuringly, the departure lounge was still congested with people waiting to board and the all-important door to the air bridge was still open! No words spoken because of our heaving chests. We looked at each other. Our grins broadened. We did not miss the plane. We had made it!!! Beaming at each other, our heavy breathing, our raised pulses, our annoyance of rising panic all gradually began to subside. Exhaling calmly, we moved slowly forward to the boarding pass scanner.

Fourth glitch: documentation challenge.

Boarding pass and passport in hand, we place submit our documentation to the scanner. Red light flashes and a long beep sound! An attendant pulls us to one side," Sir, *Madam, we need a document check please."*

Frantic panicky words race through my mind. 'Didn't we just go through all that security? Didn't we just submit to immigration and a full body screening? Didn't we just have our photos checked at security? We are who we are … we had no time in this mad rush to hand them to anyone else … "*Oh, come on … what could possibly now be wrong?*". All those indignant angry thoughts flashed concurrently, silently, as I smiled meekly and ever so sweetly at this male attendant.

Our attendant scanned his computer screen, our passports, our names, walks away to another computer, scans them again, walks back to us in the now very lonely empty departure lounge bereft of the people who had already boarded the plane, leaving us isolated. Then, with no word of explanation, he handed us back two stubs of passes and waves us on! Totally confused, we walked down the air bridge onto the plane.

But that is okay!

I can see the lovely Hawaiian flight attendants in the cabin entrance ahead.

I can feel the blue sky of Waikiki beckoning.

I can feel the holiday about to begin.

The host smiles at us with an 'Aloha…'

A flight steward looks at our tickets and directed us to the right.

I looked at Marc. I looked at our passes. The problem was, because of the business class seats we had saved for, we were supposed to be entering from the sky bridge towards the front of the plane and turn left. That was not happening. I do not know why he directed us the other direction. Aware of the stunned disbelieving looks on our faces, the steward looked again at our passes and without a word, changed his direction to the left, and redirected us to where we were supposed to sit. I wonder whether it was the added tinge of rising annoyance in my face that gave it away??

Fifth glitch: Boarding Passes are incorrect.

For the first time we noticed that our boarding passes were for different seating rows. I was nowhere near my husband for this trip!!! The prospect of a nine-hour plane flight seated next to an absolute stranger was the final straw for me. I could not do this!

After everything we had planned from time allowance to seats, this could not be real. Tears welled. It all had simply got the better of me. I lost it and began to cry. With tears running down my face, we appealed to the flight attendant, explaining in an emotional voice our pre-flight trials and now this final mix-up, this could not be happening! I just wanted it all to stop!

Do you know on that traumatic day, for the very first time, someone actually turned to me and started to help? With her beautiful Hawaiian accent and smiling face, she turned to me and announced loudly, *"It will be alright"*. It was. The male stranger who the airline had ticketed to sit next to me for the flight kindly agreed to swap seats. As the plane took off, Marc and I were in our new seats, 'together'. Hawaii, at long last, here we come!

* * *

You would think that was a once off. Something that could simply not occur yet again. Well, think again!

It is one year later.

The hustle and bustle of Christmas traffic and patients gone, our staff have had their leave and it is now our turn. All those various aspects of 'being away and what to do if'(for 10 working days) had been discussed; handover completed, that last-minute packed-bag check done, tickets and passports in hand confirmed. Our plans and preparations and vigilant checking of time allowance and tickets were all completed twice…three times. Two weeks holiday ahead, and we were ready!

Even though we had planned and confirmed when we booked and paid for these tickets' months prior that we would be seated together, (checking numerous times after the last fiasco,), when we did our *final* check online a few days prior to departure we discovered that we were not sitting together but seated apart. Only by a few rows but seated apart. It was quite a shock … AGAIN! So, forty-eight hours prior to boarding we tried to check in. But this was not possible, as every time we tried; the once friendly online check-in site was saying, *"Please contact staff at check in"*. Concern setting in, Marc stayed up and placed a late-night phone call to the flight service desk to talk to a service person at 2:00am (with a wait of 1 hour 45 minutes) only to be informed they could not help us or do anything about it either as the actual boarding pass aspect was locked.

Taken to the airport, kissed relatives goodbye, we walked hand in hand, off to the sunny blue sky yonder … but with my heart in my mouth. I was hoping and praying that the attendant there would see how upset I was at being seated apart! The counter was empty as we had arrived with a number of hours to spare (I wonder why??). Eventually a lovely service attendant arrived anxious to assist us, looked at our passes, then smiled comfortably to reassure us. Calmness began to descend in thinking this is going to be 'okay', to then only be informed that "I was alright to fly … "All good to go … but one hiccup, my husband could not get into Canada as his Entry Visa had not been approved".

(That was why we could not get the boarding passes or check in.)

But we were confused and quite astounded.

Our visas had been completed months before and were there in our hands. Therefore, we could not work out why the ban to go was on Marc only. On closer look at both the Eta Canada form and Marc's passport, with the attendant's assistance, we realised that one letter, one small letter on our paperwork stood out now above all the rest. It was different to what was on his passport. There was a M written instead of an N! That one small, tiny letter made all the difference of us going or staying!

What do we do?

Panic?

Stress!

Feel like screaming?

Oh, all of the above!

We could not believe it. After months of meticulous organisation to eliminate any possible hiccups after the last debacle, this one small, miniscule misprint of a letter was leaving us stranded at the airport!

Many other passengers behind us were now lining up. We exited the check-in counter to sit down to attempt to ring the Canadian consulate in Sydney to find out what to do! To our surprise, (or maybe not,) there was no answer except a recorded tone advising us to '*press this, press that, 'press that one … press that once again, don't forget that one … which one do I press now …*'to finally get through to the actual site to then hear a recording that "*the reception could not help us with Visa requests or concerns.*"

What do we do?
Breathe deep!
Very deep.

Marc then logged onto Google via his phone to redo his application. Success as it was accepted! But accepted and being approved were two very different things. The application would not be approved for 72 hours! Both our hands shaking, despair really setting in, contemplating our situation, Marc saying the gentlemanly thing of, "You can still go etc" (as if I would – what was he thinking), then Marc reads the tiny, microscopic, small print, *'If you have an American passport, you do not need a Visa!"* Thank God for his Dual citizenship!

Smiles of relief emerged knowing that Marc can actually enter Canada and I would not be on my own, (not that I had any intention of going by myself anyway and leaving him behind to explore a whole new world!) It was such a respite to our travel troubles. Back into the line again, no longer the first in line as we had been, but at least back in the line. We finally get to the check-in counter, and we hand the documentation over, only this time, Marc goes on the flight using his American passport and I go as Australian. With a smile from the same attendant who had denied Marc before, approval given and our domestic and international flights boarding passports were handed to us. My breathing was a now a little easier (well a lot actually).

But not for long!

Passing through security, I quickly scanned our boarding passes checking the rows. This time for the international stretch, not only were we sitting apart in separate seats by a few rows as previously thought, we had now been allocated seat numbers in completely different parts of the plane. Not only separated and travelling alone, but we had single seats in two different sections of the plane. He was on the upper deck, and I was on the lower deck!

This time I cried. I truly cried. Not just tears trickling silently down, my face was contorted red and blotchy. You know that kind of crying where you have to actually go to the ladies to recover! I truly could not believe we were going through THIS again! Our much-needed time to be together, sharing our international flight and relaxing into holiday mode, was instead now going to be seated next to a stranger for 14 hours, hearing him (or her) snore, chat incessantly, and probably even Fart. How delightful was that going to be! It would be laughable if I were not so upset! I could not believe this was happening again. All our months of planning had gone right out the window.

My darling husband seeing how distressed I was, moved to a domestic airport service desk and discussed the situation with the attendant there. She, of course, could not do anything about it but this time instead of checking a computer, actually rang and talked to the flight supervisor of the international flight we were travelling on to Vancouver. Marc was then notified *"the flight manifest was full … (in my upset brain to mean no empty seats) but they would try and sort it".*

Well, you can imagine by now my faith in ground-based airline staff had wilted and faded dramatically, so both the wait in the lounge and the domestic flight itself to Sydney was a rather tense one. I asked Marc numerous times to tell me exactly what she said … you know word for word … just to be explicit! Just to make sure he had not left anything out! Marc was his cheerful positive self and encouraged me with optimistic thoughts of … " *They will move someone"* … *"there has to be single people on the plane"* … and *"anyone next to either of us is caught in being in a seat next to a stranger too so, of course, swaps could be done, relax …"* … you know those conciliatory wonderful encouraging words you share with a troubled stressed pent up emotional soul?

How could I possibly think about relaxing?????????

Generally, I do not get phased easily, my saying is generally '*It is as it is*', but this time I was agitated! Perhaps because it was the second time this had happened or maybe it was what going around in my head. I was listening to him and breathing deeply to calm myself down, thinking rationally and logically it would only be for 14 hours apart and then we could be together. But those unpleasant thoughts of envisioning what our trip was going to be like kept jumping bleakly at me.

Of sitting next to a perfect stranger, for 14 hours trying to be polite. Of making small talk to that person, I really did not want to be near in the first place.

Of not being able to share a wine with my hubby in the romantic gesture of being 'together' on our planned escape. Instead, I would have to cradle the wine to myself and get slowly drunk as my despair raged through my head (and my body) trying to make the best of a bad situation that we had not planned for.

Of 14 hours of climbing up and down (or staggering in my case as it may have been) between decks to say, "Hi", to each other. Of sleeping beside someone I really did not know … and what was even worse … oh, even worse than all the above, was the thought of having to crawl over a stranger to get up to the go the toilet!!! After all that alcohol I would have consumed in my despair … many, many, many times!

Our Domestic Flight landed.

Sydney sparkled at us as we made our way, (no, rephrase that, sprinted) to the service desk for our international leg. Tears already in my eyes, emotion churning my stomach flipping it upside, downwards, sideways, every which way, with its cartwheels of stress and anticipation. Then stepping to the service desk, a huge breath taken in, we were greeted with a lovely smile and two new boarding passes. *"Here you are. You are in Seats 11 J and K. 'Together!"*

"Enjoy your flight!"

All that anxiety. All that brewing of a stress ulcer. I am sure I had one!

* * *

What have I learnt from this experience? To know that sometimes even though it does not appear to be so at the time, with a lot of faith, everything can still turn out okay in the end as it did with us. You can then sit back and enjoy what is ahead! Not to mention, a bit of retail therapy helps immensely to consolidate that feeling as I did afterwards in the Duty-Free Shops at the airport!

Things happen outside our control and no matter how much we plan, prepare, check over and over again; uncharted challenges can still occur. But as was said in the movie, The Best Exotic Marigold Hotel, "*It will be alright in the end, and, if it is not alright, it is not yet the end.*" We both know it is definitely not the end! We have so much more to do! But I think we will go back to planning our trips with a travel agent!

Obstacles don't have to stop you.
If you run into a wall, don't turn around and give up.
Figure out how to climb it, go through it, or work around it.

Michael Jordon

Chapter Seventeen

The Turn of The Key

For this story, you will have to bear with me for a little as I set the scene for the next challenge. My story may start to sound like a boring travel journal, but I promise, I will try to keep you interested.

In preparation for our travels to Italy, Marc and I had completed a sixteen-week course in basic Italian language. Marc attacked the grammar and was much braver in 'having a go' in actually 'speaking' Italian than me, but, when pushed, was not as good as me at 'understanding' the spoken Italian. We were fine when together in that Marc spoke in broken Italian and then I heard the response and translated the Italian answer back into English. With this picture in mind, stay with me as we ventured to Italy and into Rome!

Rome. What can be said about Rome that hasn't already been uttered by others more eloquent than I am?

Rome is the Eternal City, remaining today a political capital, a religious centre, and a memorial to the creative imagination of the past! And oh, such history! Is there really anything else better in life, to be surrounded by history, so close, actually touching history? After all, travellers flock from all over the world to look at Rome's PAST, not its present. No, it doesn't have a Times Square like New York, or a Piccadilly Circus in London, or a Sydney Harbour area that is alive and buzzing with the pulse of the present, because people go to Rome for the history. And we were there for exactly that reason!

To begin with, immigration at our arrival in Rome was quite noteworthy in the nonchalance of the immigration official. Truth be known, the official was actually talking to the chap next to him and only just glanced at me briefly and not at all at Marc when he stamped our passports. For neither of us, did he compare our physical images to our photos! There was also No-One doing any surveillance of those passing through the 'Nothing to Declare' part of customs! Admittedly, that was quite a decade or so ago but, I truly wonder if it has changed at all.

Our first experience of Rome was the traffic.

Traffic in Rome seriously followed the rule of 'nerve', since the road rules seemed to be only suggestions, not mandatory. Vehicles turning rarely indicated they were doing so, and less so if they were only changing lanes. Although I must say that lane changing is a misconception since there are no lanes, just vehicles occupying their own chosen paths. This was apart from the highways called Autostradas where cars flew along at a minimum of 140km/hr in lanes no wider than normal street lanes in Australia.

If I had to typify my image of a street in central and historic Rome, it would be a narrow cobblestoned road lined by cars parked on both sides. Any gap too small for a car was filled with mopeds, leaving just enough space left down the centre for one car to pass, provided, of course, the driver did not mind occasionally scraping the paint off the sides of their car.

I have previously discussed pedestrian crossings in New York, but I must mention the Roman pedestrian crossings. These crossings were lines painted on the road as normal, but I think that they were there really only for decoration! Where walkers walked, it was wherever they could squeeze themselves through or, if they did not mind the odd close call with a passing car, in the middle of the road. Even at lights in Rome, those crossing were unquestionably only for the brave, because Italian car drivers obviously have only a low opinion of pedestrians and simply go through red lights. In Rome, to cross the busy road, you step out at your own risk. I personally believed that stopping for pedestrians was only a 'suggestion' begrudgingly adhered to when that walker had enough 'nerve' to step out into the traffic flow – head peeking, feet moving just to see if the cars would stop for him or her. Believe me, ducking in and out of traffic was a game of hit and miss. In this case 'hit and run'! An amazing and terrifying experience all rolled into one breathless ball of anxiety, wondering if you were going to be hit! Of course, Marc thought he would try the New York venture of stepping out, but it did not work. In New York, there, they would stop but here they just tried to run him over! We even saw locals being hit by passing cars as they attempted to cross on the regulated crosswalk! Combine that with the Italian language complete with obligatory gestures flying everywhere, it essentially was a true game of 'Survivor'.

But Rome itself was an amazing city. Sometimes, I cannot find the right words to describe Rome. It illuminated the beauty, the chaos, the mismatch of elegance and decay that was around every corner. Definitely we had to visit the Colosseum and many travel diaries and blogs have talked about this huge monument of such historic notoriety and presence and we followed their advice!

We had booked into a guided tour, but Marc definitely had a much better deal than me as he visited all the levels of this historic location. Unfortunately, not long after we had arrived at the Colosseum, I felt unwell, clammy, and shivery. Luckily for me, I did manage to make it for most of the tour's first tiers and underground section. Sadly, when it came to the last section of the high part, I stayed within the boundaries of four walls of a toilet inside the Colosseum (You must think I seem to have an attachment for foreign toilets.). Perhaps not quite the same shared experience of the Colosseum as the average tourist and I would definitely not recommend this part as an alternative tour!

Rome is also not like Paris where you could sit, and watch people go by. We did however manage to sit outside a café with our Italian espresso and cappuccino in hand in tiny cups (which is another story) looking across the cobblestoned piazza at the Pantheon. Interestingly, we had forgotten that even at a bar (cafe), if you sit at a table, you have to pay extra for your espresso – *le coperto*. I wonder what the Italian phrase is for deep vein thrombosis. Maybe 'not sitting' is a good thing after all? For us, we had no chance of getting that disease, as in our four days of meandering and residing in history, we walked to a long, long list of the usual tourist destinations.

It may be a little tedious here for some readers at the moment, and if you can prefer, you may skip these next two paragraphs, but for the interested traveller reading this, our 'traveller walks' included the Campo di Fiori (open air market), Piazza Navona (once the site of artisan marketplace but more akin to sideshow alley at a carnival), the Pantheon, Trevi Fountain and the Spanish Steps. Being with Marc, obviously we included some extra sites a little off the usual tourist route such as the Churches of San Pietro in Vincoli that contained a statue of Moses made by Michelangelo, San Luige del Francesca (built by the French) Basilica San Maria Maggiore, San Croce in Gerusalemme and the Cathedral San Giovanni in Laterano – said to be the Pope's cathedral which we could well and truly believe given the opulence and the amount of gold leaf throughout the interior! Most intriguing was the Porta Maggiore, the main gateway into ancient Rome. The remaining walls and gateway gave us an image of how glorious historic Rome, complete with centurions guarding the walls … on this actual wall … may have looked. Yes, you could say, I was in love with Rome!

Rome definitely has a LOT of churches. I wonder why?

We could see why the richness (as well as the corruption) of the Catholic church during the Middle Ages created the fertile ground for Protestant faith to take hold. We went to *many* churches, and, during our wanders, we saw numerous more small churches tucked into strange places.

One of the churches we did visit was St Clementine, a church built on four levels. That is: the modern level church was the present basilica built just before the year 1100 during the height of the Middle Ages. This was built on top of a medieval church that had been a 4th-century basilica. In turn this 4th century church had been converted out of the home of a Roman nobleman that had served as an early church in the 1st century. And adjacent to this 1st century church was a Mithraic temple that coexisted with the early Christian church until Mithraism was outlawed in 395AD. Below this layer was a fourth layer of buildings that had been destroyed in the Fire of Nero in 64AD. That was what Rome is like! History on top of history! How exciting!

We explored by ourselves the lower unused layers of this Church, by winding our way down to the bottom story. As we descended you could really sense that this place definitely had a spiritual presence. We could 'feel' why three religious meeting places had been built in succession on this site! As we had not been told how to turn the lights on, it was not quite the normal lighted journey of exploration usually enjoyed by tourists. By the time we reached the deepest layer, the light was at best, twilight, and at worse, pitch blackness. As we walked, all I could do was tightly grip Marc's hand and 'step out in faith' (pun intended). This was quite a different 'dark' to the sleeping type as this particular pitch-black, engulfed me, creating the illusion of stepping into an unknown abyss of darkness. Surrounded by this blackness, submerged in spiritual auras lingering since Roman and Medieval times, I felt extremely claustrophobic. Even more eerily, as we groped blindly our way into one room, we could hear the water rushing beneath our feet in a subterranean stream. Would the next step have us fall into this hidden waterway to be carried away to ….? Even Marc finally admitted defeat and we slowly retraced our steps back to the higher levels.

Many kilometres later of sightseeing and plunging through the labyrinth of narrow cobblestoned lane ways that make up the old Rome the time comes to move on. Sadly, but still excitedly, we departed the

Timeless City, to venture further into other Italian culture and history.

Hiring a car in Australia is relatively easy. In Rome, it also seemed somewhat straightforward.

The paperwork for the hire car was uncomplicated except we were just warned to make sure we stayed at hotels with their own parking areas. But we noted the hire care company did not even provide a rough paper-based map with the hire car. You have to remember this was the time before mobile phone-based GPS or google maps! But Marc was positive with his cheery statement of, "*No worries, we have our own preloaded GPS on our NavMan!*" And then it happened.

Ready to go, seat belts on (a must in Rome), engine started, and we plugged in our GPS in the car. It refused to turn on. No power light lit up. Nothing happened. In light of our previous observations about traffic and driving in Rome, Marc was adamant that he was NOT going to try and navigate the way out of Rome without a GPS. Even our B & B Italian host had said in an earlier conversation that he himself would not try and navigate a car through Rome without a Navman. So, being who he is, Marc tried to troubleshoot and found the fuse in the GPS was broken. Now remember we have had lessons so in his broken English/Italian, he tried to ask the garage attendant where to buy another fuse. Unfortunately, the answer in Italian was far from helpful, "*Negozio non vicino da qui*" (No shop near here). Marc was still adamant he was not going to try and drive anywhere without a GPS or a paper map. Given the nature of the surrounding driving frenzy, I did not blame him! Although double parked on the road, our car luckily, was not hindering the flow of traffic, so we had time to organize some sort of solution. We had already decided that the other cars could just weave in and around us even if we had been in the way. (Oh, that's right, nothing to worry about … they do that anyway!)

Two problem solving heads together, firstly, Marc deduced we needed something to conduct electricity. What else! The only small metal objects we had with us were the metal staples in our travel documents. After all, who normally carries electrical wires with them? Secondly, how do we hold them in place in the fuse holder? Well together with Marc's Swiss Army knife and a Band-Aid from my bag, (never travel without a Band-Aid in your bag), we were able to stick those two straightened staples to the side of the dead fuse. Not prepared to rely purely on Marc's 'MacGyver' skills, I tried invoking Divine intervention before we attempted Marc's repair!! Frustratingly, it did not work. So once more trimming the band aid down further in size, we attempted again this time combined with A LOT MORE prayer, (I mean, after all - we were in a Catholic country), and it worked. The GPS sprung to life and said to both of us, "Hello" – in English! We had fixed it! And off we went! Tell me, what better way to navigate through Italy in a small tinny two door car, than with a GPS Navman held together by a Band-Aid and two staples? (I must comment here that same repair continued to work for another three years until our dash mounted GPS disappeared for good!)

Italy loves its history. Italy is definitely built on history.

Its old cities are on hills. Around the old cities are walls.

Around some of those walls are the expanded modern cities.

The retention of those walled cities was very evident in Tuscany and Umbria, including Assisi and Sienna plus many a smaller town like Monteriggioni (used in many Spaghetti-Western films in the 1970's) and San Gimignano. When first viewing the walled cities, they quite reminded me from my childhood of the biblical song, *Joshua fought the battle of Jericho, and the walls came tumbling down.*' Hopefully not when I was standing on them!

Walled cities have many, many steps! As in previous stories told, steps are like a magnet to Marc. He just has to climb them to find out where they may go even if the 'where' turns out to be nowhere interesting at all or dead-end. For a person who is not that particularly fond of cats, in this regard, he is very much like one. A cat just has to climb as high as it can go, even if it cannot get back down again.

Assisi alone had plenty of stairways to tempt Marc and we climbed many an ascending alleyway during our brief stay there. In this city, the layout of the medieval town on the hillside together with the narrow spiral staircase to our second floor B&B, certainly provided enough exercise for the both of us.

Now remember our lessons we had undertaken prior to travels where Marc spoke in broken Italian, and I translated the heard (or written) Italian response back into English? Well, this was one time where it all fell apart in Assisi.

We were stranded outside our locked accommodation trying to converse on the telephone with the non-English speaking caretaker. Marc's Italian vocabulary had hit its limits, and being on the phone, I could not hear the Italian responses to assist with translation. After much language fumbling, eventually we gained entry and enjoyed rooms at the top of a beautifully restored 12th century house. The room was on the top story and accessed by a VERY narrow spiral staircase totally unsuitable for allowing the carrying up of a normal sized suitcase. The higher you went, the narrower it became. I would certainly hate to have something to drink and then try to descend those stairs. They were so narrow, so tiny, and so tightly spiralled! But such a beautiful place to stay in this special city.

Deciding to look for fortified towers and cities, after Sienna we headed to Monterriggio which is a walled small medieval town. This town was also mentioned in Dante's 'divine comedy'. Probably little has changed since Dante wrote about it in his poetry. Since it has been basically untouched for near a thousand years, it is used often in movies. This was a fascinating place consisting of a small township with a high thick wall surmounted by fourteen towers. We climbed up along the walls and as we viewed the countryside outside, we tried to imagine medieval times when this town was part of the northern protective defences for Sienna.

From here, to warm up, after a few more toilet stops for me (Italian food having its effect on me … again) we headed to San Gimignano, another medieval walled town much more frequented by tourists. (How do I know this? Because you had to pay for the convenience of using the toilet! See I was learning!)

Judging by the large number of parking spaces available outside the city walls, San Gimignano must be wall to wall with tourists in the on-season - literally given that it is a walled town! The fact that it was winter and cold, few tourists were there that day. More steps (you really had no choice). More walking uphill (again no choice) All quite worth it as we delightfully enjoyed local Tuscany treats of Bucciarelli and Cavallucci biscuits. These are sweet biscuits, one with spices, the other sugar based and both 'quite moreish' and accompanied by a very strong cup of coffee that I shared with Marc. The shopkeeper spoke English very well but indulged us in our attempts at Italian. See, we were using our Italian lessons! Again, Marc talked, I translated! (DO remember this distinction.) But it was also so, so, cold. The temperature had dropped dramatically, and I was finding it quite difficult to enjoy the views being so cold.

With very few tourists, there was very little open. Other than the cafes, all we could find was a museum dedicated to medieval torture implements. Not a museum we would normally have gone to visit, but being that it was all that was opened, being in the off-season, and needing to get out of the cold to warm up, we ventured in.

What a shock!

As a visual person, it was extremely repugnant for me.

Seeing various sorts of torture instruments accompanied by pictures (including some real photographs reinforcing the fact that torture still goes on today) did not leave anything to my imagination.

When I had read history books and Philippa Gregory-style novels that talked about torture, I would imagine in my head the use of torture techniques and the means spent by the Inquisition to extract confessions. As a reader, it seemed 'foreign', 'ancient' and thus sanitised – not 'real'. They were my own mental images. It was what I envisioned in my mind through the words portrayed .... a little like you reading my stories! In the bowels of that museum, no windows and being stone cold, we descended further and further into the innards of the dungeons of ancient times. We were confronted with so many of those instruments of torture, all organised and displayed with visual descriptions and images of how they were (are) used. It made the brutality of the punishments, and the forced confessions viscerally real.

Emotionally and mentally, I truly began to be affected by those exhibited instruments of torture. Seeing those agonizing devices, the actual photographs and explicit pictures of use, my stomach churned and tossed, and I found I could not take it anymore! My head and heart began to react, and I began to heave. Combining that with the effect of the deepening dudgeons, my recent history with Italian food and numerous trips to the restrooms, I ultimately had to leave that gruesome sight to desperately seek fresh air, even if it was cold. Rushing back up the steps to the middle layer of the building, I literally sprinted to the toilet, urgently needing to relieve myself in a safe private place!

This was one single toilet.

This toilet was inside four small walls – a chamber, within this medieval torture museum.

This toilet chamber itself contained cruelty related artefacts, obviously stored ready for display in the actual museum.

As I relieved myself, those artefacts in that toilet surrounded me,

Yes, I gained Release! Physically. Keeping my eyes closed, mentally I was not so sure!

Breathing deeply and feeling somewhat alleviated, I went to leave.

I turned the key.

The key did NOT unlock the door!

I tried again. I tried once more. No matter what I tried, the key would NOT open the door. I was locked in!!

Alone, sealed in that toilet chamber, surrounded by those cruel artefacts!

Of course, I was calm, cool, and serene.

Of course, I chatted politely to Marc outside the door informing him in quiet terms of what the problem was and calmly asked for help.

Are you serious! No, it was nothing like that at all. I was absolutely the opposite.

There I was, in an anxious, dishevelled state of mind, being held captive, bolted inside this solitary toilet chamber. There I was, in a strange non-English speaking country, quite sure those grotesque horrible torture instruments and implements were approaching, ready to pounce, drag me back into their medieval world! And no matter what I did, the key that would release me from this small toilet torture chamber room would NOT UNLOCK THE DOOR!

No way of climbing under or over!

No windows!

No way out!

Just four, floor to ceiling, closed-in walls!

I was walled in a toilet, in a walled museum in a walled city in a foreign country and I could not turn the key! Trapped!

As panic set in, continually trying to get the key to unlock, I commenced loudly banging on the door, calling out to Marc, shouting dramatically to my beloved who was there, *free*, outside this toilet chamber to, "Get Me

Out! Get me Out". I know I am amusing you. I can hear you laughing. But in reality, it was not a pretty sight both visually and auditory!

Marc went and found the sole attendant, the sole NON-English-speaking attendant, at the front desk. He explained in broken Italian to her what the problem was. She replied to him in 'rapid' Italian how to solve the crisis through her verbal instructions, "*Giri la chiave due volte e poi giri delicatamente la maniglia*".

Remember my comments about our Italian lessons and the way we worked together ... Marc speaks in broken Italian, and I translate the heard (or written) Italian response back into English. Remember, it is me who translates the spoken Italian in English? In my horror state, I truly doubt at the time, that I could have actually calmly translated *any* Italian words into English. Obviously, being not in the right frame of mind to decipher what I had heard through the door, I was not calm enough to rationally understand what she/Marc was telling me to do!? After all - think about where I was! I was busy trying to turn and twist the key, but it would not open to let me out of that medieval toilet torture chamber!

Eventually, Marc himself was able to translate the attendants "*due volte*" into English. As I frantically continued to turn the key back and forth with NO success, calmly and slowly Marc's words started to break through my panic. He kept repeating the words. "*Due volte*" meant I "had to turn the key TWO times" for the door to unlock!

Two times? Really? Crazy country ... who ever heard of turning a key two and half times to get out of the loo! I was quite sure I only turned it *once* to lock it when I went in. Breathing erratically, I eventually turned the key twice in the **same** direction. That second turn of the key released me, and the door opened!

I WAS FREE!

Liberated from my own Toilet Torture Chamber Horror Movie.

I raced outside to calm my nauseous shaking body.

Back to normality!

Back to stability.

Back towards our small tinny two door car with GPS Navman held together by a staple and a band-aid to drive away from that walled imprisoning city!

As I stood outside San Gimignano in the freezing conditions, as I *freely* breathed in the fresh chilling air, I vowed I would never ever lock a public toilet door again!!!

And, do you know, to this day of writing, I still do not lock a public toilet door but use other measures!

Yes. This was a memory of my travels to treasure always!

Not actually quite a warm happy one for me, but I am so glad you have probably enjoyed a really good laugh!

Chapter Eighteen

Too Hard To Hold

In case you are thinking I am obsessed with toilets, I am not, but realistically speaking, for many people and especially older women like myself, no matter where you are, when you need to go to the bathroom, you simply *have* to go! Going to the bathroom is essentially something everyone has had to do since multi-celled organisms existed, even if it is in a Torture Chamber Toilet!! So, conceivably, while we are on the subject of toilets, let me share with you some more 'travel toilet 'stories!

As a child, every time we left the house, my mother would ask me*: "Have you gone to the bathroom? This might be the last time you have a chance to go as we don't know when the next stop will be."*. For me, this was the norm, even though I knew we were going to venues such as the shopping centre or to church where I knew there were public toilets. However, I did the right thing, I was a very obedient little girl, and went to the toilet before I left the house and in reverse, before I left to come home, because *"you just didn't know if the bathroom at home was going to be free!"* That was a long time ago but even now, when I leave to go somewhere, *I 'have to go to the toilet!'* What is interesting is that my doctor husband has informed me medically, because of my childhood experiences and that conditioned training, I cannot now concentrate my wee. This means for me, when my bladder is even a little bit full, I have the urge to go! Quite a hinderance when travelling!

My mother was also a little fanatical about how to use public bathrooms.

When I was younger, she would take me into the public stall, teach me to wad up toilet paper and wipe the seat. Then, she would carefully lay strips of toilet paper to cover the seat. Finally, she would instruct, "Never, NEVER sit on a public toilet seat". Then she would teach me 'The Stance'. This consisted of me basically balancing over the toilet in a sitting position without actually letting any of my skin (and definitely not my nether parts), contact the toilet seat. Not an easy way to pee for a little girl believe me, but it was something that I was taught to do, and I guess it became habitual. Even into my adult years. In my more 'mature years', 'The Stance' taught to me by my mother has become excruciatingly difficult to maintain, especially when one's bladder is full (… or half full in my case).

Female amenities are a story all of their own.

Generally, when you have to 'go' in a public restroom, you usually find a line of women in front of you that makes you think there must be a half-price sale of something desirable going on in there. But like every other female, you wait and smile politely at all the other ladies, who are also mentally crossing their legs and smiling back you so politely, while chatting and laughing quietly about the "always the long queues in women's toilets" or making comments such as "only three toilets!". I always find how amazing it is that the male toilets are always empty and the female toilets full! If you are a female reading this, you will totally understand exactly what I am saying.

As you enter the restroom, you check for feet under the stall doors. Everyone is occupied. Eventually, it is your turn. A door opens and by that time, as pressure has mounted, you dash in, nearly knocking down the woman leaving the same toilet stall. As you enter, you find the door won't latch but it doesn't really matter. (In my case, after my torture chamber toilet venture - that definitely does not worry me!) Before you sit down, you try to hang your bag on the door to keep it off that 'germy ground'. After all, you don't know what has been on the floor before you (according to my mother anyway). Then as the urge to pee demands become even stronger, you pull down your underpants, and adroitly assume 'The Stance'. Ahhhh, relief!

But then halfway through, your thighs begin to shake. Thinking of your mother, you would so love to sit down on that public toilet but had not taken time to wipe the seat or lay toilet paper on it. Instead, you maintain 'The Stance' as your mature thighs experience a quake that would register an eight on the Richter scale. To take your mind off your trembling thighs, you reach for what you discover is an empty toilet paper dispenser. In your mind, you then hear your mother's voice saying, *"If you had tried to clean the seat, you would have KNOWN there was no toilet paper!"* And your thighs shake even more.

You remember that tiny tissue you blew your nose on yesterday - the one that is still in your bag. That will have to do. You crumple it in the puffiest way possible, but it is still smaller than your thumbnail. Right at that time, someone pushes open your stall door because the latch doesn't work. Just like you in that long line-up of women in that 'only three-cubicle' amenity, they are probably desperate to go too, but had not seen your feet. But with that impact of the door hitting you, you toppled backwards against the tank of the toilet and slid down onto the 'hazardous' toilet seat! You bolt up quickly, knowing all too well that it is now simply too late. Your bare bottom had made contact with every imaginable germ and life form on the uncovered seat because YOU never laid down toilet paper - not that there was any, even if you had taken time to try. If she knew, you realized that your mother would be utterly ashamed of you because you were quite certain that her bare bottom *never* touched a public toilet seat ever because, *"Frankly dear, you just don't KNOW what kind of diseases you could get from sitting on a Public toilet."* By this time, the automatic sensor on the back of your toilet is so confused that it flushes, sending up a stream of cold water akin to a fountain, followed by a vacuum that suddenly sucks everything down with such force that you grab onto the toilet paper dispenser for fear of being dragged off to the Underworld.

Relieved somewhat, you open the door to rows of those smiling desperate women who were still waiting to pee. You walk to the sink to wash your hands but cannot figure out how to operate the faucets with the automatic sensors. Running your hands backwards and forwards pretending the water is flowing and then holding a dry paper towel, you walk past that line of women, some at this point no longer able to smile politely, cross-legged, and still waiting. As you exit, you spot your husband or partner, who has since entered, used, and exited the men's restroom and, while waiting for you had read a whole copy of the Old Testament, wondering why it took you so long!

Scrubbing my hands furiously together with the pocket sanitiser from my bag, I now understand why women go to the restroom in pairs. It is so one can hold the door closed and hand you Kleenex tissues or such under the door. And that is all within the confines of my home country!

If you have ever travelled overseas, then you must know that bathroom facilities and the rules concerning them vary wildly from country to country. If you have not, let me enlighten you on some of them!

I have definitely had my share of using public toilets in a country different to my own. Whether, due to an overly full bladder on a 'long-haul' trip ever praying for the over-eager driver to pull over, or it may have been a few hours after a somewhat dodgy tasting skewer of unidentified food with an unknown fat content that I chose to eat anyway, chances are, regardless of the country I was in, I was forced to head to the nearest available bathroom, irrespective of its cleanliness. As stated before, when you need to go, you *really* need to GO and nothing will stop you!

Did you know that some large cities, such as Paris and Vienna, are dotted with coin-operated, telephone-booth-type WCs on street corners? To use them, you inserted a coin, the door opens, and you have 10 minutes of toilet use accompanied by 'Sinatra Muzak'. I am musical but have to admit, it was rather disconcerting to have to pee to a classical piece of music. As the song built into an orchestral crescendo, it was definitely not easy to relax that already constricted full female bladder. Other times I have had versions of Frank Sinatra crooning as I 'sat' there in my private booth of relief. Believe me, I really love music just not peeing to it. It is quite hard to stay in time!

Don't forget that as the doors of this type of public booth close behind you, a sweet, pre-recorded voice ominously informs you, *"The door is now shut; you have 10 minutes"*. When said in a different language with an indecipherable number of minutes you hope it was *at least* 10 minutes. Many times, as I listened to the music playing, be it classical or crooner, I have had immense fear of not finishing what I needed to do in the required time and have watched for an unseen mechanism to open my booth door. I can just imagine it. The door opens up and there I will be perched on a seat, in all my glorious, exposed state for the outside world to see me peeing! What a lovely sight!

I must mention in Chamonix, France, in an earlier life, I did have the unexpected surprise of sitting on a heated toilet seat! As the 'cold' of the intense wintery weather hit my bladder and the call of nature dictated to me, "Right Now", I entered into one of those coin-operated, telephone-booth-type WCs. As the music played it was such a 'shock' to my cold 'toosh' to feel the luxurious heat of warm soothing metal melting the ice of my nether parts. The only trouble with that heated toilet, I did not want to leave! It was so welcoming! But, wary of those dix (ten) minutes, I reluctantly relinquished the warmth to spare possible embarrassment.

Looking for and actually finding public toilets in a foreign country with its different language is also an interesting exercise. Such as trying to actually find the WC or "vay zay", (as it is called) in Austria. We had discovered in our travels when you have that urgent need, and a toilet cannot be found, signs can be deceptive or outright tormenting - they are wrong or simply in most cases just disappear. You espy an initial notice and an arrow to pointing in a direction … you emit an initial 'sigh' of relief … but they have fooled you … the signs disappear leaving you to wander around aimlessly looking for the WC. while holding on tightly to your bladder, crossing your legs as you try to walk quickly, in the hope of finding this well-hidden but much needed amenity.

Do you know how difficult it is to walk cross legged in a strange city very fast??

* * *

You know I really hate boats!

I mean not the boat itself but being on a boat on the water is definitely not my favourite pastime! None-the-less, in our travels in Helsinki we tried special something different for us, a lunch date on a boat. This was not a façade; this was a real boat.

Marc had seen a wooden schooner moored at the harbour. It had a menu on a stand at the end of the gangplank. However, there was nothing about the boat that appeared like a café/restaurant, except that particular sign displayed. You had to actually walk onto and into the boat. Undeterred, Marc tried the door to the aft cabin. It opened, and he stepped over the high sill and went in. Ahead was a steep ladderway that went down into the dark hold. There was no room to pass another person. Marc, again, unfazed, climbed down. The restaurant part was below deck.

I still had not even entered the upper cabin. In fact, I could not even lift my leg up over the doorway sill! I was already feeling ill with the thought of going down inside a boat, and this feeling was not improving. I did venture down where I was greeted by a sailor who led us to the bow. Seated, comfortable, warm, enjoying our last day in this country, we ordered the soup. When it arrived, I was rather perturbed to see that my meal was moving. No, there was nothing alive in it, but the ship was rocking because I was actually swaying with the motion of the water within the bowels of this boat where I could not see the horizon. The food was swaying in front of me.

The soup was absolutely beautiful. Truth be known, it was probably one of the best fish soups we had in our Nordic travels, but I was quite concerned wondering would it stay where it was supposed to stay? But conversation, ruminations of our time in Helsinki, exquisite food and banter, my digestive system eventually settled, and I relaxed to enjoy my food and time together. Unfortunately, after we had left the boat to walk off that wonderous meal, 30 minutes later I was attacked with a colic feeling in my stomach and that urge to go … as in, I had to go 'right now'!

We were in a strange country, a different city from before and had no idea where the toilets were. Thinking laterally, we tried desperately to find the nearest public toilet in the park nearby. Espying them, I ran only to find they were LOCKED! By this time, I was quite desperate with my bowels turning to jelly accompanied by that urgent need for a toilet immediately! Running down the hill away from the park towards the shops, I spotted a café that was so full of people, I was sure they would not notice another person running straight into the bowels (oh, a pun there) of their huge café restaurant to use their amenities. I made it. But to be honest, only just. Commonly hard enough in an unknown city in your home country – never mind a strange one, where they speak Finnish!!!!

I will not go into the details here and I am sure you will not mind, but I felt so sorry for the long queue of ladies waiting to use this café's only female lavatory. Not to mention again in the bookshop that was two doors down as I had to go again -twice- rather rapidly after having finally emerged from the café. At least the bookstore had more than one female toilet, so I was not causing a queue as sadly had been the case for the ladies at the café. I felt rather embarrassed as I left the one female allocated cubicle in that restaurant. For the other ladies waiting, at that point of time, it was not a place I would choose to be!

A café toilet and a bookstore to the rescue but now, my eyes were feeling strange and sore. My face felt so weird, and I kept blinking and struggling to look through my eyes. When I eventually emerged from the toilet, I perceived a few strange looks from the long line of women waiting (which I thought was their shock from what had just emerged from me.) Marc asked me, "Had I been crying?" Apart from the initial angst tears my answer was, "No".

In the lift mirror going back down to the street, to my horror, upon seeing my face, my skin was red with swollen bags under my eyes that looked like I had not slept for six months. Both my eyes were all puffy and red and almost closed shut. At the same time, my face and lips were tingling and going numb. Truly, I looked like I had been punched up by my husband! No wonder the women waiting outside the toilet had looked so concerned. Oh, what fun! Swollen eyes, numb face and lips and bottomless gastro.

Marc went back to the restaurant to find out what the magic ingredient was that had made the soup taste so wonderful. He was defensive and we remain ignorant of what to avoid in the future!

* * *

Not living in a snow or even a cold area in Australia, I have so loved the fall of the gentle snow in some of the countries we had been to in our travels. It is really one of the reasons why we like to travel during other country's winters! However, cold weather brings a number of inconveniences, like having to de-ice your windscreen for a start. But have you ever noticed when it is icy, how much more you have the need to pee! As the temperature drops even further, your body temperature also drops, and the circulating water inside flows downwards and needs release. Apart from regular city parks, public buildings, or libraries (as I discovered in Helsinki) or even McDonalds in some cities, it was amusing (if that was the right word), where you can actually find 'public' conveniences!

In one of our travels, we were driving into Vienna. For some reason the GPS in our car (remember the one with the two staples and the Band-Aid? Yes, that one!) did not find the address of the Bed & Breakfast where we were staying. We were going to have to rely on finding a tourist information centre to help us to get there. Now we knew that every major city has a sign of a big 'I', that indicates which way to the tourist information centre and where usually there will also be toilets. We assumed we would find relief at the Information centre in more ways than one. Well on this particular day, in Vienna, we were wrong.

There were no right directions.

No 'Information' sign.

No public toilet!

No, not good!!!

Not having been in this city before, I never realised how huge Vienna is. After our inability to find the tourist information centre, we drove around and around this city that was so enormous. Split roads everywhere and one-way lanes and add to that, horse and carriages, trams, buses, people. Once more, we placed into the GPS "tourist information" and it began to direct us - both of us hoping we would be guided to the correct address or to our accommodation. As you would expect, by now I needed desperately to go to the toilet. What else!

Squeezing my pelvic area tighter and tighter, I began to feel quite nauseous in holding on with the urgency getting stronger to pee. This added to Marc's stress of trying to drive under those tight city road conditions, going nowhere, the tourist information centre not appearing, even though we passed the 'I' arrow a few times, and his wife holding on tightly, crossing her legs in the car, breathing heavily as if she was in labour. Eventually amidst this traffic chaos, I spotted a WC sign near a city park! Marc double parked the car across from the recreational area. I had to cross multiple lanes of traffic and dodge the traffic, but I could see those two glorious WC structures in front of me. Breathing a huge sigh of relief, I grabbed the handle, only to find it LOCKED! They were both locked.

Please tell me, what vast municipality of both residents and tourists locks its many community WCs in a huge public park? I was beginning to think that these people in Europe were Sadists! I imagined them secretly watching, laughing, enjoying the tourists' pain and torture as we struggle fervently to find a public toilet, while all the time they caressed a hidden golden key to the amenity in their pockets!

By this time, I was in a lot of pain from my bladder.

The ever-thinking Marc discovered a parking garage (six floors underground) to which we drove around and down to park. I was now desperately looking at the backs of those parked cars we were continually passing, as desirable enough for me to stop and pee behind. I was at the point where I really didn't care. Parked, doors opened, I raced to the top of the garage, literally dashed up the steps of the six floors in the fastest time ever, to eventually find the WC at the top floor of this underground parking garage. Rapidly removing all my winter gear obstructing the gap between my bladder and the toilet. I have never seen anything so more inviting! I think Marc, gladly paid the euro for 'parking' just so I could just use the lavatory!

* * *

Some public toilets in Europe, typically those found in train stations or near tourist attractions, often have a box and turnstile to collect the fee to enter. Sometimes, an attendant stands guard to collect that small fee to pee. Having the money to pay is one thing. Having the *correct* change in the *correct* currency on you is vital. Many a jump from leg to leg has been undertaken as we tried to find a 'change person or machine' in order to use a public amenity. We have now learnt in all our travels to have some small change always available just for that special unplanned moment in time. However, the whole concept of paying a woman (usually older) or sometimes even a man sitting outside a public toilet just to do my business remains still weird to me.

In some of the places we visited, you paid your coins to enter and from the attendant you were allocated a predefined amount of toilet paper (never more than 4 squares). This initially came as a shock to me because I am quite accustomed to deciding for myself how much toilet paper I personally require on an ad-hoc, case-by-case basis. After all my mother showed me what to with the toilet paper and how to use it when I was a child! But there, I really had to be careful with how I used those four tiny squares in those public amenities!

Then there were the times when after you paid, the attendant handed you a receipt. I seriously cannot possibly think of a situation where I would need substantiated evidence or an audit trail proving that I had been to the toilet. Oh well, I guess, in case of an emergency it can act as that makeshift fifth piece of toilet paper!

In Salzburg I had to pay for public amenities. The normal female line up time of waiting awaited. My turn, I hand my money to the attendant. Normal? Yes. Nothing wrong with that. But here in Salzburg, this attendant not only took my money, but also opened the door, wiped the seat, smiled at me, and then left. I think it took me a few minutes to relieve myself after my shock of this kind of an employed paid job! I do hope she washes her hands for her sake!

Obviously, I really object to paying to use some toilets due to their condition, but others were okay. By now, I understand and accept the concept of paying for the use of public amenities is necessary, regardless of their condition (as if us women really have a choice!).

* * *

With any public amenities, there are language barriers.

In the English language alone, there are many words not only for the bathroom, toilet, lavatory, WC, but also for 'Men' and 'Women'. Not so long ago the doors of restrooms were marked "Ladies" and "Gentlemen", but it is safe to say that both of these species, in the old-fashion meanings of these words, are extinct. Instead, many public places now resort to pictograms to designate what the gender preference (or both, and neutral) is for each toilet. When you are home in your familiar environment of language and country, you simply take it for granted and know where to go, which door to push open. When in a foreign country, if it is endorsed with a picture accompanying the foreign words, you comfortably ascertain which door to push open. That picture on the door assists your understanding. But, in overseas countries where you do not know the language and are reliant on signs, and there is the need to attend to toileting in a public place, such as a café or restaurant, and there are no pictures on the toilet doors, what do you do? Such as the words *'Dyrholm' and 'Baum'*. In all honestly, tell me, when looking at these two words, which would you choose? Which door would you push when you are looking for your gender appropriate amenity!!!!

As I pass into each new country, I have to quickly learn the many new names that could be used outside a public amenity to denote male and female. Often there are no pictures on the door to assist me and it is just a calculated guess! Many a time, by the visual look of the word, I got it right, but at other occasions, numerous quick turn abouts have been undertaken. Such as wandering into the men's room by mistake, see what is happening there, realise I am in the wrong place, blush profusely and leave rather quickly. Then at other moments, when I thought I had the gender correct, felt safe and relaxed in my own toilet stall, I heard the distinctive sounds of a male in the adjacent cubicle. Wrong again! I had chosen badly. OH, so still and oh so quiet would I sit until that unseen man had finished his business before I would peek out of my own door hoping no other male was there before quickly disappearing back into the corridor feeling somewhat flushed! Quite embarrassing!

Then there was Iceland. Tell me, which toilet door would you enter into with only words displayed of" prúðmenni " *or* "*hefðarkona*", "*salerni*" *or* "*snyrting*"? My point exactly!

Sometimes, the actual facilities are quite different!

In Canada, travelling from one frozen area to another, I once again had the urge to pee. No, this urge was not near in a warm shopping mall nor near a park convenience. This toilet stop *needed* to happen between Jasper and Lake Louise where there were long distances of nothing but National Parks. No villages or small towns available. The only toilet found was almost head high in snow, I needed to push my body through the snow just to get to that simple wooden shelter. The, not to mention the countless layers of clothes that had to be dismantled just to expose the nether regions to the sub-zero elements! Quite amusing! But, when you have to go, you have to go!

Public amenities in Finland were basically non-existent! Very few between towns and cities. You manoeuvred along the long, long roads in this country lined by endless trees, occasionally interrupted by a frozen lake or two and even more rarely, a barn or a farmhouse coming into view. But there was never an official toilet stop or a much-needed rest area. So, what do you do when that urge to attend to nature happens when you are out and about in snow covered Finland? You find a 'P'.

What is that you say?

Yes, you find the blue letter 'P'.

Usually in Australia, the sign P means parking. In Finland, likewise it also officially meant where you could park your car on the country roads. But we discovered that the locals read it differently.

As far as my female bladder (and Marc's too) was concerned, when there was no fuel station in sight, no town in view, when we saw a 'P' sign, we would pull off and park on that white snow, search out a tree or something to bare our bottoms to the freezing earth behind and then ease our very full bladders. Discreetly turning the white snow into patches of yellow snow.

And, as both of us stood or squatted, we would discover quite amusingly that we were not the only ones who had rested here and performed likewise. Significantly, at each of our 'P stops', we would note many patches of yellow discolouration in the snow. Hence, we learnt, at least unofficially, in Finland, the Blue 'P' sign on the side of the road had quite a practical other meaning.

Marc and I definitely left our mark of Australian heritage on Finland's territory.

I am sure you must be thinking why I seem to be fixated on writing about amenities. But be honest, male, or female, young or old, whatever country you are in, the bottom line is, everyone at some time, wherever they are and whatever they are doing, needs to go to the restroom. The simple truth is that they are a necessity. When that necessity has arisen in my travels, I have faced various noteworthy and at times humorous experiences. I am extremely sure that as future travels continue, I will encounter more diverse and amusing 'necessity' stories to tell! There will be plenty more!

Oh, by the way, I did give up on the 'Stance' that my mother insisted I do as a child and tried unsuccessfully to continue as an adult.

It was Too Hard to Hold.

Chapter Nineteen

Just Look for The Lake. Ok, Which Shade of White Shall I Look For?

Being frozen is cold.
Being frozen with your best friend is an adventure.
So romantic, being wrapped in a world of white.

I am the most romantic person out. I love romance and stories of winter and mulled wine and snuggling up with the one you love as you gazed blissfully out from the warm fireplace to a crisp clear white, frozen, scenic landscape. You know, I really enjoy being in the snow because it is so different from where we live. Many of my stories and challenges written are about snow because it is entirely different from our hot part of the Southern Hemisphere. I love so much the fall of the gentle snow in the countries seen so far, the beauty of their winter landscapes, the crisp whiteness of their virgin snow, the Christmas lights tinkling against the silvery countryside. Add to that the enjoyment of the warmth of hot chocolate melting any tiredness and coldness away as we watched the snow falling through our windows, such as our stay in Akureyri in Iceland, trapped by snow falling. All we could do was watch it and enjoy! Everything that we have seen so far in our travels showed that wintertime in the Northern Hemisphere is a beautiful time of year and suited for our short burst of travels. We love it!

Finland is only 50 minutes by plane from Sweden. An international trip from one country to another, but so close. The plane trip is even shorter than going to Sydney from the Gold Coast (800kms). But you should have seen the aircraft we were in! It was so tiny, I truly thought I could see the rubber bands as they spun the propellers around! On the plane, with the other six passengers, the roar of the engine began. But there was ice, and we were not ready to fly yet, because first they had to wash that ice off the wings! Not quite the scene to engender confidence, as I peered out the window through the darkness of the morning to view that machine hosing down the plane! My simple questioning mind asked my husband what they were doing, and his reply did not fill me with confidence. I kept thinking about the air disaster shows I had seen on television where ice on the wings had caused a crash! But what could I do, sitting in a small plane while watching the ice be washed away? Surely these are locals. They know what they are doing. Or so I hoped …

Surprisingly, or maybe not depending on your disposition, we did successfully rise into the air on our flight heading to our next destination.

Stepping out from our warm comfortable hire car, the iciness and severity of a Scandinavian/Finland winter, flew at me, permeating through every single layer I was wearing! Try standing in the middle of a strange town, as you step gingerly over ice-glazed roads, struggling in the bitter wind that is ravaging your poor tired-feeling very, very cold body at that moment, as you slip and slide on white streets. The wind going straight through you … to the core of your essence …

Being frozen is an adventure??

Being frozen is romantic?

Being wrapped in a world of white?

Being besieged with subzero weather I walked, or in my case, slid sideways over the ground, along icy roads, and paths, constantly wrapping my jacket around me even tighter to eliminate one small draft that was allowing that tiny bit of wind to chill my body even further. I fought my way in the wind to find those 'must-do things' listed on the travel brochure. This was not my vision of a romantic frozen world of white! Arendelle in the movie Frozen looked so much cheerier and Elsa the main character did not wear many layers at all. But here, the wind grabbed at my face, the cold soaked through my winter gloves, my eyes watered from the freezing cold. Thoughts of my Australian family and friends came to mind, who time were at that time saturated in an intense heat wave. At that moment, I was quite sure I would gladly swap my conditions! I was with my best friend, yes, we were having adventures, but why did it have to be SO cold ... she said between chattering teeth! In all my snow experiences, this was a 'cold 'I had not ever experienced, and it did bother me. a lot! (Sorry Elsa)

And we crossed the Arctic Circle.

For me that was most exciting. Like the photo I had taken as a child of placing one foot in the states of NSW and the other in Victoria – well I did the same here. The same scenario where I was actually standing inside the Arctic Circle in Finland ... 66°32'35" latitude north on this Earth. Dumb I know, but it was a great feeling as I knew I would never be that far north again!

Finland is such a beautiful place. The white scenery of snow-covered Northern Finland meant that it was really only one shade - white! There were the trees. Yes, there were the constant trees. There were Pine trees and Poplars and when you get tired of those, there were Poplars and Pine trees, all covered in white. Snowflakes glistening on the once green branches. Branches covered now with white icing! Everything was just so WHITE!

In Australia, in winter our lakes are still blue! Lakes are not white! But in Finland, … when Marc was trying to follow map instructions, he said to me, *"You just have to look for the lake".* I simply laughed. "Where? Which shade of white shall I look for?"

Actually, our challenge for that day according to the map we were following, was about 18kms north of where we were staying in Inari, Finland. This was to look for a German Graveyard that was supposed to be in a forest. The significance of that graveyard is it is a memorial to the Germans who had lost their lives fighting on the Finnish eastern front against Russia in World War Two. We felt it was worth looking at. So, into the woods we went. Just for something different!

Walking into the white world of the unknown, visions of Red Riding Hood crept to mind. Her red cape and hood flowing around her, Granny baking her pies, waiting for her granddaughter not knowing what was just around the corner. Walking through the woods on that track - where we really were not sure of our bearings (*the 500 metres track according to the map seemed to stretch to a further than 500m,*) The weather became increasingly icier, the snow was now lightly falling – probably from the trees who were spreading their branches towards what they thought was the sun. Do you know I had quite forgotten what the yellow ball of sun looks like this far North in winter? We were in the middle of nowhere, not any other human being around, and we continued to stroll further into the woods. The words from the musical came to mind, "*The way is clear, The light is good, The woods are just trees, The trees are just wood. I have no fear, nor no one should*". "Good thoughts. Good thoughts", I said to myself as I followed Marc through those long, tall forest trees, across that silent frozen landscape, on an unknown, unexplored deep snow track. I did contemplate - where was the wolf skulking around the corner? Was he watching his meal come closer?

It was so White.

It was so Silent.

Unadorned Silence.

As we came through the woods, ahead was a camp, complete with a volleyball court, a snow-covered volleyball court that is. That seemed quite out of place in this environment particularly in light of what we were searching for. An open-air shelter stood in front of us, however, someone had used it recently as there was a cup half filled with frozen red wine and the remnants of a campfire. It felt like we were in those television murder mystery series where forensics had determined that human existence had been or was still somewhere around! It turns out we had come across a deserted summer camp.

Backtracking we found a lesser used side trail in the snow. Following it we practically stumbled across a large rectangular building! Of course, the war memorial had been there all the time. You just had to turn to face a different part of 'white'.

Remember those horror movies on television where you see the character go to push open the door and as their hand reaches the handle, it seemed to open by itself. That dark door into a dimly lit catacomb, where it slowly creaked open, beckoning the caller to enter its shadowy existence? Well, I came to the locked bolted solid door of the memorial and to my horror, the door fell open in front of me, all on its very own. Marc said the look was priceless as both fear and shock were expressed on my face. All that was missing was the sinister music. Pushing open the door even more slightly, I felt like I was personally engulfed in those horror movies! What was I going to find as I inched my way cautiously through that huge iron door?

No lights to assist us, but once our eyes became accustomed to the shadows and the dark, you could see rows of concrete slabs. In that silent world of white, etched into the memorial concrete of those slabs were the names and ranks of approximately 2,500 Germans who had died. Sad. We wandered around in silence then left the memorial. And outside, to add to the poignant moment, was a tall iron cross silhouetted against the silent white scenery. One singular cross standing high surrounded only by white. Another heartbreaking reminder of war.

And out of the woods with its quiet blanket of snow we departed.

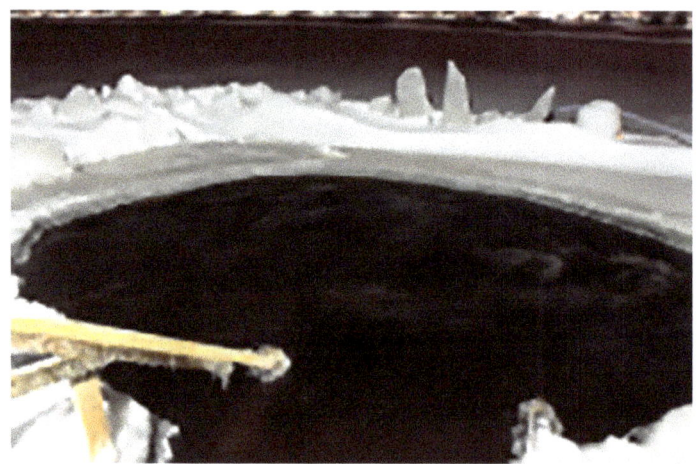

In that far northern winter wonderland, we found so many unusual things. Like numerous camping grounds, seemingly never-ending icy snow-covered roads that stretched for kilometres and kilometres bordered by landscape of snow-coloured trees and sprinkled with lakes that had completely frozen. We also discovered a water hole in the ice – where they kept the water agitated to stop it from freezing. That one was not far from our hotel. It even had a sign that articulated, "Winter swimming", complete with instructions in English! Tell me, who in their right mind would venture, at that time of year, under those wintry conditions, into that swirling water of death in nothing but their bathers! Not me!

The whole world around me was white. I truly felt I was in a different world! In fact, as my shivering chattering teeth informed me, I was sure I was. Marc, sensing my discomfort of cold eventually eased my suffering chilled body, by taking me to our hotel accommodation for the night. Slipping into bed, I was so cold as my internal core heating had shut down and I needed such a lot of help warming up!

However, I must say, that in my distress of' the cold' in that world of white, and the serious moment of that memorial, Marc did make me laugh. We slid over many icy paths on our small adventures, and I was constantly telling him to be careful, to prevent broken bones. As my own little screams of stress from my slippery slides permeated his hearing, I was always told, *"Remember, as you slide and slip that it is a controlled slide"…*

Miraculously, I did not fall. Not once. That was a blessing!

But Marc did … another patch of ice and over he went. Sliding so beautifully along the road on his bottom, legs contorted up in the air, not a quite 'controlled 'slide as he might have liked! Oh, how I laughed! As he stood up after his glide on the ice, I asked him to do it again because I did not get a picture! Funnily, he did not oblige me! I wonder why!

Oh, and by the way - we did eventually find the Lake from the map! Yep - you guessed it. It was White!

> To have a collection of memories that tells you who you are and how you got there whatever way you went ... is intriguing.
>
> — Rosecrans Baldwin

Chapter Twenty

Frozen in Time

"A picture is simply a memory frozen in Time"

Digressing from my winter snow travels, when you think of a castle, what comes to mind?

Does your imagination bring to life dreams of towering castles, picturesque backdrop of lush trees and snow-capped mountains and dancing princes and princesses? Do you see images of royal weddings, vast ballrooms, and glowing chandeliers? Do you see a princess who wears a beautiful dress with a sparkling tiara, glass shoes, and long white gloves? Do you think of Cinderella and her glass slippers? Do you see her entering the castle that is ablaze with music, warmth, light, and colour?

To the average person, 'castles' portray fantasy. They embellish a romantic view of the life of kings, queens and nobles from years gone by. They convey to the viewer that dream world promoted through media, of a realm where beautiful characters lived in those amazing structures, surrounded by glamour and opulence. Dwellings where young girls fantasise of marrying their handsome princes and then 'living happily ever after.

Is that your image of a castle?

Reality is much different.

Castles were originally made as fortresses. In truth, the majority of castles in medieval times were never built for a king or queen or any other reigning monarch. Most castles were in fact built for noblemen! In the days when it was still customary for a king to lead his troops into battle, directing his forces on the battlefield, the king rewarded loyal, brave, courageous soldiers or knights for their devotion with a nice, fat chunk of land. That knight or nobleman then built a fortress or castle as his proof of ownership and power, all very important to a feudal lord in the medieval period to protect his fiefdom.

But castles were actually damp, dirty, and not the most comfortable of places to live in. Contrary to what imagery you may have in your mind, castles were large, dark, draughty, and very cold. Windows were often small, with wooden shutters, or if the nobleman could afford it since glass was very expensive back in the medieval period, with leadlight glass-panes. The small windows meant it took at least three or four candles to produce enough light to really read or sew or do anything else by.

Can you imagine trying to read when the lighting came from the meagre natural sunlight coming through small windows or from light given off by candles or from an open fire

Castles were often very smoky. Most rooms in those castles would have had massive fireplaces. The Great Hall of the Castle would have had a large open hearth to provide heat and light (at least until the late 12th century) and later in time, a wall fireplace. This large hall was the focus of hospitality, celebration, and what pleasures of life that were available in a medieval castle. Depending upon the wealth of the occupant, they would also have had huge tapestries on each wall to help insulate the room against too much cold. The central fireplace was the only available means to warm up these large stone-lined room during winters – winters where it could frequently drop to several degrees below freezing. Unless you were draped from head to toe in furs and standing near this large fireplace, can you imagine how icy it would have been? I feel so cold just thinking about it!

Can you imagine how they would wash?

There was no running water.

If the noble person wanted a bath, and especially a hot bath, the servants had to heat the water over a fire, lug it upstairs to the bathtub, fill the bathtub, make the temperature right for the lord or lady, put the soap in (if you actually had any), then the noble person would have to strip naked, wash, dry then replace the many layers of clothing again to keep warm. Then the servants would have to bail out the entire bathtub by hand with a bucket! As a servant to be clean, the best that may have been managed would be a basin or small bucket of cold water and a hurried 'wipe over'. Then, often as not, the same outer clothes would be put back on. No wonder they didn't bathe every day! I would have to say that with my two regular showers morning and night I am not sure I would have coped.

However, when it came to sanitation though, things were always truly disgusting. Most toilets in those castles were nothing more than small antechambers, basically a bench with a hole in it or a long line of benches with nothing to separate you from your neighbour as you went about your business. Any waste which passed through the hole, the privy seat or that squat bench would end up in one of two places. If the castle had a moat around it, the waste probably ended up in there. If it didn't have a moat, or if the privy hole ... or whatever you used was located somewhere without access to the moat, your bodily waste ended up in the cesspit at the very bottom of the castle. I guess you could say that the cesspit was an early septic tank!

Sorry, but in line with all my other stories, I have to think about backing myself up to that hole in the wall to empty my bladder or bowels. I cannot! Can you imagine your rear end hanging out from a 'window' where the contents of your toilet would simply fall, usually from a great height, into that cess pool or into the moat surrounding the castle? *Gardy Loo - Watch out below*!!!!! And don't dare drink from the water in the moat

No, the image of castles portrayed to us in our imaginary world of fairy tales like Cinderella and Sleeping Beauty, glamour and grandeur are not quite the same as their reality. Yes, the Lord and Lady were granted the 'luxury' of their own rooms, usually at the top of one of the towers in the castle. There, they could enjoy privacy, a semblance of comfort, and usually a greater deal of warmth and sunlight as heat from the Great Hall would rise to warm up their private chambers, but that was about it! Overall, in contrast to our modern standards of living, most medieval castles would have been incredibly cold, cramped, totally lacking privacy, been disgustingly smelly and likely home to more than a fair share of rats, lice, and fleas!

In light of all this negativity about castles, why am I so captivated by castles, by their stones, by their structural designs and cultural idiosyncrasies, their positioning in the landscape?

Is it because whilst Australia is an ancient land, it is a young country with few old buildings? Is it because we visit architectural history far older than our own to see these amazing, fabulous fortresses? Was it because, as I took my first step into each old castle, my imagination transports me to a world of the past, sending me on an enchanting journey to discover ancient history, medieval traditions, and spectacular architecture? Is it because, as I meander quietly through their aged stones I am conveyed to past worlds of extreme piety, noisy witch burnings, violent executions, clever folk heroes, mythical villages and charming towns, countless legends of brave knights fighting and bloody wars, of anecdotes of the rise and fall of many kings and queens who commanded these large strongholds dotting the countryside landscapes? Was it because their stone old stories reached out to me to say … *"Here I am, Come and see my strength, my character, my history …?"* I do not know but yes, most definitely, those castles we saw oozed allure and anticipation! I can visit churches and temples and after a while, they all look the same, follow the same pattern, the same design. But a castle … well, to me, a castle always simply unique – built to adapt to the landscape, to the type of warfare of the time, and to the wealth and power of its builder!

To me, the past is bought to life as their ancient stones brimmed with mystery and stories so far removed from stodgy old history textbooks. They are a visceral reminder that quests, battles, and chivalry aren't always the exclusive province of fantasy novels or fairy tales but were actually real. In those now silent halls, it is so hard to grasp just how bustling that same castle would have been at the height of medieval times.

Even though this chapter holds nothing humorous, I knew I had to record my thoughts because each castle we visited, in different countries, from great Gothic structures perched on hilltops to simple tower houses and to everything else in between, each one had a story. I heard and felt their stories suspended in front of me, swamping my imagination in enchantment of diverse images and scenery. And I loved each and every one we met.

For example, what about their clockwise spiral staircases?

Think about what foot trod those spirals. Who was that figure all those years ago who ascended or descended before you? How exciting!

We learnt many castles' spiral staircases were fashioned in a specific way and Marc and I climbed so many of these spiral staircases in our travels. Though it was not always obvious to the eye, most of these staircases were actually designed clockwise. They were built this way for safety, to make it harder for a right-handed attacker coming up the stairs to swing their sword. Think of those movie scenes where royalty is at the top of the spiral staircase and guards raced down those spiral sculptures fighting to their deaths defending their King or Queen. Think of the famous Three Musketeers.

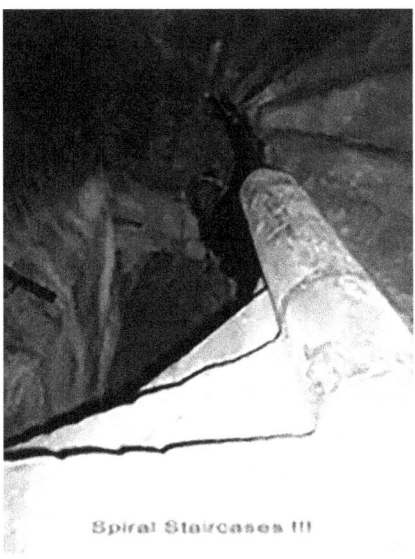

Spiral Staircases !!!

With all those castle spiral staircases, the stairs not only tested your fitness with their short treads and high risers, but also tested your vestibular system. After several turns on the stairs, I would begin to feel the whole world spin and that had nothing to do with me being on my honeymoon or being of 'my age'! Many a vertiginous imbalance was endured by us both due to climbing three or more stories, spiralling round, and round and round and round as we ventured off exploring unknown rooms and halls. Many a moment paused to have our breathing regain control while at the same time pondering how they managed to do all this with only candlelight and in long skirts!

Can you see the fairy-tale character, Belle from 'Beauty and the Beast', in her yellow ball gown, descending those spiral steps to meet her Beast?

Can you see yourself descending that same spiral staircase in your own beautiful gown, feeling, and seeing the fabric swirl around and around as the material spreads out before you?

Can you see yourself stopping at the end of that staircase that led into the brightly lit Great Hall to meet your suitors or to curtsy to the waiting crowd before you?

Oh, I can! I definitely can!

Duane Castle, Scotland, is a castle that had been nominally built in the late 14th century by the 1st Duke of Albany, Robert Stewart. (For Monty

Python fans, this was the castle used in the Holy Grail film!). As was the custom of the time, it was built to cement an image of authority and good governance. What was most impressive to me with this castle was the huge kitchen with its enormous fireplace and the size of the Master Bedroom. Access to the master bedroom was, of course, via a very long spiral staircase from above the inner hall. I am sure that meeting conjugal duties after this steep spiral climb would have tested any master's fitness! Did you know in this particular castle we saw a document written where the woman calls down to her man - *"Are you coming up to bed to make love to me?"* His reply was, *"You can have one or the other"*! After going up and down those staircases myself, I can truly understand why! I also wondered how quick it would be to race up those spiral steps to go to 'the bathroom' ... or, better known as the 'hole in the wall'!

Medieval Castles were more than just large fortresses with massive stone walls. They were ingeniously designed fortifications that used many brilliant and inventive ways to protect their residents from attacking enemies. Much thought, creativity, and planning went into the designs. Each castle was a structure totally designed right down to the last detail, from the outer walls to the shapes and location of stairwells all carefully planned to provide maximum protection to the inhabitants. A medieval castle was so much more than just a large glamourous citadel with massive stone walls around it.

What about their Secret Passages?

Many of these castles had secret passages and they served a variety of purposes. Secret passages could lead to secret chambers where people could hide, supplies could be kept or a well for water accessed. Some passages were designed as tunnels that opened up a distance from the castle so inhabitants could escape during an attack or get supplies in and out during a siege. How exciting, how romantic, and how terrifying as well! Can't you imagine fleeing and quietly hiding and waiting silently in those secret passages and rooms using only a flame torch to see? Can't you imagine discovering those old secret passages and wondering whether they led?

Travels, Challenges.....Marc!!

Predjama Castle in Slovenia was a wonderful example. This castle is the largest 'cave' castle in the world. It is described as 'A Fairy-tale Castle Embraced by Rock'.

Why is it called a cave castle?

Because this impregnable medieval marvel has been perched in the middle of a one hundred and twenty-three-metre-high cliff for more than eight hundred years. The whole structure was designed in 1311 with layers of defensive locations extending back into the cave behind it. To me, it appeared that this castle simply jutted out from the rock and was 'attached' to the mountain behind.

This castle had its own quite unique mystery and intrigue, and for us we excitedly ventured into exploring its unknown qualities. One of the 'qualities' that added to its clandestine feeling was a network of secret, mysterious underground tunnels at the rear of the castle that connected the castle with the cave directly behind and beneath. There are actually a set of steps that lead through the mountainside to open on the other side of the ridge away from any aggressors. This secret 'back door' allowed the castle owners in the past to survive sieges of up to a year by allowing supplies to be snuck in without the attackers ever knowing Exploring those secret passages was so exciting and yes, my imagination went overboard!

Predjama Castle was certainly very distinctive from other castles we had seen, not only being a cave castle, but because its location meant it never would have been able to be warm or dry. In fact, it would have been quite miserable to live in. Can you imagine what it was like in the past? This huge castle inside this enormous wet cave? Even though modern-day owners had repaired it quite well and replaced roofs and walkways, you could never envisage the idea of the rooms ever being warm.

The stairwells, we were bold enough to try, were always wet and full of pools of water. When we were walking through their corridors, the damp was even more penetrating and drips of water from above were fair game. It was not pleasant at all when a stream of ice cold-water would run unexpectedly down the back of my neck! Neither were they tiny 'drips'. Instead, think of a drainpipe leaking where quite significant amounts of water could suddenly fall from the roof of this castle to land startling onto your warm body! (Do realise we were exploring this castle in winter). Also, I wondered where the excrement would go in this castle built into this solid huge rock at Predjama. I really don't know. I actually don't even want to think about it.

Even though the intricacies of the mystery of tunnels and walls were riveting and fascinating, I just could not imagine myself living in Predjama Castle. With the continual sound of dripping running water beside me all the time, I would be constantly running to the toilet. In fact, when we were there, it was so cold and so wet inside the castle and extremely chilly. By the time we left, I really had to pee! This was the first time in this specific castle I had to use a squat toilet. Sound easy??? For the male perhaps, but not for females and, definitely not in winter.

In that cold wet castle in a cave, envisage trying to drop the bulky layers of warm clothing without letting any of them actually touch the not particularly clean or dry ground. Then, having effectively tied your lower legs together, try to squat over this square ceramic tray there in the floor. Under those conditions with the cold air from outside swirling around you, and with that occasional drip from above or worse, splatting on your bare behind, try to relieve yourself without missing the hole or, worse, peeing on or in your shoe. Once that task was done, try to clean yourself up. Then as you are ready, pull up all the layers of winter clothing you are wearing while keeping your backpack and the back of your coat high off the ground, so it does not get wet (or more wet!). Presentable once more I walked out smiling into that stark cold air that hit me all the more since my nether regions had not re-warmed yet! The only positive aspect was that the toilet door there had lipstick on the front, so I had known which toilet door to use! Males you have it too easy sometimes!! Now visualise trying to do this same function in those long, beautiful ball gowns of Cinderella's time? How would you keep them clean? Oh, by the way, it has been said that the legendary rebellious knight Erazem of Predjama who withstood the imperial army's siege of this amazing castle for over a year, reportedly died, while using a toilet after a betrayal by his servant. I am so glad I did not use that particular toilet!

Slovenia held many intriguing castles. An hour's drive from the capital Ljubljana is Lake Bled. Here, a medieval castle was built on a precipice above the city of Bled. It is the oldest Slovenian castle with the first written documents about the castle dated 1011. It is perched atop a steep cliff more than 100 metres high overlooking the lake, and I guess it is built, as a medieval fortress should be, with towers, ramparts, courtyards, a chapel, a terrace offering magnificent views, moats, and a drawbridge! How exciting! And so definitely old with the parts we were able to visit 'relatively' unchanged since the 16th century.

The trek up to the castle is via a series of steps that, although switch-backed' essentially went straight up. The guide from Lonely Planet labelled the steps as a 'tortuous path straight up from the town' and I would agree sincerely! We had steps, steps, and more steps! There was the additional ascent over the moat up into the castle on what seemed to be a 45-degree inclined path. You can imagine what walking that was like! Even a Czech sporting team that arrived to view the castle at the same time we did, were breathing extremely heavily when they appeared at the top. As I dealt with my own middle-aged gasping and panting and strained muscles, seeing this group equally puffed and out of breath made me feel so much better!

Marc however, experienced walking this twice. Why, may you ask?

On the way home, going down from the castle, we went to take a photo of those amazing steps on the hill below the castle and Marc then realised that he had left the big SLR camera in the amenities. It was not left in the lowest toilets in the castle but further up in the section rising from the lower yards to the upper terrace. So, he ran all the way back which was truly straight up, sincerely hoping that it was still there and not stolen. Me, always in support of my husband, ran slowly, or rather I walked slowly back to the entrance gate. Being so steep, I just could not do it as a straight run. The gate keeper had left Marc through without too much delay and he had continued his 'sprint' to the upper reaches of the castle. Luckily, the camera was still there on a ledge in the toilet. Marc walked slowly back to me a little sorer in the knees after the run up!!! Nothing like a little bit of 'extra' exercise! These days, we just use my iPhone for photos - it is lighter and stays handy in your jacket pocket!

There was also the magic of another castle - the Tower of London.

For me, this was exhilarating. I had always wanted to see this castle as it is a recurring icon in the numerous historic novels that I have read over many years. Before me, this powerful historical tower rose tall and strong, standing as a mighty fortress above as the mist rising from the Thames encircled its grey beauty. Such a terrifying, magnificent sight to see!

The Tower of London, and its White Tower, an imposing structure, is in the middle of London, right beside the river Thames. It was built in the fashion of concentric castles - a castle within a castle that greatly increased the defensive capability of the fortification, as attackers would have to breach not one, but two sets of formidable stone walls. With its huge expanse of stone and mortar and many turrets, I could almost see history visually emerging, drawing me in, beckoning me to enter this grand castle with its ensemble of royal buildings dating from the 11th to 16th Century.

The Tower was a dynamic and changing project for many rulers of England, as monarch after monarch added walls and smaller towers (actually a total of thirteen inner and six outer) and finally encircling it with a moat whose water was delivered by the Thames River.

Did you know that although Henry VIII used it as a prison, he continued to use it as a palace and entertained guests? Some guests came with gifts of animals. These gifts were kept near the drawbridge where Henry built Lion Tower-a Zoo where roaring beasts would greet visitors. Can you imagine that!

For me, just walking through that entrance, seeing the immense stonework, espying the site where Anne Boleyn and Catherine Howard were beheaded, knowing this was where Edward and Richard, the young princes, disappeared from one of the tower rooms to strengthen Richard III's claim to the throne, was all simply absorbing and unnerving in a grim grotesque way. Crossing the moat which opened to the Thames River through the Traitors Gate, we thought of the many prisoners bought in that way on a barge, possibly to die within the Tower's walls.

Walking quietly through the grounds I could feel the procession of kings and queens on their barges making their way to this grand 900-year-old fortress built initially by William the Conqueror! I could sense the apprehension and fear as Anne Boleyn entered the grounds to be imprisoned for treason, then executed by the man, she had married only three years before. I could see her being taken from her stately Hampton Court Palace to this cold stony majestic structure and then later, see her kneeling upright in front of the crowds as she lost her head with a two-edged sword. As our guide gruesomely informed us, the swordsman was so swift that when he lifted her decapitated head to the assembled crowd, her eyes were open, and her lips were still moving in prayer!

Sitting in the church near the tower from under whose floors 1500 bodies have been exhumed and only thirty-four identified (including the bodies of Anne Boleyn and Catherine Howard), it all felt so real and so very horrific. Yes, a grim and ghastly place to visit but so exciting for this amateur historian. As the cold fog and mist surrounded me, an eerie feeling enveloped. While sitting there, I pondered that we were actually in the 'presence' of Royalty … even if they were dead! I could hear their voices praying silently. I could hear the weeping of their servants. But how I relished each room, each wall, each dark murky corner, each story associated with each chamber.

Smarmore Castle in Ireland held a different plethora of fascination. This time though we didn't just visit it, we stayed there!

This castle basically is a fine period house steeped in history and charm, incorporating the Tower, which dates back to 1320. It is located in Ardee, a town in the Irish Borders, about 45 minutes north of Dublin. This was the final residence of our honeymoon in 2009. Tell me, what better way to finish our honeymoon trip than to stay in a castle!

Excitedly, we stayed in the *highest* room in the *highest* tower of this castle! Can't you see me lying on that luxurious four posted bed in the highest room? Can't you see me gently reclining on one of the gilded chairs in the morning reading alcove by the windows? As I sat in the 'blue room' with my new husband, I reflected that the only thing missing were the long gowns and candlesticks to complete that fairy-tale picture. Yes, here as the enchanted lady of the castle, I could quite see myself in a long sweeping ball gown. This scene definitely appealed to my amorous side by ending our honeymoon with this romantic stay in this castle.

I must confess that I do have a definite lack of direction. I can walk into a shop, turn around and walk out the same door and turn in the wrong direction from whence I came. No idea where I am! So of course, old castles with their winding stairs, multiple rooms and the many refurbishments over the centuries make a particularly interesting combination for me. I generally stay close to Marc when we visit locations I am unfamiliar with, but I still get lost. (Maybe it is because I am 'upside down' on the' other side' of the world? That is my excuse anyway!) At Smarmore Castle, I made so many wrong turns usually ending up in quite a different part of the castle to where I thought I was going. With my bad sense of direction, I became disoriented many times trying to find my way back to our tower room!

Today it is a 22-bed drug and rehabilitation centre. Imagine that! I am not sure that trying to find your way back to your bedroom in this twisting winding castle with its many stairwells would help your attempt at alcoholic rehabilitation!

Schloss Metzen, an historic Austrian castle is situated in a forest on a small hill near the village of Brix Legg, in the Tyrol region of Austria. We stayed here too as an unexpected wedding anniversary gift from my husband on one of our later travels.

The image of our rental car turning into a long windy driveway surrounded by white mist and clouds of fog is one I can still see. Out of this enveloping mist, appeared this castle. Its tower stretched high above us, its turrets formed peaks around it, all complete with tall gates and crest. This was a real medieval castle, and I was going to sleep here! We truly were in our own castle in the cloud!

Although I was so excited, I tried to appear nonchalant, we followed our young host in meandering all over the castle, down many stairs, out through numerous courtyards, through various doors, onto more set of stairs up and down again and into a beautiful breakfast room. This breakfast room was complete with its own chapel. It had an all-embracing cross and huge crucifix of Jesus hanging on the front wall. It really threw me into the Philippa Gregory novels of the royal families going to chapel to kneel on the cold stone floors to pray for many hours, before they 'broke their fast.' Once more, following our host, down more steps, across a courtyard and up more spiral staircases and there it was. Our own castle room.

The door opens. Before me is the most magnificent room with lounges table, king size bed, huge wooden carved wardrobe, fireplace, gilded chairs, enormous, curtained windows furnished with lamps sitting in the long narrow windows. (By the way, the bathroom was modern and held a double size bath, a double size shower, a separate square toilet and bidet, complimented with heated flooring … not medieval authenticity but in the cold wintery weather of Austria in December, I most certainly appreciated it). I was surrounded by aristocratic splendour. There in that particular room, in that Austrian castle, once again I was transported back to imagery of opulence and wealth. In that beautiful room, as I curtsied low to my 'husband and lord' (just- for- that- day -mind- you) and sat beside him in the high-backed lounge, all demure and angelic, I felt I had travelled back in time to medieval ages of lords and ladies. Of course, to complete the picture all I needed were the long dresses and ermine minks and if they had been hiding in that carved wardrobe, I would have donned them. All this is quite visually hard to describe to you, my reader, what I saw and how I felt in just this one room of this magnificent castle, but I hope you can see what I have presented.

Travels, Challenges…..Marc!!

At the gate house entrance to Edinburgh Castle

In our travels around castles, we also saw those must see 'tourist traditional castles' like Edinburgh Castle. This castle is one of the oldest fortified places in Europe and was home to kings and queens for many centuries. I mean, when in Scotland you have to see this castle don't you? With a long rich history as a royal residence, military garrison, prison, and fortress, it was so alive with many thrilling tales. When you walk down the Golden Mile and climb Castle Hill, you are actually walking in the footsteps of soldiers, kings, and queens – and even the odd pirate or two.

We were fortunate by being able to spend some time with the guard in the Honour Room. He knowledgeably rattled off the history of the Scottish and English aristocracy, the impact of about Anglicism and Catholicism, the litany of who had been married to who and why, the 'who' was sleeping with 'whom', the German influence, the French interest. It all came to life!

Then there were the ruins and remains of castles where we stopped to explore.

Marc being Marc had to climb them 'just because he could!' Looking up into his face as he perched on the highest part of a derelict tower or walked like a cat on the edge of a stone wall, a former part of the strong fortress wall, all I could feel was anxiety. No - not him! But … you know my husband … what more can I say!

Many other different castles come to mind such as Calgarff Castle and Glenbuchat Castle in Scotland that consisted of predominately the ruins of the lowest part of the walls of 13th century castles. These castles showed the defensive strategies used at that time for their bows and arrows. Urquhart Castle retained enough walls to get an impression of the castle including a four-story tall tower providing a grand view of Loch Ness! It was a shame that the English blew the structure up!

One castle worth mentioning was the Rock of Cashel.

It is a historic site located at Cashel, County Tipperary, Southern Ireland. The Rock of Cashel is known as Cashel of the Kings. (The Gaelic word Cashel means stone fortress or castle from the Anglo-Saxon world). This castle was where one of the original kings of Ireland set up a stone fortress on a rock in 432AD but by the time the great grandson inherited the property, he decided he was not going to live on this cold wet place and instead, donated it to the local church!

It really was a most spectacular archaeological site on a prominent green hill, banded with limestone outcrops, rising from a grassy plain and bristling with ancient fortifications. All the remaining ruins of this 'castle' were the relics of the church but the dampness, the green mould and the weathered sandstone of the walls were amazing. The water was literally running down the insides of the walls and it was NOT raining outside. Can you see this picture? On the day we were there, a late June (summer) day in Ireland, it was quite uncomfortably cool, and oh, how quickly my skin colour had changed from its normal shade to blue as I started to shiver with cold. The guide beside me had similar hair colouring to me and looked at me remarking that, *with my heritage I should not be feeling the cold as I had obviously descended from the Vikings*". She actually thought we were Irish. It came as a shock to her to learn we were from Australia. By the time we had meandered around this old castle, the wind was so cold, so icy I could not feel my hands. It definitely did not help my demeanour when our lovely guide informed us that "summer was actually present last week, and we had all compared sunburn". I remember thinking, we were in southern Ireland, were we not south enough? Didn't the birds fly north in summer for the warmth? I believed at that point of icy time, I had it all wrong as my blue lips and numb hands told me so!

Turku Castle, founded in the late 13th century and still in use today, is the largest surviving medieval building in Finland. This castle has played many roles, from defensive bastion, luxurious palaces, the seat of government, to a prison, warehouse, and a barracks. In this castle, we roamed many rooms and walked up and down spiral staircases to view this amazing medieval relic and were not disappointed. Even more romantic, as we sat on the thrones as the King and Queen we were surrounded by a world of white. That was a first time for us. We were in a real castle, on and in, a cloud of snow. Tell me, what could be better than that??

Yes, castles for me are intriguing and amazing places.

Castles tell their stories, of tales, of relics, of legends, of people. They hold so much antiquity, so many memories, so many stories. They romanticise the Cinderella story, the Sleeping Beauty world, the domain of Anna and Elsa and Arendelle, and aside from the Disney stories, they also reflected the harsh real world as it was, as they lived. Their history danced from the pinnacles of the many castles we saw. It bounced off their shattered walls, their broken towers, their sweeping remnants of stairs and all had their own, individual story to tell.

I was so captivated.

I am still captivated.

I am still enthralled and mesmerized.

From the touchstones of their ruins, their narratives, their world of romance and war, of ancient passages, we had truly made a pilgrimage.

And you know what, we still have so many more to explore!

Twenty-One

Sometimes You Win, Sometimes You Don't!

In all my travels, with Marc, I have slept in various places and forms of accommodation. Some I was happy to do, others – not so sure but I will try all forms MOST of the time.

We were in Sweden, for a very short stay.

Of course, we walked our usual ambulatory explorations around the old city and the new areas. I mean … I am travelling with Marc! However, the highlight of this city, apart from its age and architecture, I must admit was the Ghost Tour that entertained us one night. Of course, the history was skewed *slightly* by our guide … but he was so animated that you truly believed every word he said! It was an English *tour (probably would have been a little hard to be part of the Swedish one so we chose this instead)*.

Callum, our guide, bought everything to life as we walked around the old town for two hours following him like sheep on an extremely cold Saturday night. The group followed him through the lanes and alley ways of the Gamla Stan (the old part of Stockholm) like lost sheep, hanging onto every word he said as he bought the medieval times of the old town to life! My imagination was so confronted as I heard tales of beheading, limbs being cut off, witches being burnt, soldiers plundering, kings and queens ruling, complete with humorous embellishments. Yes, a definite must do if you ever one day decide to go to Stockholm. Such exciting grim ghoulish stories, but I am sure that the children who were with us in the group might have had nightmares that night! I also enjoyed the 'Grugg' (mulled red wine) after the tour to warm us up!

Now as Sweden was going to be our halfway point, we both decided it was a chance to recoup for a few days from all our previous travelling with its early morning flights, long drives, busy days, wet, cold, snowy weather explorations, and hours of walking and to just let our bodies have a chance to relax and wash away any wandering grimes.

For these restful few days, Marc had chosen a place in Stockholm that was dingy, dark with narrow stairs and small rooms – 'historical' he called it. I had chosen a luxury hotel with wide windows, king size bed, bath and beautiful ensuite complete with linen service.

What do we choose?

Guess who won!

Luxury!

Oh yes! Bring it on!

The beautiful Hotel Diplomat lay waiting for us with three whole days of indulgence! And did I indulge! Hot soaking baths, lovely suite, full length balcony windows that opened; a huge bed to stretch out on, coffee and tea when you wanted it. Such divine luxury. And yes, I will admit unreservedly, I thoroughly enjoyed every luxuriating moment!

But did I really win? Because I must ask you a question …

When you are in this beautiful hotel, on a winter vacation, what would you expect to be doing on a calm, somewhat sunny cold late Sunday afternoon? When can you see the flags outside your room flapping furiously as the wind caught their tails? When you can observe the sun slowly taking a break from the sky as it graciously retreats complete with its small amount of warmth signifying the afternoon is passing by?

Perhaps you would be reading a book, or lazily sharing a glass of wine? Sharing a coffee? Even taking that much needed 'little' nap on that luxurious day bed. Perhaps you could be writing an email home or simply enjoying the warmth of the room you are in and those surrounding pleasurable thoughts in your head? Yes, these are undoubtedly all excellent ideas and probably what the average person would do to enjoy a cold winters weekend afternoon in a cold city, particularly after the scintillating ghost tour of the night before in freezing conditions.

But what was I doing?

No, not any of those suggestions.

I am far away from my luxurious hotel that I had 'won'.

Instead, I was sitting on top of a tour boat, seated on a deer skin, wrapped from head to toe in my layers, and enfolded in a red blanket which was trying hard to lure warmth to remain in the crevices of my freezing body while the cold wind whipped straight off the Baltic Sea attempted to turn any centimetre of my hidden heat into icicles!

As I smiled into the camera, blustery headwinds were beating my face and swirled further around and down my body into any free, once warm, air space as I sat atop this icy cold tour boat which *slowly* navigated its way around the harbour in the *late* afternoon as the sun was setting in Stockholm, Sweden, on what Marc insisted was a 'must do' boat tour! "The Best way to see Sweden", our guide informed us.

Do you know, after our boat tour around some of the islands in that freezing winter chill on that lazy Winter's Sunday afternoon, I was absolutely, unreservedly, bitterly icy. I was actually so cold; my toes and fingers had lost all feeling; my face was aching and even my backside and nether parts had turned blue! It took so long later for Marc to warm me up!

In all honesty. if I was a male, my 'balls' would have been so cold they would have extricated themselves and flown all the way back in Australia long before the end of that tour!

Yes, some you win.

Some you lose

In Sweden, I am not sure which one I achieved?

I do believe the Jury is still out on that one!

Twenty-Two

The Lighter side of Travel

For just another minute. let me take you away from the normal travel monologue to talk about something a little different.

We often talk about 'Jet Lag' when we travel.

Some suffer from it greatly and others do not. But it is part of what you may experience when you undertake long-haul international travel. Some travellers take a sleeping pill to assist in coping with long journeys like when you fly from Sydney to London. Others cope with jet lag by whatever manner they know how at the end of their journey. Because our sleeping patterns are all mixed up from the travel and time changes, we simply say to others to explain what may be seen to them as erratic behaviour, *"Oh, I am just suffering from jet lag."* I tend not to suffer with it when we arrive at an overseas destination but feel it more on my return trip home. It also depends upon the country and what is the season and time of year.

But what about *light dark* lag? Strange term I know.

The official name is called Seasonal Affective Disorder!

Now that is something that I can talk about, and is not related to Jet Lag but rather, to seasons. I am not turning medical, but do you know that 'Seasonal Affective Disorder' is a mental health condition that is triggered by the changing of the seasons. In simple terms, the season can affect your mood, in particular create depression, and it shifts with the various seasons. While medical experts do not know the exact cause of 'SAD' (as it is called), it is believed to be linked to reduced exposure to sunlight during the shorter autumn and winter days.

Being theoretical here, 'Light' has a profound effect on your sleep and your mood. Our body's internal clock uses sunlight to time various important functions, such as when to wake up, when to eat, when to go home from work and when ready for bed. When you are exposed to light early in your day, this stimulates the body and mind, encouraging feelings of wakefulness, alertness, and energy.

But for some people, the season of winter when there are lower light levels and shorter days, this lack of daylight can lead to symptoms of SAD, basically making you feel rather down and depressed. (SAD what a good abbreviation!) Rather like that feeling you can get when it is cold, dark grey overcast outside and you do not have that normal 'zing' in your step but instead, can feel down and despondent, that is what it is like. I actually have a close friend who goes through this here in Australia. Every winter she goes rather flat in her mood during the winter months when the sun goes down early and rises late. It really affects her. Her mood changes noticeably in this time of year in that she always feels down and discouraged. For Marc and me, heading to the northern hemisphere in the months between December to February (our usual time of travel re our work commitments, not to mention out desire for a complete change of season) we have personally experienced those changes of variance of sunlight. One example is our venture into another realm, to Reykjavik - the capital of Iceland.

Do you know that it is possible to explore a new city when the sky is dark? When the streetlights are still shining, the reflections of the buildings in the lake water are sparkling, twinkling their coloured Christmas decorations and lights at you, while the sky remains so black. So, you say, "Nothing new, we often go out at night!" But you would be quite wrong. I am describing 10:00am in the morning in Reykjavik in January. Walking a major city of a country at 10am and it is just like night. So strange!

Reykjavik was such a pretty city compared to the dull and grey drabness of London (where we had previously been). We loved the history of London, but this place was remarkable! Even though it was many weeks after Christmas, the city of Reykjavik had left all their Christmas lights up and it appeared like a fairy city. But even without those lights, the buildings themselves were painted in bright colours and the whole place was incredibly attractive. It was here, in this city, we experienced our seasonal change, probably because it was quite unusual walking around the city in the dark, the sun having not come up yet nor showing any signs of ever rising either!

In Iceland, at that time of year, the sun did not rise until 11.30am and then set again around 3pm. Not much daylight, but a twilight until about 4pm and then dark once more. Deciding we were not going to let the dim hours control our sightseeing, we daily ventured out into the morning shadows and explored. I have to admit, getting out of bed was hard as it was still so black and dark, and my body simply wanted to sleep some more! (Personally, I enjoy the winter months at home as I can sleep. It is soooo dark). Most days, we were completely wrapped up in winter gear because the wind was blowing, and the rain or the snow was either falling, or threatening to fall. Not exactly good days to be exploring but do I need to say anymore since I was travelling with Marc? However, we had been warned that the winds in Reykjavik could be extremely strong and believe me, we felt them one day.

Did I say strong? Not quite the descriptive word I would use as we were swooped and thrusted along the footpath, blown sideways with snow and ice particles landing on our faces. Sound fun? Not quite.

We travelled around the lake, walking in the blackness, and made our way up to the National Museum, where we learnt much about the history of Iceland. Lunch was consumed at the museum (even though the sun had just risen, and it really should have been breakfast) while we watched the world outside change so quickly as the sun pushed back the shadows.

After lunch (nee breakfast), we started walking back to our lodgings … when suddenly everything went white. I initially did not know what had happened but then I realised that, for the first time, I was caught in a snowstorm flurry! Even though we thought we knew where we were, we were actually lost in the whiteness.

The 'strong' wind pushed and propelled me with huge gusts, almost able to pick me up in the air, forcing me away from where I wished to go. Marc grabbed me and stopped me from flying high in the sky (just like Dorothy and her house in that tornado,) and pulled me into a side alley to shelter out the 'storm'. All those 'lost dying' movie scenes of Everest and Antarctica came rushing back to me. I clearly felt myself unsettling as this storm of white so quickly engulfed and seized us. And then, just as quickly as it came, it went! Gentle snow still was falling but the flurry part had gone, and once again, we found ourselves back in 'known' territory but this time, with daylight to accompany us home. Quite a scary moment there, I must admit.

I have to ask, what else do you do when the small amount of sun sets so early, but you are not quite ready to go back to your cabin? You visit 'The Penis Museum". Yes, you heard correctly. A museum full of different penises. The Icelandic Phallological Museum contains a collection of more than two hundred and fifteen penises and penile parts belonging to almost all land and sea mammals that could be found in the world. Definitely, just what a girl wants to see!

How do I describe this 'delightful' place!

I actually cannot describe what it felt like while walking around all the 'exhibits' preserved in formaldehyde. You will just have to use your imagination although, unless you have been to this museum or have had an interesting earlier life, I am sure you do not have enough images of enough different penises from enough different species for your imagination to do this exercise justice! For me the experience was a challenge like no other. Though he is a doctor, even Marc learned a few things about penises that had not been included in his *human* anatomy lessons such as that some species actually do have real bones in their penises – hmmm, think about it! I even found out that there is a man who has bequeathed his 13.5-inch specimen to the museum upon his death. (And I really needed to know that! Why?) I think that is all I need to say about that particular excursion in Reykjavik!

There is the opposite to winter solstice.

Light at the wrong time of night can effectively alter the body's internal 'sleep clock' that regulates sleep-wake cycles. Ultimately, when there is insufficient darkness throughout the night, this can lead to frequent and prolonged awakenings or even total lack of sleep. Long periods of light up to eighteen hours a day, and light exposure even at night, can encourage alertness and make it so much harder to fall or remain asleep. Well, that applies to me.

I am one of those people who need the dark to sleep because, if it is not dark, I cannot sleep properly or deeply. To sleep, if I see a patch of light, I need to cover it up. I am that individual who places bags and all sorts of things against the curtains or the window or whatever light is flashing in the room to stop the possibility of even a tiny crack of light being seen. If there is the slightest splinter of light attempting to gleam and sliver through that tiny crack, to me it becomes a monstrous annoying luminous spotlight pointing directly at my eyes. I have to block it out. Cover up all the windows. Never mind if I cannot breathe without fresh air, I just need it to be dark. As a result, I adore hotels and cabins where there are 'block-out' curtains so when the light switches off, all you can see around you is – ABSOLUTELY NOTHING. So, imagine my dilemma, as part of our wonderful holiday, when we headed to the northerly situated Orkney Islands in June/July,

It was summer when we arrived in Stromness, Scotland. It was one week away from the summer solstice and the perfect time to get out and about and enjoy everything the Orkney Islands had to offer us. In contrast to our stay in Reykjavik, Iceland, in January where it was dark for most of the time, and we had to get up in the blackness to catch a few hours sightseeing in the day, Stromness had very long days, short, bright nights, and a calendar full of festivals, events, and activities. What better way to spend part of our honeymoon/holiday than right there on those beautiful islands?

The Orkney Islands were truly full of unspeakable beauty and achingly stunning coastal vistas and definitely home to areas of great archaeological importance. You know I really love history and am now going to bore you about some of the amazing prehistoric sites we experienced. (If you don't wish to read any of this information, you can now move on further in my chapter).

For example, *The Tomb of the Eagles*, was a Stone Age tomb that revealed an amazing collection of bones and artefacts built some 5,000 years ago. To enter the tomb, you lay on a trolley and pulled yourself along with a rope. Actually, quite hard for someone who is claustrophobic, but I managed to do it! Marc even crawled into a side-chamber in the tomb where there was no light. Not me. Are you silly?

The Standing Stones of Stenness was an amazing monument where stones measured up to six metres tall. When we were there, only four remaining stones were left but not bad considering since they had been there for over 5000 years.

Then there was Maes *Howe* which was among Europe's finest Neolithic burial chambers, a fascinating chambered tomb that predated the Egyptian pyramids. Built around 3,000 B.C., this mysterious structure featured remarkably sophisticated stonework. On the outside, the chamber looked simply like a large, grassy mound but when you entered through a 14.5-metre-long passage it was perfectly aligned to function as a calendar. This meant that on the winter solstice, the sun shone straight down that opening and illuminated the back of the central chamber. In the summer solstice … well we were there to find out what happened!

Worth mentioning is The Stone Age village of *Skara Brae*. Being 5000 years old, Skara Brae was perfectly preserved in a sand dune until 1850 when it was found after a storm ripped of the top off the dune. Unlike the burial chambers and standing stones that make up the majority of the amazing archaeology of the Orkney Islands, Skara Brae was unique in that it offered us a glimpse into Neolithic everyday life since we were able to see the houses and living areas as they were all those years ago. A captivating glimpse into the past!

For me the highlight was the *Ring of Brodgar* which is one of the most iconic symbols of Orkney's rich prehistoric past. It covers an area of around 13,500m² and is the third largest stone circle in the British Isles. Historians believe that the site probably dates from between 2500 and 2000 B.C. and would once have contained about 60 different stones. This is a most mysterious historical attraction and an area of spectacular natural beauty.

As we left the car and walked up the hill, in front of us, were 27 huge standing stones that formed a perfect circle with a diameter of about 104 metres. This circle we were observing on that special day simply created the perfect stage of one of the oldest stone circles in existence. It is so hard to describe! Quite an unbelievable different experience from Stonehenge because at the Ring of Brodgar you can truly walk casually amongst the stones unimpeded by any barriers – really feel the impact of the site!

If you have watched the recent TV series Outlander or have read the books, you will understand that to me the stones bought all that much-loved work of fiction into a real time and place. Standing there, in those Ring of Stones, I felt, like the character Claire, with her experience of touching the stones and going back in time. If I simply placed my hands on one of those enormous structures, I could be transported back into an unknown time period and place in Scotland a few hundreds of years ago.

Dare I touched one, and see? I am still here so guess what my choice was?

Now Orkney summers are extremely long, with almost continual daylight. At the midsummer solstice, the sun rises around 3:00am in the south-east, before setting again at around 10.30 pm, in the south-west. The summer sun shines for almost 20 hours and finally sets but remains just below the horizon. This means there is no true darkness - simply a period of extended twilight, known in Orkney vernacular as the "simmer dim".

When we were there, the sun was above the horizon for over eighteen hours, so we experienced constant days of dawns at 3:30am and still staring out the window at midnight and being able to clearly look clearly out to sea. A wonderful time to be on holidays when you could fit so much into your travelling and see so much more in the 'Daylight glow'! We were told by our hosts, that in the next week, at the summer solstice, they were going to have a game of Midnight Golf! Can you imagine playing golf at midnight when it is so light?

But there was a price to pay for those long hours of summer light.

According to experts, symptoms specific to summer-onset seasonal affective disorder (SAD), may include having trouble sleeping (insomnia), poor appetite, weight loss, agitation, or anxiety. As your waking and sleeping patterns are affected by the changes in the length of the day, some find it extremely difficult to sleep without the comfort of darkness. In a nutshell, this means when it should be dark and you are seeing daylight, your body gets confused about when to be awake and when to be asleep. That was most definitely me!

In the Orkneys, I was really enjoying everything, but felt tired, could not concentrate effectively, and remember things. I was not down or depressed nor did I lose weight (that was such a shame as I could have handled that one). Most definitely, I could not sleep due to the amount of continuous sunlight consuming my day. Even though in our B & B I was in bed trying to sleep, the room did not have block out curtains. With my craving of darkness, my body and brain were saying, "It is still daylight, you should not be in bed … wake up!" So, no sleep, or the lack of effectual sleep, made this person not a nice person at all. This affected how I felt, what I thought and how I interacted with other people and in my case, the 'other people' was my husband. On this holiday, on our honeymoon, and the new bride became rather feisty, snappy, ill humoured, simply because it was too bright for too long and my body clock was completely out of whack with not getting enough sleep! Poor Marc! So, he decided he would assist my sleeping pattern, to give me a good nights' sleep. Oh, such a lovely man. (Or maybe he was tired of my feistiness!)

It was 9:30pm - normal bedtime for us at home. Gently he cued me for bed. He created a gradual darkening environment, played soothing music with its gentle rhythms and mesmerising voices. Heavier towels or such were placed over the existing curtains, obliterating every little crack of light that possibly could enter, bringing any outside light to non-existent. It was such a calm sleep-inducing seductive environment, and I was gently being lulled into the sense of 'night-time', telling my body that 'it was ok to stop and sleep now'. The room was dark. My back being massaged by husband's strong warm hands, lulling me further into a natural sleep pattern. My brain began to inform my internal clock it was dark. As my breathing became regular and I gently drifted off into a much-needed full night's sleep, at that cusp of almost asleep, with the room so dark, so peaceful, when I was feeling so drowsy, … nature called! *"I'll be right back"*, I whispered to my husband snuggled against me, and I rose from the darkened peaceful room to open the door …

Our B & B did not have an ensuite. We were at the top of the guest house and the bathroom was around the corner. So, to attend to bodily functions, you had to leave your room to go into the hall then down to the bathroom…

I opened the door. Instead of what my brain was seducing me to believe that it was night-time and that I was meant to be asleep, bright sunlight from the dormer window in the hallway hit me straight in the face. My brain quickly reversed from that seductive moment to knowing that, NO, it was not night-time at all. IT WAS DAYLIGHT! Hello, summer night world, I am AWAKE again! And that was the end of that! I laughed all the way back to our room. Poor, Poor Marc! All his seduction undone by the sun.

Did I sleep on that trip at all? Eventually I did!

I had to learn to adjust to this lack of darkness. I did learn to cope with my 'new normal sleeping pattern' of not slumbering till 11:00pm and then waking at 3:30am with the bright sunshine but then lulled my body back to sleep by dozing in bits and pieces until 7am! That was the new norm for me as I gradually trained my body to do this, and I did survive! It is amazing the things you can do when you try hard enough. Another obstacle overcome!

Travelling overseas near the winter solstice is a challenge all of its own. Leaving your cabin or motel room to drive to the tourist destination in the dark can be hard as you would much prefer to lie in your bed in the warmth, and sleep until the sun rises but only for a short few hours. But it is doable!

Travelling overseas near the summer solstice should be a time of joy and renewal. The Midnight Sun is one of those rare experiences that requires no money nor any prior preparation to enjoy in full. But continuous summer sun is also a challenge. It can sap your energy as you are constantly feeling tired while the sun is still blazing outside into the late hours of the evening. And you do have to sleep!

So, a word of advice.

If you are ever travelling in the northern hemisphere near either of the two solstices, to enjoy your summer or winter holiday more fully, try to avoid any of those associated fatigue issues linked with SAD sleep disturbances and changes of seasons.

How?

Don't forget to pack a torch.

Or

Don't forget to pack those block out curtains!!!

You Will Definitely Need Them!

To accept the challenge of the unknown is accepting the challenges along the way, choosing to keep moving forward, and savouring the journey

Roy T. Bennett

Twenty-Three

Here Comes the Sun

"Here comes the Sun, and I say It's all right!"

Did you know that in our own home country of Australia we have also had the pleasure of experiencing some magical moments! Such as The Northern Territory. This part of Australia is a vast area of land, with much of that earth being remote and inaccessible.

Can you envision ancient shallow caves with rock art that echo the deep rich culture of Australia's First People? Try and visualise deep blue skies above, as the scorched red earth rests beneath towering stone escarpments. Consider salt-water crocodiles as they wade portentously along the banks of dark ominous rivers. (Do not be confused with their diminutive fresh-water relations who tend not to see humans as convenient suppers). Picture tantalising beautifully clear pools fringed with cycads, pandanus and paperbark trees tempting the unwary to have a swim. That is one vivid way of describing this tropical end of my home country.

Another way to portray it is as HOT!

Exceptionally Hot!

Yes, Darwin the capital city of Northern Territory, was exceedingly hot. For me, to walk out from the cool air-conditioned doors of Darwin's airport into that overbearing world of heat was such a shock. And it was only July. The middle month of our Australian Winter.

I normally reside in a warm sub-tropical environmental paradise part of Australia where winter is not really cold. Quite different from the southern part of Australia where my relatives and friends live and who regularly complain about their cold and envy our warmth. Therefore, I probably should not be commenting upon the heat, nor complaining given our 'warm winters'. But this was a different *heat*, found in the middle of winter, and was certainly something I had not expected to experience! As we left the air-conditioned airport, with the sun burning intensely through our clothes. I truly could not imagine being here in the summer months! Officially this was Northern Territory 'dry' and 'cool' season. But I certainly did not experience 'dry' as we went for our 'small' experimental walk around this, for us, previously unexplored city of Darwin to get our bearings.

Initially, our walk took us towards the Darwin Convention Centre and the waterfront stretch where we soaked up the sand and the greenness of the water surrounding us. Our little walk ended up in a Marc type of *'I wonder where this goes'* and *'let's see where these leads'*. We meandered vertically up a winding tree-covered staircase and found ourselves on an open unshaded road heading down into the CBD of Darwin. Somehow, for a dry heat, I was certainly very 'wet' by the time we returned. No sunscreen, face red, feet blistered, hot and quite, quite, quite uncomfortable!

But why were we here?

Work of course!

My husband was attending a Rural and Remote Medical Conference for four days at the Darwin Conference Centre and he asked me to come along with him. Knowing that he would be attending various conference/workshop sessions during the time we were here, I decided I would just have to simply swallow my disappointment and my regret about myself not being physically at work! I realised I would just have to 'suck it up' and do my own work through logging in remotely as I sat by myself under the palm trees overlooking the waterfront lagoon. As hard as it might be, I was sure I could handle that! True to my word, as I looked out from under my own personal area of shade beneath the luxurious palm trees swaying in the slight breeze, the sun shining down brightly, releasing its generous rays of beams and shadows (and HEAT), and watched the children and adults happily swim in the (croc-free) saltwater lagoon, situated between resort and privately owned apartments on one side and the ocean on the other, I was seriously so much feeling my 'disappointment' of not actually being at work scenario for the next few days. Can't you?

Darwin is a different city.

At the risk of sounding again like a travel log, this city has so many churches, and I mean huge churches for a small population. They all seemed to be centralised in one location - not too far from the other. You certainly had a choice of where you would like to go if you attended church! The most fascinating structure-wise was the Anglican Cathedral. The church itself was so enormous that I wondered if they ever actually did fill it up on Sundays. It had three glass sides with almost one side of the front facing wall that looked like a sail or waves. This held the remnants of the original stain glass window from the church before it was hit by Cyclone Tracy.

Darwin is no stranger to cyclones and for those readers who do not know this historical event, Cyclone Tracy hit Darwin in the small hours of Christmas Day in 1974 and was amongst the most destructive ever recorded in Australia. Wind gusts reached 217 km/h before the anemometer was destroyed, with those gales extending to about 40 kilometres from the cyclone's centre. Sadly, 71 people were killed, 145 people seriously injured and more than 500 receiving minor injuries. Sombrely, it devastated 80 per cent of the city and was definitely a statement in Australian history! I personally remember being in Sydney and hearing the news broadcast and not quite believing it had happened. Something I will always recall!

The city itself for me, was not at all interesting.

There was very little in the CBD of Darwin and basically the main street Mall held very few shops. Gift and souvenir places were quite obvious and aimed at the conventional tourist and cruise ship's passengers for their 'Day in Darwin', but for the run-of-the-mill person, the day-to-day shopping franchise stores were minimal. As I write this today, I wonder if it has changed at all? However, one thing that did stand out was the colourful array of clothing hanging outside the shops.

Darwin has a busy indigenous community and, in my limited time there, I noticed that the clothes the indigenous wore were bright and colourful, choices also shared by some of the white community. I loved the reds and bright colours! But Darwin's *fashion* definitely is not a statement compared to Melbourne or Sydney. Chic gives way to comfort, and footwear is limited generally to thongs or leather sandals – not a stiletto in sight. I am sure that there were venues where the locals dressed up in full attire, but this was not the 'norm'. The female attendees at Marc's conference were in contrast generally smartly dressed, including dress shoes, as they walked to the convention centre. You certainly could identify who were the visitors and who were the locals.

It is a relaxed city, almost akin to that 'Fijian time' feeling.

Sitting at the waterside, 'working', while my husband was busy indoors at his conference, various shapes and sizes were spread out around the lagoon, lying unashamedly in the vast natural space given to us. Assorted moulds and designs of both woman and men. From an unassuming woman's perspective, most of the woman shapes were definitely leaning towards the larger side. I guess, they did not mind that their bodies did not represent the 'magazine-idolised shape' as rolls of excess weight were easily seen and displayed! Even the young girls in their bikinis were generally 'larger' than what I saw elsewhere. Perhaps that relaxed feeling and environment was due to the fact they did not have to be competing with the thin anorexic 'in-crowd' women so obvious in other capital cities. There was no *need* to be trendy, to be *that* thin person. It was so wonderful to see. I assuaged they wanted to be who they were with the weight and style they wanted to be. I so admired that! I happily acquiesced, in my stage in life, I would fit in quite well there with my own belly roll overlapping my stomach and thighs!!! Oh, you ask, what was I wearing? A sarong and absolutely nothing on my feet imitating the locals! Of course!

Still sounding like a travel log (my apologies,) Darwin did have its good points. It could also be classed as a romantic place with its amazing sunsets and outdoor movie cinema

In our stay there we walked to Mindil markets and afterwards went to the adjacent beach to watch the legendary and remarkable sunset that graced the western sky at this beach every night! Armed with Sushi, fried rice, and skewered prawns from the local market, we sat down with many (many) others on the sand dunes and observed the sun slowly vacating the sky.

Living where we do in our own sub-tropical paradise, this sunset should not create such a reaction. However, in Darwin at this beach, the redness seeped from the heat of the day, re-arranged herself, cooling the world down, stained and dyed the evening colours of purple and bluey black. That unusual merging of colours and blaze of brilliance, as the veil of light diminished in stages from one huge red ball to one pink pinprick, to then float away to reveal stars, was nothing short of amazing. Then, like a dream, it was gone, the sky faded into darkness and all about was shadowy. That wonderful dreamscape moment when the darkened world seemed infinitely greater was a moment when anything could happen. When anything could be believed in! Romantically, Marc and I sat together and watched that last vestige of sun lingers on the horizon. Something to be said about romantic tropical sunsets. Certainly, not a bad location to be for our 'working' holiday! I could handle that challenge easily!

After the compulsory conference attendance, we had agreed to discover more of the Top End. So, medical conference over, we headed down the Stuart Highway leaving Darwin to the Arnhem Highway towards Kakadu National Park. Amazingly the speed limit on those very straight and long, long, long, but not particularly wide or smooth, roads was 130kms per hour and we were doing that. Whenever we had to slow down to 100, it seemed so slow! (Quite amazing, how you can so easily become accustomed to the faster speed). We met a few road trains (semi-trailers pulling two more trailers) going in the other direction and we both deemed how interesting it would be to attempt to overtake one of them going in the same direction as you! But as a whole, the road was exceedingly long and boring, and that intense sun shone brightly into the car! But along the way, tourist expectations were well met, as we viewed aboriginal rock art (incredibly inspiring), crowded like piles of sandwiches in rock galleries.

Those images definitely encouraged the imagination of the viewer in surmising how these ancient people had survived, in those harsh climatic conditions and habitats, to tell their stories from their dreamtime. To share their stories in a form that has survived to be amazingly communicated with the rest of the world centuries later. We were certainly listening!

But it was still so hot!

Everyone around me, including my darling husband assured me this was the best time of year to see the Northern Territory of Australia and, in particular, Kakadu National Park and the township of Katherine where we were going later. However, even though I was loving what I saw, I was sure at that point of time, the weather was great for those who absolutely (1) loved the burning heat, (2) adored flies and other insects settling on your skin all day and (3) generally enjoy bathing in the whole sun/heat-drenched filled experience of a so-called Northern Territory 'dry' season!

With the sun shining down on my covered head, hair tied back, a much needed but most hated object - my hat – on my head, beads of perspiration swam together and then assembled into rivulets that poured down (dripping) from the top half of my body. Perspiration slowly merged with moisture pooled from my lower half as I looked up at my husband who smiled and took a most 'glowing' picture of me standing in front of some amazing Aboriginal artwork!

Eventually, sundrenched, soggy, and shimmering in sweat, we arrived at the Aurora Kakadu resort and campsite and the resort's air-conditioned room engulfed me with her swirling reviving cool arms. Tantalizingly, only twenty metres away from our bedroom, a sparkling blue pool brilliantly beckoned and called my name enticingly to submerge myself into her civilizing liquid. I quickly acquiesced. As I relaxed in the pool and the warm humid night began to smother me with its nightly heat, no relieving breeze came to help me breath, and beads of moisture settled in place upon my face, I reflected of my jacket and scarf occupying space in Marc's backpack because *"I thought I might be cold."* Cold???

I ask again.

This is the dry season?????

I wonder what it would be like in the 'wet season'? To be here, when the rains and humidity were highly intense and dankness and constant clamminess was cemented firmly not only on and in your body, but in your mind, your soul, and your spirit day after day after day after day and continued endlessly for six long months? No wonder they say people go "troppo" up here! (Apparently that is what happens to the human brain in the 'wet'). After my short experience, I believed if I were here in the 'wet season' as opposed to the dry, I most certainly would be one of the first ones to crack. That is if something that had already melted slowly into a blob and liquefied on the ground could actually crack! But immersed in the 'cool' liquid of the pool, my heated apprehensions melted away, I was ready to meet further exploration and additional hot days ahead in the Top End of Australia!

* * *

When I was teaching at school, or when we went to official presentations, administrative functions or even church gatherings, they always began with a 'Welcome to Country'. This phrase, well my understanding of it anyway, was perceived as acknowledging the indigenous landowners and to recognize their presence on the earth. I understood this as a ritual or formal ceremony that non-local or non-indigenous can show respect for Aboriginal and Torres Strait Islander heritage, and their ongoing relationship as traditional owners of the land. However, in my short time in the Top End, I was given a different insight into what this 'phrase' – welcome to country, truly means.

On one of our tours, our Aboriginal guide, explained that although my perception was accurate, '*Welcome to Country*' was so much more than simply a 'welcome to the area and acknowledgement of the traditional owners.' He clarified this was because 'country' to the aboriginal included *"the sky above, the blue in the sky, the ground below, the earth, the waterways, the clouds, the water in the waterways that feed the earth, and the natural beauty of the surrounds that they live in."* With that concept in mind, I certainly developed a different understanding as we ventured further into other areas in this Top End.

Katherine Gorge in Nitmiluk National Park, Katherine, (located 340km south of Darwin), is characterised by limestone formations with bubbling thermal springs and plenty of convoluted cave systems. This Gorge is actually a series of gorges on the Katherine River and borders Kakadu National Park. However, the big question for us was not 'whether' we should actually experience the world famous Nitmiluk Katherine Gorge, but '**How** do we view it'? By this I mean, did we walk, canoe, boat or fly around the 12km-long series of 13 stunning gorges? So, we decided to experience it initially by helicopter! What a mind-blowing experience! So many images come to mind as I now struggle to write about the beauty, the natural surrounds, the sky, the water below of the Jawoyn Country. But let me start at the beginning!

You already know from previous stories, as much as I enjoy the scenery, I get quite nervous flying in helicopters, but as this was the best way to see this spectacular natural phenomenon, I thought I would just do my best to enjoy it. Yet, my nerves had already overtaken me as we drove in the car the 20 odd kilometres to the Nitmiluk National Park where we were to take off. On our way driving along the road, my darling husband espied the body of a small plane carcass hanging vertically in a tree and nonchalantly commented about the dramatic ending to that plane. I could have slapped him. Of course, that comment *really helped* my nerves!! What was worse, as we arrived at the tin-hut that represented the helipad administration, I spied a small helicopter on the helipad, and assumed that was the one we were to fly. That flying machine in front of me was so small and did not have any doors at all! In that particular helicopter were two passengers already in place and secured with one harness to stop them from falling out. Witnessing this unappealing prospect, I glanced at Marc before my nerves did the most awful things to my bowels.

Off to the toilet I went again … and again … and yes, again! Oh, a goose would have been so proud.

My nerves were somewhat dispelled with seeing the lift off, of that particular craft and the arrival of the actual helicopter that was for us.

It was still small but as I understood it, only Marc, the pilot and myself would be the occupants. The reassuring part for me, there were doors! Big blue beautiful ones that closed and locked you in! I was given the front seat beside the pilot, (probably so I had the vantage view of seeing where were going to crash) and after securing ourselves with headsets and harnesses, in our small, encased world of rotors and steel, we flew high in the sky. Our pilot took us along the entire Katherine Gorge - all thirteen gorges.

Words cannot really communicate those amazing views!

This breath-taking Katherine Gorge with its sheer size, countless waterfalls, array of wildlife and unique gorges was astonishing. What sets Katherine Gorge apart from most other gorges, is its unique zig zag formation, as the gorges cut their way through the landscape, creating an unusual pattern in which the rivers follow beneath. To see the river twisting and winding its way along the rock valleys with the sheer sandstone cliffs framing the clear green water; to perceive that river at its narrowest and then at its widest points; to simply gaze from the heavens above at this natural waterway so long, so huge, no manmade buildings around at all, was to see the beauty and exquisiteness of nature at its finest here in Australia.

Not only did we have the opportunity to enjoy this picturesque experience, with permission granted by the Jawoyn Aborigines we were also honoured to explore rock art in their natural settings without any barriers. To be able to physically climb up and over rocks, lie down and scramble under a ledge to actually perceive the rock art painted on the roofs of those ledges hundreds of years old; to climb and wade across the tops of small waterfalls and plunge pools to view different artwork depicting the food and fish that sustained the indigenous people of this land, was truly hard to define. Each picture drawn on or in these rocks told their own story, and believe me, there were so many stories to be told! Kakadu with its fenced-protected art was incredible but this natural non fenced viewing was absolutely magical!

And our magic extended even further!

Our small helicopter landed securely at another isolated site adjacent to a plunge pool below a small waterfall. The water was crystal clear with reflections of variant greens. Alone, next to this pool, as you looked up to the sky, you could feel the protection of those giant boulders. You could sense the tranquillity of the cliffs that enclosed that small waterfall and natural lake, as images of the sky and surrounds reflected and danced on the water below. Isolated, not one other human around.

To our immense surprise our guide informed us, *"I will be back in 45minutes, this is all yours."* And as he departed, he called out over his shoulder, *"There are no crocodiles this high up in the gorge".* (A very important piece of information in this part of the world).

So, what do we do?

In front of us was this beautiful intimate pool surrounded by clusters of various shaped sandstone boulders and cliffs that encompassed and protruded from the earth. It was now our 'private pool'. Well, obviously, we sat down and revelled in the gentle breeze and natural surroundings and tranquillity of that magical place and dipped our toes then feet in the water, all sedate prim, proper. Isn't that what you are supposed to do? Not Marc. Not my husband. He stood there, tested the water, stripped off totally naked and plunged with everything hanging loose, into those clear waters. I laughed as his white bare bum undulated visibly as he swam gently away from me across this clear green pool. I viewed my professional doctor-husband swim and then climb out of the water to sit naked on the rocks, to lie there in his natural glory, soaking his white body in the sun.

What do I do?

From this side of the clear water, the little girl inside me peeked out, and said to no one listening, "Ok … why not?" and I followed suit!

Off came my clothes. My very white body glided into the water to gracefully swim and float (at least in my mind's eye anyway) across to the same rocks. Now there were two white bodies draped across those rocks surrounded by clear light green water. A La Naturale! Yes, the 'Mermaid like' photo of this *'grandmother come mermaid'* 'complete with all her rolls and bumps and lumps was taken.

We now absolutely understood why the guide had left us on our own! I have to ask you, what better way, to really absorb and assimilate that sense of nature around you, to be 'welcomed by country', as you glide naked in that pristine clear water; to feel at one with the water in this absolutely perfect environment.

What an indulgence! It was so exhilarating. It was so wet!

It Was So Cool!

In time, my relaxed feelings about communing with nature eventually did shift, due to the coolness of the water. Shyness and trepidation came closing in, hand in hand with concerns of possibly being caught naked by our pilot. This disquiet forced me to leave the calmness of the water, to dry with conventional method of the towel left for us, and to redress in my normal garb, once again all 'prim and proper'.

No, Marc did not mirror me. Instead, still naked, he much preferred to let nature do all the drying by lying spreadeagle on a warm rock. (What else would you expect!) Approximately 50 minutes or so later from our initial plunge, our guide returned. By then we were both seated on the rocks groomed and dressed. The Perfect Couple in the Perfect Picture being Perfectly Professional once again!

We followed our special private exploration of the Gorge with a sunset dinner cruise.

Can you envision the experience of the charm of a sunset in the Aussie outback, set against the dramatic backdrop of the Katherine Gorge? We sailed along the Katherine River on a three- and half-hour sunset cruise and sipped sparkling wine and watched the sunset over the rugged landscapes of the Nitmiluk National Park. The water below our boat was smooth, not even a ripple. A most satiating factor for someone who does not like boats! Our journey meandered around the waterways of this natural gorge, of its sheer cliffs, small sandy freshwater beaches, waterfalls, and rock pools, presented with Nature in all its glory. Our boat swayed, sashayed, and floated gently on the gorge, and drifted alone on the water for the moment with no human hand guiding it. I really cannot verbalise the feeling of harmony, of immense natural beauty.

How can I share the Listening to the music of the water as it flowed around you?

Watching shadows lengthen.

Seeing the sun lower further in the sky and reflecting on the water as it prepared to rest its shimmering heat on the earth below. Hearing the silence of the immense cliffs that loomed above you as you observed the night sky ablaze with stars.

How can I depict in words, the full moon casting illuminated shadows over the deep dark water, that held you throughout that non-existent timeline of where you are standing? That same moon's glory lighting those deep waters around me.

Tuning out from the noise of our open-air dinner, wine, and small chatter, I breathed in the moonlight, the water, the beauty, the peace, the calmness of those natural surroundings. If only we could package it all in a box, wrap it with a ribbon and take it home!

And it did not end there. A short trip (in Northern Territorian terms) of one hundred and fifteen kilometres took us to Mataranka. The small town of Mataranka, south of Katherine is home to the Bitter Springs Thermal pool, where the Roper River meanders through waterholes, tumbles over rocks and natural dams.

How do I describe Bitter Springs?

Formally, it is a crystal-clear natural spring of warm waters surrounded by a forest of pandanas palms. If you are not the adventurous type, there is a stairway entrance to the main pool where you could just loll about, soaking up the effects of the luxuriant 34 degrees Celsius spring water. Another way was to wade from the side into the warm waters of the Spring, and drift with the dawdling current that connected the two swimming areas to the exit ladder, on the walkway that circled the Spring area. But how do I genuinely describe Bitter Springs?

I certainly cannot imagine why the word 'bitter' would even be part of the name, or in any sentence associated, as the experience we had of these calm waters was simply sensual. There was nothing bitter about it at all! What was interesting to see was as numerous, busy, noisy, chatty travellers approached those waters, conversations lapsed, as the peacefulness hugged all who stepped into those gentle waters of Bitter Springs. Noisy interchanges quietened. Sounds became harmonious, singular and at peace ... all one with nature as countless hours 'floated' by.

Imagine laying back, your eyes to the sky, your body completely immersed, gracefully floating in that warm spring fed water? Imagine surrounding yourself in the vast calmness as it cradled you in its thermal water's embrace of sparkling green and blue water bubbles, contrasted only with the darkness of ferns, lilies and other aquatic plants that edged those waters, fringed by paperbark and palm forest. Can you feel the placid warmth as it lapped around you, over you, under you, as you inhaled the serenity of this amazing water world?

Oh, we did!

Such peace, such harmony, such serenity, such a different holiday from the diverse challenges faced in all my previous trips and holidays with Marc. And as the short twilight descended, as day gave way to night, wet, wrinkled, and totally waterlogged, reluctantly, we re-entered the normal world.

To think that people pay exorbitant prices, to attend a day spa, to attempt to replicate in a short amount of time, what the tranquillity of nature at Mataranka and Katherine Gorge gave us for many hours for free. I know which one I preferred!

I can now say that on this day, we definitely believed we had been 'welcomed to country' – in all its' glory and meanings.

The Calm.
The Peace
The Tranquillity …
Before the storm.

Twenty-Four

The Calm Before the Storm

Have you ever been afraid?

I know that is quite a silly question coming from me who has been confronted with many trials, ordeals, obstacles and at times, fearful moments with Marc. We all have fears of some sort, some more than others. But what kind of 'afraid' have you been? What kind of fear has held you trembling or desperate for courage? What kind of fear has immobilised YOU in some way? To be really be afraid of something.

Many people suffer from irrational fears.

Dictionary speaking, an 'irrational fear' is a type of fear that one experiences that does not necessarily have any basis behind it. These can be spiders, edges of cliffs, heights, snakes, needles, claustrophobia or being locked in a public toilet! (Hey, been there, done that!) But they are the things that make you jump, feel hugely uncomfortable, terrify you or just turn you into a blubbering mess for no good reason 'except they just do.' Often, we do not know why we have this fear as they are quite illogical. We all have them. I certainly do. Apart from being locked in a public toilet, I have a number of them. The biggest one for me is spiders. Those horrible insignificant, sometimes hairy, eight legged things that are important in the natural eco system.

For me, a *good* spider is a *dead* spider. I clearly remember sitting for hours without moving to watch a spider crawl across the room, settle in one space, as I waited for my late husband to come home to kill it. I did not take my eyes off i, but I was not going anywhere near it. I remember gassing myself as I sprayed another spider with so much insect spray that it turned white, and I ended up rather green, lying on the couch. Even today, when I walk through a web you should see me tear viciously through the strands of my hair trying to get whatever spider that 'might' be in my hair. I am like a ninja! I am so frightened of them. I have scratched my legs in the same way trying to get any possible spider off me. No, not a pretty sight.

Then there are the rational fears. These are fears that are very real. Those are things that could actually happen and kill you, like car accidents, train wrecks, drownings, earthquakes, tsunamis, and bushfires. And of course, crocodiles!

The Crocodile!

A Cold-blooded reptile who looks at you with those unblinking eyes. Not just those silly American alligators, but the saltwater Australian crocodiles that can be up to nine metres long, stand one point five metres off the ground and can chase you at up to fifteen kilometres per hour on land. If they can do that on land, just imagine what they can do in the water!

Did you know that in 1985, Eco-philosopher Val Plumwood in her story, "Being Prey", was seized by the legs, in a red-hot pincer grip of a crocodile, and whirled into the suffocating wet darkness below? While being churned under water within that crocodile's jaws, the report goes she came to the realisation, that for the crocodile she was food, merely a piece of meat. You think so? Good judgement there! Personally, I don't think I would have had time to think at all. I would have been too busy screaming! Yes, Crocodiles are a rational fear. Because Crocodiles are very real.

As a reptile, crocodiles loom large in the human imagination. It has been used as an enemy in children's stories like Peter Pan.

As a young child, I thought crocodiles lived under my bed and if my feet hung over the side, they would get bitten off. For a while, I slept in a ball and would jump clear of the edge when getting out of bed. I have no idea why I ever had that kind of fear because I actually lived in the middle of suburban Sydney, a mixture of cars and concrete, where there were definitely no crocodiles! Naturally, I grew out of that fear. My childhood fear subsided and became quite non-existent, because as an adult, apart from the movie, *'Crocodile Dundee'*, and Steve Irwin with his *The Crocodile Hunter television* shows, the extent of my personal interaction with crocodiles had been viewing them on television or in zoos. You know, me on one side of the wall, them on the other and plenty of concrete barriers in between. But all that changed as we were acquainted with those creatures in a morning cruise in the Top End, along the East Alligator River. (Why on earth they call it Alligator River when it is actually full of crocodiles, I have no idea). Here, I was presented with this very real fear as we were given the privilege (if you could call it that) of coming close to crocodiles in their natural habitat! I was given my first sight of a crocodile in the river, 'Up Close and Personal' as the catchphrase goes.

The thought of being a step or two down from the top of their food chain wasn't something that I was liking one bit. Our guide had also brilliantly informed us that crocodiles were capable of reaching speeds of up to twenty kilometres on land and, chances are if you tried to run away, you would lose miserably. Personally, I would think that you probably did not have the chance to run at all, because if you were actually that close to see this monster on land, it would be definitely too late! We were also informed that they could lay motionless for hours in the shallows of murky water (similar to where we were,) waiting for some poor soul to come near, to then spring up with blinding speed, trap their prey, drag them into the water, and proceed to tear them apart or, employing their deadliest of all its tactics, the 'death roll'. My imagination went berserk as our guide painted the picture of being held underwater, literally held down by roughly 1600 kgs of crocodile, being spun around and around, adding to your blood loss, pain, and disorientation … ultimately drowning. In other words, it's over. Crocodile wins. Human loses. Standing on the edge of the murky muddy water hearing this, I stepped back quite a few metres from the edge. Quite A Long Way!

Within the confines of a small boat, sitting on murky, muddy water later, where I could not see the bottom or surrounds, I had to admit that I was quite terrified. Even though my brain logically told me I was safe and contained, just like my childhood fear, I really wanted to curl up in a ball as tight as possible, tuck legs arms whatever I could under me, and as far away from these predators.

All our eyes peered at the water.

And there it was!

The creature, that crocodile that survived whatever killed the dinosaurs, was there edging closer and closer to our boat, right near me, and definitely real.

At first it looked like a log. But this log on the surface developed eyes! Those eyes (probably to better place it all in focus) gleamed as it tilted its heads upwards to see prey above the horizontal plane. I was sure those eyes were looking directly at me!

As the crocodile lingered beside us, the other passengers on this small boat sitting precariously on muddy, murky waters all raced to that side of the boat desperate to see. The Crocodile This turned our floating platform into an unbalanced vessel filled with excited tourists all taking photos of that drifting green-eyed 'log', whilst simultaneously, threatening to tip all of us into the crocodiles' habitat. And our guide kept saying, *"Please be careful ... don't tip the boat!"* Well, I can tell you, that did a whole lot for my confidence!

Being a sucker for punishment, that evening, we were once again within the confines of another small vessel, but this time for a sunset cruise.

It was picturesque as we viewed a different sunset, birdlife, sea eagles and jabirus, in their serene, beautiful natural environment. As my husband sat beside me, hand in hand, snug, secure, it was rather a tranquil calm world, a peaceful relaxed romantic twilight. I could continue to be romantic, but this was a different image, because we were there to view more crocodiles in a boat on a different waterway.

Even though we were in a placid world, my hand was frozen to the inside of the boat, hanging on tightly to the steel rim to keep me from falling into the water as we espied many, many crocodiles on the banks and in the water. They were creeping slowly, slowly gliding, their eyes round and large watching us as they perhaps stalked their prey for the night.

While looking at those glowing eyes, we were told that crocodiles have 'small brains but are not simple-minded, nor stupid and are extremely good at learning'. They watch and they learn. I could only assume that while no crocodile was going to start thinking about the problems of relativity, I did wonder, as they watched and waited patiently, visibly ready, to pounce in this calm quiet environment, what they might be thinking. Were we on the menu?

They slowly glided beside the boat, submerging their bodies underneath the water, their heads rising gracefully as their one green eye looked languidly at you, as you seized that opportunity, to take that close up, never-to-be-forgotten photograph. Actually, Marc did, I was too busy holding on, or better put, gripping firmly, to the side of the boat.

Then in the midst of that silent eerie world, suddenly we were loudly interrupted by a thrashing of a crocs tail on the side of the boat. The eerie silence was split with shrieks from other passengers as they moved rapidly away from side to side, as many tails of crocodiles violently collided with our small boat in this entrapment body of water. Thrashes of tails, screams of humans, what a great combination! I can tell you, it did absolutely nothing for my already stretched nerves! As the sounds quietened and the crocodiles slid back under the water, what did our guide tell us? Lurking beneath the muddy swirling water of the Yellow Water Billabong and floodplains were many, many, many crocodiles that we could not see. Not just one … numerous.

Not the kind in Crocodile Dundee for the films. Not the kind in the Australian Zoo in enclosures and fed meat each day.

Real crocodiles in their natural habitat.

Crocodiles who were waiting for you to lean just that little bit too far over the edge of the boat.

Crocodiles who were waiting for you to extend your arm out, just that little bit further, to then take you from the boat into their jaws and roll you to death

And if you did accidently fall in, well, you had about five seconds before a croc got you.

Tell me again, what am I doing here?

Oh yes, just the kind of holiday I wanted.

* * *

In the Top End of Australia, the air temperature and humidity of the twilight in that boat had risen far above the range for comfort. It Was SO Hot! It was steamy, sultry, blistery, muggy and the air around us was listless. The waves of heat rose off the water surface like flames above a roof. As I sat there, rivulets of sweat poured off me, soaking and clung to my shape. Perspiration dripped from me that reduced my ability to do anthing physical or even to think.

All around me was cool, alluring , enticing water that could chill my hot, sun-soaked drenched body down.

Should I go for a swim?

I don't think so.

I think this time,I will simply pass!

"How doth the little crocodile
Improve his shining tail,
And pour the waters of the Nile
On every Golden Scale!
How cheerfully he seems to grin,
How neatly spreads his claws,
And welcomes all who fall in,
With gently smiling jaws!
(Lewis Carroll)

As we get older, we understand more and more about, it is not what you look like or what you own, but what you have become.

Being older creates more challenges, and character is formed by those challenges faced and overcome!

Michelle Bandyk

Twenty-Five

*The Old Grey mare ...
No. she definitely aint what
she used to be ...*

*"You cannot help getting older, but you don't have to be old.
Getting older is an adventure, not a problem.*

It has now been almost fourteen years since I first met Marc. I am fourteen years older. Fourteen years since the stories for this book began! Yes, both of us have grown older! But have we aged?

Of course, in the physical sense we have, but mentally - no! Even though this 'old grey mare 'cannot move about as nimbly as she once had when she had first met Marc in her late 40's, she is still travelling. The most important aspect is that her mind is still as young as it was when this whole journey began all those years ago! Simply "more mature". Fourteen years later we are still having our walking adventures. Definitely, a little slower at times, but it is still happening. Let me share with you two journeys.

'Bushwalking' is the Australian word for hiking.

It is walking through bush, at times, in undeveloped land, on tracks, or cross-country generally in large national parks which preserve those scenic and rugged areas in their natural state. Fitness campaigns extol the physical health benefits of hiking, and regular walkers need no convincing of the many quality-of-life benefits they obtain from this relatively 'easy' activity. Interestingly, when I was researching for this chapter, I found a summary of responses from hikers of why they bush walk. These included: *"To Escape from stress"; "Challenging yourself"; "Fitness", "Exercise"* and *"Companionship"*. So, you would agree with my research that these are good enough reasons to go bushwalking? Well, I will let you decide!

Before I launch into this story, I have to ask, what is it about men that they must constantly prove themselves that they can do something? When on a break from work, why can't they just take the straightforward way out and relax and rest? Why is it that they, "Have to do this!" I really don't know! But in all honesty, likewise, tell me, what is it about me that I cannot say, "No!"

It was my husband's 63rd birthday and we had previously booked a most beautiful venue about 130kms driving from home, in Queensland, in the mountains, at a place called Binna Burra Lodge. We were welcomed with a luxurious view high above the rest of the natural world. Our 'Sky Lodge' accommodation was complete with fireplace, food, and wine. It was the most romantic venue for his birthday. Even more noteworthy, almost fourteen years ago, in our phase of that 'getting to know you' part of our relationship, we had previously stayed there. We had formerly walked similar tracks together, celebrated by our very first romantic dinner in front of the fire. So, this weekend was actually in fact, a trip for both of us down memory lane. A special occasion to celebrate. What more could we both want?

It was such a warm welcoming place and I felt relaxed and calm. But on that birthday weekend, with the cold weather settling in around us, stretched out in our luxurious cabin, the fireplace embers glowing, wine in hand, I had to ask Marc that ill-fated question, *"What would you like to do?"*

A slight pause, his eyebrows raised, his face uplifted, his eyes lit up, the smile beamed broadly across his face and as quick as the words were out of my mouth, I knew what his answer was going to be, "*How about something different - Let's go for a walk!*"

I groaned inwards. Oh, silly me!

You and I both know from my many previous experiences that a walk to Marc is not a 'walk' in the similar colloquial terms of amble or stroll or saunter but hard trekking on a track, but more often not really a track. My 'Marc sixth sense' told me that this was not going to be any different! But I was prepared to go.

We were both more mature and I was quite aware that I was carrying a little more weight than I used to fourteen years ago but knew I could still walk a fairly fast pace when needed and capable of walking up hills. After all, I could ride a bicycle for several hours over many kilometres and firmly believed that at 62 years old, all this time later, I could still walk those tracks! Knowing I had been the *silly one* to ask *that* question, I considered positively, that for the two of us, within this walk, there had to be romance there, as it would be an 'active walk' down memory lane, to not only remember past memories but to make, for us, new ones. I am certain that you are never too old to set a goal and attempt to accomplish it! Even though it was a long period of time between our original trek here and this current one, as it was his birthday, what he wanted to do, who was I to argue! Wasn't I nice?

Our track started benignly, reasonably broad, and only rising gently. The air was cool, the company pleasant, the bush and bird life sounds were faint but distinct. The track before us was enjoyable. We talked as we walked. We held hands. Just like our very first walk! The first turning point came. The rise steady. But of course, the track became narrower, less well kept. The 'grade' unfortunately started to dip down, indicating that we were going to lose some of that altitude we had already gained, altitude that we would undoubtedly have to reclaim before rising any further. Another turning point appeared and the track degenerated into what is called a 'Class 5' track.

Now to give you an understanding of the various classes of tracks, Class 1 and 2 are easy, graded tracks on formed roads or paths that are maintained on a regular basis and are clearly signed. Then you have Class 3 or 4 which are unsurfaced tracks that are generally distinct, regularly inspected and where the navigation is usually obvious to follow. But what class of track were we on? Class 5. A class 5 trail is "a trail not constructed or maintained. No signs or markers provided except where necessary to minimise environmental damage. Trails may range from clearly visible footpads to indistinct overgrown routes, muddy sections, steep grade, and numerous hazards such as fallen trees and rocks". Are you now getting the idea?

I guess I should not have thought it would be any different. This trail, by the way, was not the one we had trekked all those years before. It was in the same area but went in a different direction.

At times, it was not clearly seen. Not wanting to be separate from the track, the rainforest had preferred to wind its snake vines around trees and onto the 'path', resulting in the gentle blend and merge of the two realms of nature together. Hence, our route narrowed, became rougher and in places quite slippery. At times, the edges of the track crumbled. That was when I could hear the silent voices of those steep ravines to the side of me, calling like sirens, beckoning the unwary (me) to slip and fall to my death. Yes, fourteen years later, my imagination was still just as active as to 'what could happen to me!' Hanging on tightly to an overhead vine or a tree buttress, I quietly (and fearfully) traversed this 'track' on the edge of that world, while challenging myself to not look down as I followed Marc. Trusting Marc, walking behind him, I had no idea where the track or trail or whatever we were on, was heading. I could not see it at all! I also figured that if we were going to fall off a cliff - he would go first and break my fall for me!

On the higher gradients, numerous fallen trees were in the pathway. Each had to be climbed over or, even more arduously on my knees, climbed under. But have you ever tried to climb over a huge stump of a fallen tree encompassed with vines when your muscles were quivering?

You see that trunk there in front of you. As much as you would like it to do so, that tree torso was not going to pick itself up and move out of your way, so you had no choice but to conquer it. Well, I had to do more than conquer it, I had to overpower it! I raised my leg. One leg went over. The other one eventually surrendered its stretched muscles to the tree trunk, and inopportunely that was it! I was straddled there, my legs dangled on each side of the tree trunk, my lower half stretched wide and apart. I was physically stuck and could not move either way.

My husband called from in front of me, those encouraging words, *"It's like dismounting off a horse"*. 'Really'? Dismount? I could not see or feel any stirrups on that tree horse! I simply could not get my leg over that Clydesdale-type tree animal as I worked hard to dismount from its enormous torso - my legs swinging from side to side as I tried to escape that bush horse saddle. Success eventually gained as once more my feet connected with the damp earth soooo far away. Conquered! But, NO, nothing graceful about getting off that horse!

What about bending down and moving under a fallen tree that was too high to get over and you have to go under? Easy? Better than going over and getting stuck! I already did that! Stooping down, bending my knees I attempted to navigate under that wreckage of nature! But tell me, have you tried doing this with a backpack on your back? You bend down, inching under, almost crawling, almost there, that sense of achievement beginning as you wriggle your way while your muscles were wincing and cringing, assisting you in that baby crawl position. Beginning to rise to my former glory, I smiled and breathed happily, thinking 'I did it', another obstacle overcome! Then all of a sudden, that backpack, like a tightly coiled spring suddenly snagged on that same tree pulls you backwards, cheerfully saying, "Hey! Did you forget about me?" No, not quite as easy as you might think!

Causeways also had to be negotiated with their slippery moss-covered rocks. The logical side of my brain told me I have walked on similar before, and I just witnessed Marc cross those exact same rocks with ease, but my 'older' 'risk-assessing' part of my brain breathed, 'one slip off those rocks and you may break an ankle and that would be simply disastrous'. Or what if I fell and slipped off the edge of that tropical forest world to slide down to the ends of the earth and end this wonderful natural experience! That was what my brain was telling me! My imagination working overtime again! Again, I had to ask myself, "Why were we walking here on this poor type of track? This poor excuse for a track."

This trail was just endless rainforest with its large, buttressed trees, tree ferns draped in vines and Bird-Nest ferns that pushed themselves through the dense impenetrable under-growth. I must not forget the occasional "Wait-o-While" vine that reached out to grab the innocent walker, me, and keep me in their embrace for 'a-while'. (That was certainly history, all those years ago, repeating itself!). Even though more experienced than my first encounter with those 'friendly' vines, many times I still 'waited a while' to untangle myself. Sadly, our anticipated views, when they did appear, were only glimpses through the trees of the valley below, and that was when I actually deigned my quivering body to look *down*! Most of the time it was my head down watching the forest floor to espy what was waiting to reach out, grab me and trip me up! I do enjoy a challenge, you know that, and have mastered many in the past fourteen years since meeting Marc. But at that point of time, I had stopped long ago 'enjoying' that hike we were doing for any of the reasons previously listed.

I could not say this hike was for the Escape from stress; this was adding stress to more stress. I deemed I could do any exploration quite happily (and so much more comfortably) from the safety of my lounge chair watching Discovery Channel or National Geographic programs on television. I could indisputably use that method of visual enjoyment of nature and its beauty quite easily! Was I doing this for fitness and exercise? Yes, I knew I could seriously lose a few kilos, but if I really wanted to, a few weeks with a HIIT workout from a Video Tube fitness series within the comfort of my own loungeroom would do that! Was it for Companionship? I truly loved my husband and always cherished both his company and our companionable silence. But there in that rainforest wilderness where in their silence the vines reached out to grab me; where small rocks and mounds danced wildly in front attempting to trip my feet as I negotiated my path, where slippery wet earth and muddy drenched ground endeavoured to slip and skate me onto unmarked territory away from what was called a track, Companionship was not being encouraged in the slightest! Hadn't my years of experience walking with Marc told me anything? But I did persevere for only two reasons. I was doing this for Marc's birthday, and I was too stubborn to give up. And I said I would do it!

Our pace grew slower as the track became harder to traverse. The altitude kept climbing. It was demoralising to pass a sign that indicated we had taken over half an hour to cover that one last kilometre. That was not fair as my right knee had been screaming for some time but as always, my stubbornness pushed me on. Marc at least had acknowledged with a smile that "Jane was not happy right NOW" and slowed his pace to lend a steadying hand to 'Jane' across the slippery bits.

Finally, we arrived. High above the earth. The Forestry sign says, "Mt Wagawn, A place of beauty and peace." Anticipating beautiful wonderworld of breathtaking scenic views, I looked around but there was NOTHING to see at the top. Just more encompassing bush.

HOW DEFLATING.

My head drooped as my tired back and legs muscles spasmed comprehending that I had hiked all that way through overgrown, steep gradients, numerous hazards to see NOTHING? This was SO WRONG as there was always a prize at the end of any challenge with Marc! I was now beyond caring. I definitely did not feel peaceful and just wanted to go down. Back to my world of manmade comfort away from this over consuming world of nature. But there was Marc, always optimistic. Sometimes I do not know where he gets his energy from, as he pushed on, further down a ridge while I stood there and struggled hard to smile and present a positive face in order to not let my disappointment creep in. Then, with his cheerful grin, he came back with a *"found it – had to be here somewhere"*. Assisting me another 20 metres further down along the ridge, there it was. Before me, my eyes feasted upon a most striking panoramic view of the upper Tweed Valley! Mt Warning on our left and, on our right, the NSW-side of the border stretching off to the west. It was truly breathtakingly spectacular and presented an amazing natural world of wonder, of beauty and peace! (And the whole of me said inwardly, "Thank goodness!" Something had to be offered for the three hours of hard upwards trekking I had just completed). Memories renewed; new memories made! Stubbornness rewarded.

With my normal optimism returned, rugged up against the cold wind, we ate our packed lunch, took the obligatory photographs, and just sat and enjoyed the view we had worked so hard to find.

Of course, we had to go down. But the trek down off any mountain is always faster so they say, and we had experienced this in previous travels. So, with muscles quickly starting to chill and stiffen, we packed up and started back the same way we came. The same track but in reverse. The same challenges. Now, both of us with laughter as my natural enthusiasm had been restored. I mean, the track was now known, downhills always outweighed the ups, and our momentum downwards became faster closer to the finishing line. I Had Completed It (again)and proud of myself of hiking twenty-three kilometres (again), on a 'Class 5' track even more challenging than all those years ago when I was much younger! Just like our very first walking trek fourteen years ago, our hands held again and the Binna Burra Tea House with its coffee and cake (and toilets!) sang out to us marking that last part of our six-hour journey up and down the mountain!

* * *

There was another long weekend, another walking track to achieve in the same area, but under completely different climatic conditions. We had booked and paid for this 'holiday' during the previous year but due to Covid and Border Closures (ah, that is in my next chapter), it had been rolled over to this particular weekend in a less hospitable time of the year. Of course, my husband suggested we go for a walk - as we usually do. His initial recommendation was another 24km (7 hours) circuit on a Grade 4 bush track. However, he settled on a 4 hour 12 kms one, stating, "We will do the longer one tomorrow". I guess I could have said, "No", but as indicated above - when do I really ever say, "No", to Marc and walking? With the agreed suggestion of a technically 'shorter walk', I was happy to go. How wrong was I! In retrospect, I do not think there was anything 'happy' about it.

In case you think I am whining, to set the background just a little, I did inform my husband prior to this particular long weekend, that I was not physically in as good a shape as I had been on with our previous bush hikes. This time I was carrying a combination of disabilities: a damaged inflamed shoulder that had been causing pain, infirmity, and disturbed sleep for weeks, and a tender hip incurred from having over 'indulged' in walking around Sydney and surrounds, the previous weekend. This was through following my husband and his youngest son as they tried to out-do each other in exploring both the South AND North Heads of Sydney harbour on foot in the same day. I guess I should simply say, Like Father Like Son! So, I warned him, that in the past where our four-hour walks would usually take 2-3 hours (as we generally walk fairly quickly), today's walk may be longer! But he understood and was okay with that!

Having discussed my concerns and suitably 'armed' through the liberal use of Voltaren gel on injured parts, not to mention, even more liberal use on my lower legs and feet of Vick's ointment and Teatree Oil to deter the many leeches looking for a Lyndell-blood-feed after the rain, I was ready to walk. I pulled my socks up over my pant legs, placed my backpack only minimally weighted with our lunches and locked my shoulder in place in my jacket pocket to avoid movement and thus pain.

I was ready. After all, this was nothing new. I had done this before. I was prepared. But what no one had discussed or warned me about was the actual status of this particular track consequent to the recent climatic conditions.

As you read earlier, when we have completed Grade 5 ones, I have always managed to climb up and over or under the various obstacles in place, sometimes with lots of groans, grunts, and whines but I have achieved them. In hindsight, I realised why, they were dry! Today's Grade 4 track was more of an aquatic filled quagmire of mud and running water for most of the four hours trekked. It is an understatement to say I was not impressed. You have to remember, that I had only one upper limb to provide support and balance. My other hand was stuck in my pocket to protect my shoulder and was thus a liability since I could neither support myself nor stop a fall on that side. So, holding my walking stick in my one useful hand, I balanced my way as best I could through the oozing, squelchy sucking mud, even as blisters emerged on my hand from the death grip I was using to hold my walking stick.

Researchers say 'mud play' is about fun and should be a normal part of outdoor play. That 'playing with mud' we engage all our senses, resulting in a highly stimulated and active brain and ultimately reduces levels of anxiety and stress! Well as far as I am concerned that research is totally, absolutely, unequivocally incorrect. I was not here to play with mud. There was nothing nice about this mud. It was squishy, soggy, mushy, wet gooey and so slippery! It was simply sticky matter underfoot, resulting from the mixing of earth and water, which then resulted in being even more sticky and slippery as you attempted to place your foot on some form of Terra Firma to engage traction. I did not want anything to do with mud at all. If I were not a lady, I would say even more!

Yes, it did engage my senses. I was acutely aware that this was not what was planned or what I really wanted to do. I was aware that the track I had anticipated or expected had disappeared, and this quagmire of gelatinous goo was all that was left. My senses were also quite aware that one slip may result in a fall and the obvious placing of my bad arm/shoulder onto the ground to support my falling weight would result in even further pain and spasms! I did not want to 'play this game' anymore. There was nothing about this mud that reduced anxiety and stress. In fact, it did quite the opposite. I was so upset and even verbally angry at Marc (which is most unusual for me), at one point of time as I could not stretch my leg far enough apart to take that leap, he wanted me to do, over the rushing water and into the mud.

Feet heavily coated in mud and in my non waterproof shoes, my socks and shoes now full of water – oh so yuck – I navigated those rushing rivulets of streams before me.

Then, the wind came howling so strongly up the escarpment that the water draining off our plateau and from our flooded track in a multitude of waterfalls, was being blown back upwards against gravity to fall back on us from above. Those icy waters that were meant to fall safely into the valley were being recycled to fall as icy rain to fall on our heads.

This was adding insult to injury. We did not just to have walk through the stuff, it had to have another go by falling on us! I guess I should have had more sense! I guess I personally should have thought about it more! This weekend had been previously booked and planned. But locally we have had deluges of rain and flooding for a few weeks but obviously I had not thought that it would affect the bush tracks as much as they had. Silly me! My cognitive skills not working! No brain engaged there …

How was Marc with all this?

He knew it was hard going. He knew I was upset. (I mean I did raise my voice at one time as he was not listening to me!) He was always helping me when needed which is what he does. But even he fell when crossing one fast-flowing stream and plunged sideways turning onto his back hurting his bum.

Our companionship/camaraderie was still there as we shared lunch together and took the obligatory photo of scenery evidence. But this was sadly without much conversation between us. No, not because I was angry with him, or at myself. I was not angry. Basically, I was too exhausted to speak. As I walked, I had to just mentally work through what I needed to do with my feet, where I was going to place them (now they were soaked through and covered in mud), where to put my sore arm and troubled hip, how to stop further blisters from occurring on my left hand (a bandage assisted with that one), how to manage to walk through this water and mud that was always trying to trip me up and place me on my bum. That was what I mentally and physically needed to do *for me* as I traversed those four hours in that muddy wilderness.

As we conversed again on the homeward run, he laughingly commented to me how 'wives often do-what-their-husbands-like-to do hoping it will be returned in kind'. I did not comment. But on the last stretch, heading back to the accommodation, we encountered other walkers who had passed us in the morning and were now just a little ahead of us (so I guess we had not done too bad). They inquired about our plans for more walks. As I breathed hesitantly slowly beside him, my husband replied…," Oh, I think we will have a quiet day off tomorrow. Reading and some board games". Oh – Thank you!

Needless to say, there were the positives. Marc also acknowledged that it was a tough track, and although it had been hard for me, I had finished it anyway. I thought of the quote, "I love to get in the mud, to appreciate being clean" (Lailah Gifty Akita) and decided that I much preferred being clean without falling in mud at all. I decided that the only kind of mud I liked was where you are at an art studio, with numerous glasses of wine and cheese in hand, watching someone else create from it. But, in fairness, it was another accomplishment! A different challenge. Most importantly no leeches, only one that tried but failed to get past my defences! (In reality, I am not sure how I would have reacted if many of those bloodsucking slimy insects had attached themselves to my mud-soaked being! I imagine you would have heard my screams of, "Get THEM OFF!", from the place you are now reading this story!)

* * *

Aging is a natural process that everyone has to go through. As much as I don't want to admit it, even me! Growing Older is mandatory. We cannot stop that happening. It would be wonderful to live the Bob Dylan Lyrics that say, "*May we build a ladder to the stars, And climb on every rung, May we stay forever young.*" But '*Growing Up*' though is entirely optional! I have so learnt that mantra in these past fourteen years with Marc, in our travels and our challenges. We grow old when we stop playing. Fourteen years older from her first encounter with Marc, this old grey mare definitely whines at some of the challenges I am put through. However, I am not sure that I will ever stop playing when I am with Marc because, he will keep me young!

I have a positive outlook. One day when it is my turn to slip away to the hereafter, I cannot go there 'well preserved'. Just think how boring that would be. Preferentially, when that day comes, maybe with a glass of wine, or a gin and tonic in one hand, and a piece (or in my case) a whole block of Chocolate in the other, I will slide away to that heavenly walking place, singing, "Woo Hoo, here I come!" A much better idea.

But until that day happens, I predict I will continue to enjoy further challenges with Marc as they present themselves. Who knows, maybe for even another fourteen years! What I can safely say, is this Old Grey Mare (actually not grey at all but whiter and blonder) is not what she used to be. But irrespective, she is still conquering those mountains and obstacles. And … she will probably do it all again on many, many, many more 'first dates'.

(By the way, I must add that the Old Grey Stallion himself was also a bit sore as well!!)

Did we do another walk that weekend? Yes, we did.
But for that next walk, at least I knew in advance what to expect! Mud! More Glorious Mud!'

Do not wait until the conditions are perfect to begin.
Just beginning makes the conditions perfect.

Alan Cohen

Twenty-Six

Then There Was Covid!

Stay at Home!
Only Leave Your Home If You Have To!

It is Friday night.
The Television is on and wine in hand. A normal beginning to the weekend. But this was not a normal Friday night for me. I was on leave!!!

Everyone needs a break once in a while as it helps to relax, refresh, and recharge you. Working in a medical environment where life has been extremely hard, busy, and demanding, I definitely needed all of the above. I was so looking forward to the next 5 days celebrating, what was then my 60th birthday, followed by a week away in the snow at Dinner Plains /Mt Hotham in Victoria, Australia. Well, that was the plan!

My 60th birthday … a milestone birthday … was in 2020, the first year of Covid-19. All I wanted to do to celebrate this occasion, was to go to the snow, to feel the cold, to rug up in warm clothes, to sit in front of a fire warm and insulated from the cold outside and just relax. Absolutely scrumptious! By now, you know that I really love the whiteness of the feathery snow quilt on the ground as it drapes its white gloved hands on everything it touches. We don't have a lot of that in Australia, but I was looking forward to one week of frolicking in the snow in an Australian alpine village, of sliding down hills on a toboggan, of morning walks in the small village, of wearing three or more layers of clothing to keep the freezing temperatures away from my skin, of reading and sitting enveloped in a nice cosy chair followed by nights of warm fireplaces and drinking hot chocolate as I lay snuggled up in my husband's arms. Ah Bliss.

But Covid-19 changed the plans I had made.

It changed my dreams and images of what my special birthday vacation should be like, of what I really should be doing, of the one thing I truly wanted to do for my birthday. Indecision and uncertainties, followed by border closures, affected any ability, any chance for us to head away to celebrate my birthday in the only way I wished. Plane flights were cancelled. Yes, tears fell. Feet stamped. Petulant attitude expressed. But, finally growing up again, a slow resignation grew to accept the fact that this holiday was not going to happen! Covid-19 had changed so many plans for so many people but somehow, I naively had thought it would pass me by. I was so wrong!

Covid-19 Pandemic hit the world hard.

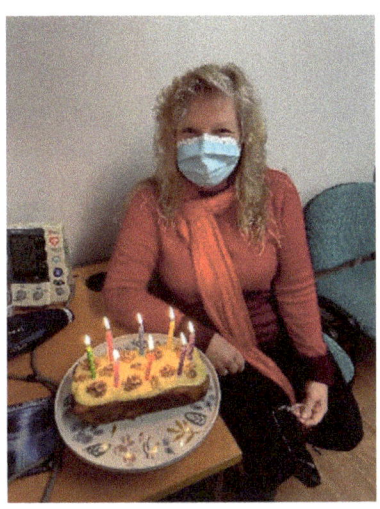

If you are reading this book and going through or went through this period in history, then you fully understand and are mindful of this disease. But if you are reading this at some time in the future, Covid-19 was a highly infectious respiratory virus that spread rapidly around the entire world. Initially the elderly seemed the most vulnerable with the highest death rate, but the virus mutated to become more infectious causing death in younger and younger adults. The disease was so virulent with no treatments, that the world essentially shut down trying to control this horrific outbreak and slow the shocking death rate until treatment could be found. Social Lockdown!

Standing 1.5 metres apart from each other; no gatherings allowed of any sort; exhortations to not visit others, even family, was the mantra from health departments. City, regional and state lockdowns around viral outbreaks were endured – with resignation by most and with protests by others causing more spread. Border Closures in Australia between states became annoyingly commonplace (this from a grandmother who could no longer see her children or grandchildren for very long time periods except via video). Regular use of hand sanitisers and the wearing of face masks became the norm. Once upon a time, if someone walked into a business with a mask on, the staff became terrified fearing a robbery. During this epidemic, someone entering a business without a mask elicited panic and unforgiving demand to leave and only return when they donned a face mask!

There was also considerable discussion in the media about the impact the virus had on mental health. Cut off from seeing family in nursing homes or hospitals or of being able to travel anywhere to see family and/or friends certainly impacted the mental state of many. While physical distancing helped to prevent people from contracting the virus, it also created other problems, including isolation, loneliness, and anxiety. It changed the way we attended important events such as weddings and funerals and seeing or visiting our loved ones. A world void of in-person socialising, touching, hugging, singing, dancing ...

But for some Australians, the restrictions governments had rightly put in place to combat COVID-19 were also a catalyst for relationships to be strengthened and reaffirmed, including developing and finding new ways to work together. We saw the renewal and importance of reaching out and being socially connected even while physically separated. Such as working and learning from home, the use of online meetings and online church services. It was a realm of webinars; video business meetings and gatherings held where participants were neatly dressed from the waist up, but the desktop conveniently hid the pyjama or tracksuit pants (or their absence) on their lower halves because no-one could be bothered whilst stuck at home. (I actually did enjoy being part of a meeting where I had coffee in one hand, and no one could see me wrapped up in my P'J's!). Irritating zoom meetings where audio microphones did not work became the norm … and the general cry of, "You're on mute!" Binge TV viewing became the regular, daily entertainment. Panic buying of toilet paper whenever a lockdown was announced became curiously expected, but quite ridiculous because if you caught the virus, you would get a runny nose and not a runny bum! (Could not quite figure that one out!) And so, my Birthday Travel Plans were rolled over and set for the next year, but this time, would include bringing my entire family in tow.

Another year and we were still hoping to travel domestically, conscious it was a daydream of times past. For many Australians, all forms of travel more than 5kms from home had stopped. In fact, travel was banned to anywhere! The challenge in the second year of Covid was even daring to make plans – knowing they were likely to be cancelled due to yet another lockdown. Sadly, trying to 're-celebrate' my 60th birthday, one year on was squashed under a Covid restriction's heavy blanket. Ten days from departure, travel restrictions were re-applied again. Heading for that departure gate for us was not going to be a choice for some time to come! Unable to travel internationally. Unable to travel within our own country. Sometimes Unable to Travel more than 5kms from your home. The challenge of serial disappointments became commonplace! Always a smile presented to the world but deep frustration simmering underneath. Disappointment of course reigned supreme for everyone, not just for us!

Here was my new Challenge! The simple challenge of being at home!

As you could tell from the chapters before, my (our) challenges had more often than not, came from our travels. From the unknown. From the risk assessments. From Marc's character of 'let's see what happens when we go there?' But for my birthday, with one week free from work that loomed for both of us, we could not go anywhere. In our own local backyard, the task presented was to make this one week off feel like a 'holiday. 'To organise that holiday 'we needed to have' when we could not physically go anywhere away from our own home. To still have 'Our holiday'

What did we do?

First, I had Marc turn off his phone – he was 'not at home'! That meant that the hospital, midwives, and medical practice could not contact him! Next, a daily list of 'activities' to make it feel like a holiday. Picnics in our backyard completed with BBQ meals. Glasses of wine and sharing time together. Walks on the winter beach (lucky enough to live in a seaside area where exercise was allowed via strolling on the beach – but you were not allowed to stop and sit – you had to keep moving!) TV series binges. Reading books.

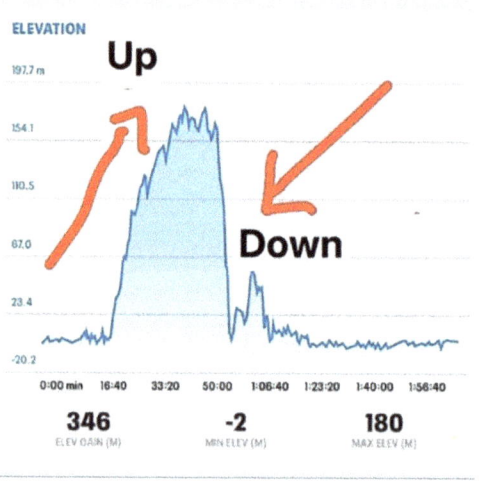

Day trips on our bicycles exploring local backroads – including a memorable navigation error on Marc's part that resulted in a substantial hill-climb and an even more spectacular, (if you can use that word), of a frightening down-hill run resulting in my bicycle reaching knuckle-blanching speeds and me suffering a subsequent minor panic attack. I mean, you do know by now what my challenges have been like over these past chapters of this book. I really do not have to tell you that! Just look at the picture here to see the gradient evidence engaged of our bike ride on that day! Definitely another tale to write about!

With Covid-19, it was a different challenge. Totally different. But in saying that, we took the time to do those things that we normally did not get the time to do!

A little different? A little less stressed? We both made that one week away from the pressure of work and patients feel like a holiday. You know, 'the holiday we had when we could not have a holiday'! No, it was definitely not as rejuvenating as most of our breaks, but we did the best we could with this task and that task was an experiment all in itself. That task was the actual challenge! Importantly, we were together, alone, without the rest of the world leaping in!

And we did it!

Covid-19 and all!

PS: By the way, I did eventually get to the snow and celebrate my 60th birthday with my family.

A few years later … but as they say - Better late than never!

Epilogue

"Do you know where we are going?"
With a mischievous grin he replied....
"No, but let's find out!"

Have I found out yet?

No, I still do not know where we are headed!

With Marc, I probably will never know.

I guess that will continue to make my life an exciting ongoing challenge!!

In reality, I had absolutely no idea what was ahead when I commenced a new relationship in late middle age to experience different situations, adapt my thinking, and to consider another's perspective were challenges all in their self. The path travelled was not always predictable and smooth. Apart from our 'travel' experiences, we also dealt with general day to day challenges and including living with Covid-19. Not all trials were conquered, and I really loathed many of them, but for those that I did face and mastered, there was that proud sense of accomplishment and many periods of delight.

In reality, I did not even have to do any of them. I did not even have to create a life with Marc. I simply could have continued on, content in my safe widowhood as I was prior. No one forced me to do any of these tasks, to meet these challenges. Even though you may have thought at times, 'she is whining again', as you read of my complaints, my frustrations, my fears, my tears, just remember, I had made all those choices myself. In each case I could either choose to scream and not do it at all, or I could choose to, with a big smile on my face, throw my hands in the air, give a happy shout, and enjoy the thrill of the journey! I am a simple, normal human being, and I did do both! Numerous times! I also had much laughter, so much fun and laughter, and I truly hope you have shared these with me!

But also remember that Marc too had to make a choice. He chose me! Every part of me!

I cannot say for certain if I will ever find out where we are heading because who knows where we will go from here? Who knows what other daily challenges two people, getting older in life, will meet! All I know is that from this point we will together continue to add more chapters to our story.

Life is full of surprises and serendipity. Being open to unexpected turns in the road is an important part of success. If we try to plan every step, we may miss those wonderful twists and turns. And as Marc says, with his mischievous grin, "let's have fun finding out".

You ask … do I have any regrets?

No! Not at all.

Not one!

Why?

Because … Life itself is a Travel…in how you get there …

Because … Life itself is a Challenge, in how you deal with things …

Because … I have met Marc!

What an amazing thrilling absolutely exciting ride this has been!

And I truly wonder … what will be next???

OH, LET'S FIND OUT!

> **THERE IS ALWAYS A NEW BEGINNING BECAUSE THE BEGINNING IS ALWAYS TODAY!**
>
> — MARY WOLLSTONECRAFT SHELLEY

About The Author

Lyndell Heyning is a writer based in Brunswick Heads Australia. She has worked as a primary school teacher and University lecturer, teaching children and training pre-service teachers in the Creative Arts. Lyndell is also an established writer in peer-reviewed international journals and regularly writes in her blog. This is her second book. Her first book "The End is Just the Beginning: A Widow's Wisdom" is available from Amazon.

You can contact Lyndell Heyning via her blog:
www.inmyownlittlecorneroftheworld.com

www.ingramcontent.com/pod-product-compliance
Lightning Source LLC
Chambersburg PA
CBHW051534010526
44107CB00064B/2722